William Drummond

The Poems of William Drummond of Hawthornden

William Drummond

The Poems of William Drummond of Hawthornden

ISBN/EAN: 9783744710732

Printed in Europe, USA, Canada, Australia, Japan

Cover: Foto ©Thomas Meinert / pixelio.de

More available books at **www.hansebooks.com**

THE

POEMS

OF

WILLIAM DRUMMOND,

OF

HAWTHORNDEN.

Dignum laude virum Musa vetat mori,
Cælo Musa beat. - - - - - -
HOR. lib. iv. od. 8.

LONDON:

PRINTED FOR J. JEFFERY, PALL-MALL.

M. DCC. XC.

A

SHORT ACCOUNT

OF THE

LIFE AND WRITINGS

OF

THE AUTHOR.

*** The following account of DRUMMOND has lately appeared, in a work privately printed, intitled, " Curfory Remarks on fome of the Ancient Englifh Poets, particularly MILTON;" and is here inferted by permiffion of the Author.

AMONG all the writers, at the beginning of the laft century, who flourifhed after the death of Shakefpeare, there is not one whom a general reader of the Englifh poetry of that age will regard with fo much, and fo deferved attention, as WILLIAM DRUMMOND. He was born at Hawthornden in Scotland, in 1585; and was the fon of Sir John Drummond, who, for ten or twelve years, was

A 2   ufher, uſher, and afterwards knight of the black-rod, to James VI.

His family became firſt diſtinguiſhed by the marriage of Robert III. whoſe queen was ſiſter to William Drummond of Carnock, their anceſtor, as appears by the patents of that king, and James I.; the one calling him " our brother," the other, " our uncle."

Drummond was educated at Edinburgh, where he took the degree of A. M. In 1606 he was ſent by his father to ſtudy civil law, at Bourges in France; but, having no taſte for the profeſſion of a lawyer, he returned to Hawthornden, and there applied himſelf with great aſſiduity to claſſical learning and poetry.

Having propoſed to marry a lady, to whom retirement and her own accompliſhments had entirely attached him, and who died after the day of marriage was, appointed, he again quitted his native country, and reſided eight years on the Continent, chiefly at Rome and Paris.

In 1620 he married Margaret Logan, a granddaughter of Sir Robert Logan, by whom he had ſeveral children; the eldeſt of whom, William, was knighted by Charles II.

He ſpent very little time in England, though he correſponded frequently with Drayton and Ben Jonſon; the latter of. whom had ſo great reſpect for his abilities, and ſo ardent a deſire to ſee him, that, at the age of forty-five, he walked to Hawthornden to viſit him.

Having

Having been grafted, as it were, on the royal family of Scotland, and upheld by them, he was a steady royalist in the troubles of Charles I. but does not appear ever to have armed for him. As he had always been a laborious student, and had applied himself equally to history and politics as to classical learning, his services were better rendered by occasional publications, in which he several times distinguished himself.

His attachment to that king and his cause was so strong, that, when he heard of the sentence being executed on him, he was overwhelmed with grief, and lifted his head no more.

He died in 1649.

In a survey of Drummond's poetry, two considerations must be had, viz.—the nation of which he was, and the time when he wrote. Yet will these be found not offered to extenuate faults, but to increase admiration. His thoughts are often, nay generally, bold and highly poetical; he follows nature; and his verses are delicately harmonious.

On the death of Henry prince of Wales, in 1612, Drummond wrote an elegy intitled, " Tears on the Death of *Moeliades* ;" a name which that prince had used in all his challenges of martial sport, as the anagram of " *Miles a Deo*." In this poem are lines, according to Denham's terms, as strong, as deep, as gentle, and as full, as any of his or Waller's. The poet laments the fate of the prince, that he died not in some glorious cause of war. " Against the Turk,"

he

he fays, " thou hadft ended thy life and the Chriftian
" war together :

> Or, as brave Bourbon, thou hadft made old Rome,
> Queen of the world, thy triumph and thy tomb.

Of the lamentation of the river Forth,

> And, as fhe rufh'd her Cyclades among,
> She feem'd to plain that heav'n had done her wrong.

Further,

> Tagus did court his love with golden ftreams,
> Rhine with her towns, fair Seine with all fhe claims ;
> But ah, poor lovers ! death did them betray,
> And, unfufpected, made their hopes his prey.

And concludes,

> The virgins to thy tomb will garlands bear
> Of flow'rs, and with each flow'r let fall a tear.
> Moeliades fweet courtly nymphs deplore,
> From Thule to Hydafpes' pearly fhore.

Perhaps there are no lines in Pope, of which the eafy
flow may be more juftly admired than of thofe in his
third paftoral :

> Not bubbling fountains to the thirfty fwain,
> Not balmy fleep to lab'rers faint with pain,
> Not fhow'rs to larks, or funfhine to the bee,
> Are half fo charming as thy fight to me.

When king James, firft after his acceffion to the
Englifh throne, returned to Scotland in 1617, his
arrival was celebrated by every effort of poetical con-
gratulation.

3

gratulation. Upon this occasion Drummond com-
poſed a panegyric, intitled The Wandering Muſes,
or The River of Forth Feaſting, in which are found
four lines apparently imitated by Pope in the above
paſſage, and which do not, in point of harmony,
fall much ſhort of that imitation. He ſays,

> To virgins, flow'rs; to ſunburnt earth, the rain;
> To mariners, fair winds amidſt the main;
> Cool ſhades to pilgrims whom hot glances burn,
> Are not ſo pleaſing as thy bleſt return.

Of theſe two poems of Drummond, it is obſervable,
that the firſt was written in 1612, the laſt in 1617:
The earlieſt piece of Waller is that to the King on
his navy, in 1625. The piece in which Sir John
Denham's greateſt force lies, Cooper's Hill, was not
written till 1640. The harmony of Drummond,
therefore, at a time when thoſe, who are uſually called
the firſt introducers of a ſmooth and poliſhed verſifica-
tion, had not yet begun to write, is an honour to
him that ſhould never be forgotten. Nor is his ex-
cellence half enough praiſed or acknowledged.

DRUMMOND and PETRARCA had this in common,
that each lamented, firſt the cruelty, and then the
loſs of his miſtreſs: ſo that their Sonnets are alike
naturally divided into two parts; thoſe before, and
thoſe after, their ſeveral miſtreſſes deaths. It may
juſtly be doubted that, among all the ſonneteers in
the Engliſh language, any one is to be preferred to
Drummond. He has ſhewn, in ſome of theſe com-
poſitions, nearly the ſpirit of Petrarca himſelf.

The

The feventh fonnet, of the firft part, has much re-
femblance to Sir Henry Wotton's elegant little poem,
on the Queen of Bohemia, *Ye meaner beauties,* &c.
Among Drummond's *Flowers of Sion,* the poem
which begins, *Amidft the azure clear—Of Jordan's
facred ftreams,* eminently diftinguifhes him, whether
he be confidered as a philofopher, or a poet.

THE

P O E M S

O F

WILLIAM DRUMMOND.

P O E M S.

THE FIRST PART.

S O N N E T.

IN my firſt prime, when childiſh humours fed
   My wanton wit, ere I did know the bliſs
Lies in a loving eye, or amorous kiſs,
Or with what ſighs a lover warms his bed ;
By the ſweet Theſpian ſiſters' error led,
I had more mind to read, than lov'd to write,
And ſo to praiſe a perfect red and white ;
But (God wot) knew not what was in my head.
Love ſmil'd to ſee me take ſo great delight,
To turn thoſe antiques of the age of gold,
And that I might more myſteries behold,
He ſet ſo fair a volume to my ſight,
   That I Ephemerides laid aſide,
   Glad on this bluſhing book my death to read.

         SONNET.

SONNET.

I KNOW that all beneath the moon decays,
   And what by mortals in this world is brought
In time's great periods fhall return to nought ;
That faireft ftates have fatal nights and days.
I know that all the Mufes' heavenly lays,
With toil of fprite, which are fo dearly bought,
As idle founds, of few, or none are fought,
That there is nothing lighter than vain praife.
I know frail beauty's like the purple flow'r,
To which one morn oft birth and death affords,
That love a jarring is of mind's accords,
Where fenfe and will bring under reafon's power :
   Know what I lift, this all cannot me move,
   But that, alas, I both muft write and love.

SONNET.

YE who fo curioufly do paint your thoughts,
   Enlight'ning ev'ry line in fuch a guife,
That they feem rather to have fall'n from fkies,
Than of a human hand by mortal draughts :
In one part Sorrow fo tormented lies,
As if his life at ev'ry figh would part ;
Love here blindfolded ftands with bow and dart,
There Hope looks pale, Defpair with flaming eyes :

                                        Of

Of my rude pencil look not for fuch art,
My wit I find too little to devife
So high conceptions to exprefs my fmart ;
And fome fay love is feign'd that's too too wife.
  Thefe troubled words and lines confus'd you find
  Are like unto their model, my fick mind.

S O N N E T.

A H me, and I am now the man whofe mufe
    In happier times was wont to laugh at Love,
And thofe who fuffer'd that blind boy's abufe,
The noble gifts were given them from above.
What metamorphofe ftrange is this I prove ?
Myfelf now fcarce I find myfelf to be,
And think no fable Circe's tyranny,
And all the tales are told of changed Jove :
Virtue hath taught with her philofophy
My mind unto a better courfe to move :
Reafon may chide her full, and oft reprove
Affection's power ; but what is that to me,
  Who ever think, and never think on aught
  But that bright cherubin which thralls my thought?

S O N N E T.

H OW that vaft heaven intitled Firft is roll'd,
     If any glancing towers beyond it be,
And people living in eternity,
Or Effence pure that doth this All uphold :
What motion have thofe fixed fparks of gold,

The wand'ring carbuncles which fhine from high,
By fprites, or bodies crofs-ways in the fky,
If they be turn'd, and mortal things behold :
How fun pofts heaven about, how night's pale
    queen
With borrow'd beams looks on this hanging round ;
What caufe fair Iris hath, and monfters feen
In air's large fields of light, and feas profound,
    Did hold my wand'ring thoughts ; when thy
      fweet eye
    Bade me leave all, and only think on thee.

SONNET.

FAIR is my yoke, though grievous be my pains,
    Sweet are my wounds, although they deeply
      fmart,
My bit is gold, though fhorten'd be the reins,
My bondage brave, though I may not depart ;
Although I burn, the fire which doth impart
Thofe flames, fo fweet reviving force contains,
That like Arabia's bird my wafted heart,
Made quick by death, more lively ftill remains.
I joy, though oft my waking eyes fpend tears,
I never want delight, even when I groan,
Beft 'companied when moft I am alone,
A heaven of hopes I have midft hells of fears :
    Thus every way contentment ftrange I find,
    But moft in her rare beauty, my rare mind.

SONNET.

SONNET.

VAUNT not, fair heavens, of your two glo-
    rious lights,
Which though moſt bright, yet ſee not when they
    ſhine,
And ſhining, cannot ſhow their beams divine
Both in one place, but part by days and nights.
Earth vaunt not of thoſe treaſures ye enſhrine,
Held only dear, becauſe hid from our ſights,
Your pure and burniſh'd gold, your diamonds fine,
Snow-paſſing ivory that the eye delights.
Nor ſeas, of thoſe dear wares are in you found
Vaunt not, rich pearl, red coral, which do ſtir
A fond deſire in fools to plunge your ground ;
'Theſe all more fair are to be had in her :
    Pearl, ivory, coral, diamond, ſuns, gold,
    Teeth, neck, lips, heart, eyes, hair are to behold.

SONNET.

WHEN Nature now had wonderfully wrought
    All Auriſtella's parts, except her eyes,
To make thoſe twins two lamps in beauty's ſkies,
She counſel of her ſtarry ſenate ſought.
Mars and Apollo firſt did her adviſe,
To wrap in colour black thoſe comets bright,
That Love him ſo might ſoberly diſguiſe,
And unperceived wound at every ſight.

Chaſte

Chaſte Phœbe ſpake for pureſt azure dyes ;
But Jove and Venus green about the light,
To frame thought beſt, as bringing moſt delight,
That to pin'd hearts hope might for aye ariſe :
   Nature, all ſaid, a paradiſe of green
   There plac'd, to make all love which have them
     ſeen.

SONNET.

NOW while the Night her ſable veil hath ſpread,
   And ſilently her reſty coach doth roll,
Rouzing with her from Thetis' azure bed,
'Thoſe ſtarry nymphs which dance about the pole ;
While Cynthia, in pureſt cypreſs clad,
'The Latmian ſhepherd in a trance deſcries,
And looking pale from height of all the ſkies,
She dyes her beauties in a bluſhing red ;
While ſleep, in triumph, cloſed hath all eyes,
And birds and beaſts a ſilence ſweet do keep,
And Proteus' monſtrous people in the deep,
'The winds and waves, huſh'd up, to reſt entice ;
   I wake, I turn, I weep oppreſs'd with pain,
   Perplex'd in the meanders of my brain.

SONNET.

SLEEP, Silence' child, ſweet father of ſoft reſt,
   Prince whoſe approach peace to all mortals
     brings,
Indifferent hoſt to ſhepherds and to kings,
                          Sole

Sole comforter of minds which are opprefs'd ;
Lo, by thy charming rod, all breathing things
Lie flumb'ring, with forgetfulnefs poffefs'd,
And yet o'er me to fpread thy drowfy wings
Thou fpar'ft, alas ! who cannot be thy gueft.
Since I am thine, O come, but with that face
To inward light, which thou art wont to fhew,
With feigned folace eafe a true felt woe ;
Or if, deaf god, thou do deny that grace,
  Come as thou wilt, and what thou wilt bequeath,
  I long to kifs the image of my death.

S O N N E T.

FAIR Moon, who with thy cold and filver fhine
    Mak'ft fweet the horror of the dreadful night,
Delighting the weak eye with fmiles divine,
Which Phœbus dazzles with his too much light ;
Bright queen of the firft heaven, if in thy fhrine
By turning oft, and Heaven's eternal might,
Thou haft not yet that once fweet fire of thine,
Endemion, forgot, and lovers' plight ;
If caufe-like thine may pity breed in thee,
And pity fomewhat elfe to it obtain,
Since thou haft power of dreams as well as he
That holds the golden rod and moral chain ;
  Now while fhe fleeps, in doleful guife her fhow
  Thefe tears, and the black map of all my woe.

SONNET.

SONNET.

L AMP of heaven's cryſtal hall that brings the
　　hours,
Eye-dazzler, who makes the ugly night
At thy approach fly to her ſlumb'ry bowers,
And fills the world with wonder and delight;
Life of all lives, death-giver by thy flight
To the ſouth pole from theſe ſix ſigns of ours,
Goldſmith of all the ſtars, with ſilver bright
Who moon enamels, Apelles of the flowers:
Ah from thoſe wat'ry plains thy golden head
Raiſe up, and bring the ſo long ling'ring morn;
A grave, nay hell, I find become this bed,
This bed ſo grievouſly where I am torn:
　　But wo is me though thou now brought the day,
　　Day ſhall but ſerve more ſorrows to diſplay.

SONG.

I T was the time when to our northern pole
　The brighteſt lamp of heaven begins to roll,
When Earth more wanton in new robes appeareth,
And ſcorning ſkies her flowers in rainbows beareth,

On

On which the air moift diamonds doth bequeath,
Which quake to feel the kiffing Zephyrs breath;
When birds from fhady groves their love forth
      warble,
And fea-like heaven looks like fmootheft marble,
When I in fimple courfe, free from all cares
Far from the muddy world's enflaving fnares,
By Ora's flow'ry banks alone did wander;
Ora, that fports her like to old Meander,
A flood more worthy fame and lafting praife
Than that fo high which Phaeton's fall did raife;
By whofe pure moving glafs the milk-white lilies
Do drefs their treffes and the daffodilies;
Where Ora with a wood is crown'd about,
And (feems) forgets the way how to come out,
A place there is, where a delicious fountain
Springs from the fwelling breaft of a proud mountain,
Whofe falling ftreams the quiet caverns wound,
And make the echoes fhrill refound that found.
The laurel there the fhining channel graces,
The palm her love with long ftretch'd arms embraces,
The poplar fpreads her branches to the fky,
And hides from fight that azure canopy.
The ftreams the trees, the trees their leaves ftill
      nourifh,
That place grave Winter finds not without flourifh.
If living eyes Elyfian fields could fee,
This little Arden might Elyfium be.
Oft did Diana there herfelf repofe,
And Mars the Acidalian queen enclofe.

                 The

The nymphs oft here their baſkets bring with
　　flow'rs,
And anadems weave for their paramours ;
The ſatyrs in thoſe ſhades are heard to languiſh,
And make the ſhepherds partners of their anguiſh,
The ſhepherds who in barks of tender trees
Do grave their loves, diſdains, and jealouſies ;
Which Phillis, when thereby her flocks ſhe feedeth,
With pity now, anon with laughter readeth.
　　Near to this place when Sun in midſt of day
In higheſt top of heaven his coach did ſtay,
And (as adviſing) on his career glanced
As all along, that morn he had advanced,
His panting ſteeds along thoſe fields of light,
Moſt princely looking from that glorious height :
When moſt the graſhoppers are heard in meadows,
And loftieſt pines or ſmall, or have no ſhadows :
It was my hap, O woful hap ! to bide
Where thickeſt ſhades me from all rays did hide,
In a fair arbour, 'twas ſome ſylvan's chamber,
Whoſe ceiling ſpread was with the locks of amber
Of new bloom'd ſycamores, floor wrought with
　　flow'rs,
More ſweet and rich than thoſe in princes' bow'rs.
Here Adon bluſh'd, and Clitia all amazed
Look'd pale, with him who in the fountain gazed ;
The amaranthus ſmil'd, and that ſweet boy
Which ſometime was the god of Delos' joy :
The brave carnation, ſpeckled pink here ſhin'd,
The violet her fainting head declin'd
　　　　　　　　　　　　　Beneath

Beneath a fleepy chafbow, all of gold
The marigold her leaves did here unfold.
    Now while that, ravifh'd with delight and wonder,
Half in a trance I lay thofe arches under,
The feafon, filence, place, began t' entice,
Eyes' drowfy lids to bring night on their fkies,
Which foftly having ftolen themfelves together
(Like evening clouds) me plac'd I wot not whi-
        ther.
As cowards leave the fort which they fhould keep,
My fenfes one by one gave place to Sleep,
Who follow'd with a troop of golden flumbers,
Thruft from my quiet brain all bafe encumbers,
And thrice me touching with his rod of gold,
A heaven of vifions in my temples roll'd,
To countervail thofe pleafures were bereft me,
Thus in his filent prifon clos'd-he left me.
    Methought through all the neighbour woods a
        noife
Of chorifters, more fweet than lute or voice,
(For thofe harmonious founds to Jove are given
By the fwift touches of the nine-ftring'd heaven,
Such airs, and nothing elfe) did wound mine ear,
No foul but would become all ear to hear :
And whilft I lift'ning lay, O lovely wonder !
I faw a pleafant myrtle cleave afunder ;
A myrtle great with birth, from whofe rent womb
Three naked nymphs more white than fnow forth
        come.

                                                For

For nymphs they feem'd ; about their heavenly faces
In waves of gold floated their curling treffes ;
About their arms, their arms more white than milk,
They blufhing armlets wore of crimfon filk,
The goddeffes were fuch that by Scamander
Appeared to the Phrygian Alexander :
Aglaia and her fifters fuch perchance
Be when about fome facred fpring they dance,
But fcarce the grove their naked beauties graced,
And on the verdure had each other traced,
When to the flood they ran, the flood in robes
Of curling cryftal their breafts' ivory globes
Did all about encircle, yet took pleafure
To fhew white fnows throughout her liquid azure.

    Look how Prometheus' man, when heavenly fire
Firft gave him breath, day's Brandon did admire,
And wonder'd at this world's amph'theatre :
So gaz'd I on thofe new guefts of the water.
All three were fair, yet one excell'd as far
The reft as Phœbus doth the Cyprian ftar,
Or diamonds, fmall gems, or gems do other,
Or pearls that fhining fhell is call'd their mother.

    Her hair, more bright than are the morning's
      beams,
Hung in a golden fhower above the ftreams,
And dangling fought her forehead for to cover,
Which feen did ftraight a fky of milk difcover,
With two fair brows, Love's bows, which never
      bend
But that a golden arrow forth they fend ;

                    Beneath

Beneath the which two burning planets glancing
  Flaſh'd flames of love, for Love there ſtill is
    dancing.
Her either cheek reſembled bluſhing morn,
Or roſes gules in field of lilies borne ;
'Twixt which an ivory wall ſo fair is raiſed,
That it is but abaſed when it's praiſed.
Her lips like rows of coral ſoft did ſwell,
And th' one like th' other only doth excel :
The Tyrian fiſh looks pale, pale look the roſes,
The rubies pale, when mouth ſweet cherry cloſes.
Her chin like ſilver Phœbe did appear
Dark in the midſt to make the reſt more clear :
Her neck ſeem'd fram'd by curious Phidias maſter,
Moſt ſmooth, moſt white, a piece of alabaſter.
Two foaming billows flow'd upon her breaſt,
Which did their tops with coral red increſt :
There all about as brooks them ſport at leiſure,
With circling branches veins did ſwell in azure :
Within thoſe crooks are only found thoſe iſles
Which fortunate the dreaming old world ſtiles.
The reſt the ſtreams did hide, but as a lily
Sunk in a cryſtal's fair tranſparent belly.
   I who yet human weakneſs did not know,
(For yet I had not felt that archer's bow,
Nor could I think that from the coldeſt water
The winged youngling burning flames could ſcatter)
On every part my vagabonding ſight
Did caſt, and drown mine eyes in ſweet delight.
                O wondrous

O wondrous thing (faid I) that beauty 's nam'd !
Now I perceive I heretofore have dream'd,
And never found in all my flying days
Joy unto this, which only merits praife.
My pleafures have been pains, my comforts croffes,
My treafure poverty, my gains but loffes.
O precious fight ! which none doth elfe defcry
Except the burning fun, and quivering I.
And yet, O dear-bought fight ! O would for ever
I might enjoy you, or had joy'd you never !
O happy flood ! if fo ye might abide,
Yet ever glory of this moment's pride,
Adjure your rillets all for to behold her,
And in their cryflal arms to come and fold her :
And fince ye may not long this blifs embrace,
Draw thoufand portraits of her on your face,
Portraits which in my heart be more apparent,
If like to yours my breaft but were tranfparent.
O that I were, while fhe doth in you play,
A dolphin to tranfport her to the fea !
To none of all thofe gods I would her render,
From Thule to Inde though I fhould with her
    wander.
Oh ! what is this ? the more I fix mine eye,
Mine eye the more new wonders doth efpy,
The more I fpy, the more in uncouth fafhion
My foul is ravifh'd in a pleafant paffion.
    But look not eyes—As more I would have faid,
A found of rattling wheels me all difmay'd,
                    And

And with the found forth from the trembling bufhes,
With ftorm-like courfe a fumptuous chariot rufhes,
A chariot all of gold, the wheels were gold,
The nails, and axle gold on which it roll'd :
The upmoft part a fcarlet veil did cover,
More rich than Danae's lap fpread with her lover.
In midft of it in a triumphant chair,
A lady fate miraculoufly fair,
Whofe penfive countenance, and looks of honour,
Do more allure the mind that thinketh on her,
Than the moft wanton face, and amorous eyes,
That Amathus or flow'ry Paphos fees ;
A crew of virgins made a ring about her,
The diamond fhe, they feem the gold without her.
Such Thetis is, when to the billows roar
With mermaids nice fhe danceth on the fhore:
So in a fable night, the fun's bright fifter
Among the leffer twinkling lights doth glifter.
Fair yokes of ermilines, whofe colours pafs
The whiteft fnows on aged Grampius' face,
More fwift than Venus' birds this chariot guided
To the aftonifh'd bank, where as it bided :
But long it did not bide, when poor thofe ftreams
(Ah me !) it made, tranfporting thofe rich gems,
And by that burthen lighter, fwiftly drived
Till (as methought) it at a tow'r arrived :
  Upon a rock of cryftal fhining clear
With diamonds wrought this caftle did appear,
Whofe rifing fpires of gold fo high them reared,
That, Atlas-like, it feem'd the heaven they beared.

C   Am dft

Amidft which heights on arches did arife
(Arches which gilt flames brandifh to the fkies)
Of fparkling topazes, proud, gorgeous, ample,
(Like to a little heaven) a facred temple.
The walls no windows have, nay all the wall
Is but one window, night there doth not fall
More when the fun to weftern worlds declineth,
Than in our zenith when at noon he fhineth.
Two flaming hills the paffage ftrait defend
Which to this radiant building doth afcend,
Upon whofe arching tops on a pilafter
A port ftands open, rais'd in love's difafter;
For none that narrow bridge and gate can pafs,
Who have their faces feen in Venus' glafs.
If thofe within but to come forth do venture,
That ftately place again they never enter.
The precinct's ftrengthen'd with a ditch of fears,
In which doth fwell a lake of inky years
Of madding lovers, who abide their moaning,
And thicken e'en the air with piteous groaning.
This hold to brave the fkies the Deft'nies fram'd,
And then the fort of chaftity is nam'd.
The queen of the third heaven once, to appal it,
The god of Thrace here brought, who could not
      thrall it;
For which he vow'd ne'er arms more to put on,
And on Riphean hills was heard to groan.
Here Pfyche's lover hurls his darts at randon,
Which all for nought him ferve, as doth his brandon.

                            What

What grievous agony did invade my mind,
When in that place my hope I faw confin'd,
Where with high tow'ring thoughts I only reach'd
     her !
Which did burn up their wings when they approach'd
     her.
Methought I fat me by a cyprefs fhade,
And night and day the hyacinth there read;
And that bewailing nightingales did borrow
Plaints of my plaint, and forrows of my forrow.
My food was wormwood, mine own tears my drink,
My reft, on death and fad mifhaps to think.
And for fuch thoughts to have my heart enlarged,
And eafe mine eyes with briny tribute charged,
Over a brook I laid my pining face :
But then the brook, as griev'd at my difgrace,
A face me fhew'd fo pin'd, fad, overclouded,
That at the fight afraid mine eyes them fhrouded.
This is thy guerdon, Love, this is the game,
In end which to thy fervants doth remain.
More would I fay ; when fear made fleep to leave me,
And of thofe fatal fhadows did bereave me ;
But ah, alas ! inftead to dream of love,
And woes, I now them in effect did prove :
For what into my troubled brain was painted,
Awak'd I found that time and place prefented.

SONNET.

SONNET.

A H burning thoughts, now let me take fome reft,
And your tumultuous broils awhile appeafe :
Is't not enough, ftars, fortune, love moleft
Me all at once, but ye muft too difpleafe ?
Let hope (though falfe) yet lodge within my breaft,
My high attempt (though dangerous) yet praife :
What though I trace not right heaven's fteepy ways,
It doth fuffice my fall fhall make me bleft.
I do not doat on days, I fear not death,
So that my life be good, I wifh't not long ;
Let me renown'd live from the worldly throng,
And when Heaven lifts, recal this borrow'd breath.
   Men but like vifions are, time all doth claim,
   He lives who dies to win a lafting name.

SONNET.

T HAT learned Grecian who did fo excel
In knowledge paffing fenfe, that he is nam'd
Of all the after world Divine, doth tell
That all the time when firft our fouls are fram'd,
Ere in thefe manfions blind they come to dwell,
They live bright rays of that Eternal Light,
And others fee, know, love, in heaven's great height,
Not toil'd with aught 'gainft reafon to rebel.

                                        It

It is moſt true, for ſtraight at the firſt ſight
My mind me told that in ſome other place
It elſewhere ſaw th' idea of that face,
And lov'd a love of heavenly pure delight.
   What wonder now I feel ſo fair a flame,
   Since I her lov'd ere on this earth ſhe came ?

S O N N E T.

NOR Arne, nor Mincius, nor ſtately Tiber,
   Sebethus, nor the flood into whoſe ſtreams
He fell who burnt the world with borrow'd beams,
Gold-rolling Tagus, Munda, famous Iber,
Sorgue, Rhone, Loire, Garron, nor proud-banked
     Seine,
Peneus, Phaſis, Xanthus, humble Ladon,
Nor ſhe whoſe nymphs excel her loved Adon,
Fair Tameſis, nor Iſter large, nor Rhine,
Euphrates, Tigris, Indus, Hermus, Gange,
Pearly Hydaſpes, ſerpent-like Meander,
The flood which robbed Hero of Leander,
Nile that ſo far his hidden head doth range,
   Have ever had ſo rare a cauſe of praiſe,
   As Ora where this northern phœnix ſtays.

C 3   SONNET.

SONNET.

TO bear my plaints, fair river cryftalline,
    Thou in a filent flumber feem'ft to ftay ;
Delicious flowers, lily and columbine,
Ye bow your heads when I my woes difplay ;
Forefts, in you the myrtle, palm and bay,
Have had compaffion, lift'ning to my groans ;
The winds with fighs have folemniz'd my moans
'Mong leaves, which whifper'd what they could not
      fay ;
The caves, the rocks, the hills, the fylvans'
      thrones,
(As if even pity did in them appear)
Have at my forrow rent their ruthlefs ftones :
Each thing I find hath fenfe except my dear,
    Who doth not think I love, or will not know
    My grief, perchance delighting in my woe.

SONNET.

SWEET brook, in whofe clear cryftal I my eyes
    Have oft feen great in labour of their tears ;
Enamell'd bank, whofe fhining gravel bears
Thefe fad characters of my miferies ;
High woods, whofe mountain-tops menace the fpheres,
Wild citizens, Amphions of the trees,
You gloomy groves at hotteft noons which freeze,
Elyfian fhades which Phœbus never clears ;

                    Vaft

Vaſt ſolitary mountains, pleaſant plains,
Embroider'd meads that ocean-ways you reach;
Hills, dales, ſprings, all whom my ſad cry con-
    ſtrains
To take part of my plaints, and learn woe's ſpeech,
    Will that remorſeleſs fair e'er pity ſhow ?
    Of grace now anſwer if ye aught know : No.

SONNET.

WITH flaming horns the bull now brings the
    year,
Melt do the mountains, rolling floods of ſnow,
The ſilver rivers in ſmooth channels flow,
The late bare woods green anadems do wear ;
The nightingale, forgetting winter's woe,
Calls up the lazy morn her notes to hear ;
Spread are thoſe flow'rs which names of princes bear,
Some red, ſome azure, white, and golden grow.
Here lows a heifer, there bewailing ſtrays
A harmleſs lamb, not far a ſtag rebounds ;
The ſhepherds ſing to grazing flocks ſweet lays,
And all about the echoing air reſounds.
    Hills, dales, woods, floods, ev'ry thing doth
        change,
    But ſhe in rigour, I in love am ſtrange.

C 4

SONNET.

SONNET.

THAT I fo flenderly fet forth my mind,
   Writing I know not what in ragged rhymes,
O'ercharg'd with brafs in thefe fo golden times,
When others tow'r fo high, I'm left behind :
I crave not Phœbus leave his facred cell,
To bind my brows with frefh Aonian bays ;
But leav 't to thofe who tuning fweeteft lays
By Tempe fit, or Aganippe's well ;
Nor yet to Venus' tree do I afpire,
Since fhe for whom I might affect that praife,
My beft attempts with cruel words gainfays,
And I feek not that others me admire.
   Of weeping myrrh the crown is which I crave,
   With a fad cyprefs to adorn my grave.

MADRIGAL.

WHEN as fhe fmiles I find
   More light before mine eyes,
Than when the fun from Inde
Brings to our world a flow'ry paradife :
But when fhe gently weeps,
And pours forth pearly fhowers,
On cheeks fair blufhing flowers,
A fweet melancholy my fenfes keeps ;

Both

Both feed fo my difeafe,
So much both do me pleafe,
That oft I doubt, which more my heart doth burn,
Love to behold her fmile, or pity mourn.

S O N N E T.

MY tears may well Numidian lions tame,
    And pity breed into the hardeft heart
That ever Pyrrha did to maid impart,
When fhe them firft of blufhing rocks did frame.
Ah, eyes which only ferve to 'wail my fmart,
How long will you my inward woes proclaim ?
May 't not fuffice you bear a weeping part
All night, at day but you muft do the fame ?
Ceafe, idle fighs, to fpend your ftorms in vain,
And thefe fweet filent thickets to moleft,
Contain you in the prifon of my breaft,
You do not eafe but aggravate my pain ;
    Or if burft forth you muft, that tempeft move
    In fight of her whom I fo dearly love.

S O N N E T.

YOU reftlefs feas appeafe your roaring waves,
    And you who raife huge mountains in that
        plain,
Air's trumpeters, your hideous founds contain,
And liften to the plaints my grief doth caufe.
                                        Eternal

Eternal lights ! though adamantine laws
Of deftinies to move ftill you ordain,
Turn hither, all your eyes, your axles paufe,
And wonder at the torments I fuftain,
Sad earth, if thou, made dull by my difgrace,
Be not as fenfelefs, afk thofe powers above
Why they fo croft a wretch brought on thy face,
Fram'd for mifhap, the anchorite of love ;
    And bid them (that no more Ætnas may burn)
    To Erimanth' or Rhodope me turn.

.   S O N N E T.

IF croft with all mifhaps be my poor life,
  If one fhort day I never fpent in mirth,
If my fp'rit with itfelf holds lafting ftrife,
If forrows death is but new forrows birth ;
If this vain world be but a mournful ftage,
Where flave-born man plays to the laughing ftars,
If youth be tofs'd with love, with weaknefs age,
If knowledge ferves to hold our thoughts in wars,
If time can clofe the hundred mouths of Fame,
And make what's long fince paft, like that's to be,
If virtue only be an idle name,
If being born I was but born to die ;
    Why feek I to prolong thefe loathfome days ?
    The faireft rofe in fhorteft time decays.

SONNET.

S O N N E T.

ALL other beauties howfoe'er they fhine
In hairs more bright than is the golden ore,
Or cheeks more fair than faireft eglantine,
Or hands like hers that comes the fun before :
Match'd with that heavenly hue, and fhape divine,
With thofe dear ftars which my weak thoughts adore,
Look but as fhadows, or if they be more,
It is in this, that they are like to thine.
Who fees thofe eyes, their force that doth not prove ;
Who gazeth on the dimple of that chin,
And finds not Venus' fon entrench'd therein,
Or hath not fenfe, or knows not what is love.
To fee thee had Narciffus had the grace,
He would have died with wond'ring on thy face.

S E X T A I N.

THE heaven doth not contain fo many ftars,
Nor levell'd lie fo many leaves in woods,
When Autumn and cold Boreas found their wars;
So many waves have not the ocean floods,
As my torn mind hath torments all the night,
And heart fpends fighs, when Phœbus brings the
light.

Why

Why was I made a partner of the light,
Who croft in birth, by bad afpect of ftars,
Have never fince had happy day or night?
Why was not I a liver in the woods,
Or citizen of Thetis' cryftal floods,
But fram'd a man for Love and Fortune's wars?

I look each day when death fhould end the wars,
Uncivil wars 'twixt fenfe and reafon's light;
My pains I count to mountains, meads and floods,
And of my forrow partners make the ftars;
All defolate I haunt the fearful woods,
When I fhould give myfelf to reft at night.

With watchful eyes I ne'er behold the night,
Mother of peace, (but ah to me of wars)
And Cynthia queen-like fhining through the woods,
But ftraight thofe lamps come in my thought whofe
        light
My judgment dazzled, paffing brighteft ftars,
And then my eyes in-ifle themfelves with floods.

Turn to the fprings again firft fhall the floods,
Clear fhall the fun the fad and gloomy night,
To dance about the pole ceafe fhall the ftars,
The elements renew their ancient wars
Shall firft, and be depriv'd of place and light,
Ere I find reft in city, fields, or woods.

End

End thefe my days ye inmates of the woods,
Take this my life ye deep and raging floods;
Sun never rife to clear me with thy light,
Horror and darknefs keep a lafting night,
Confume me, care, with thy inteftine wars,
And ftay your influence o'er me ye bright ftars.

In vain the ftars, th'inhabitants o'th' woods,
Care, horror, wars I call, and raging floods,
For all have fworn no night fhall dim my fight.

S O N N E T.

O SACRED blufh empurpling cheeks, pure fkies
With crimfon wings which fpread thee like the
morn ;
O bafhful look fent from thofe fhining eyes,
Which though flid down on earth doth heaven adorn ;
O tongue, in which moft lufcious nectar lies,
That can at once both blefs and make forlorn ;
Dear coral lip which beauty beautifies,
That trembling ftood before her words were borne ;
And you her words ; words ? no, but golden chains
Which did inflave my ears, enfnare my foul,
Wife image of her mind, mind that contains
A power all power of fenfes to controul :
    So fweetly you from love diffuade do me,
    That I love more, if more my love can be.

SONNET.

SONNET.

SOUND hoarſe, ſad lute, true witneſs of my woe,
  And ſtrive no more to eaſe ſelf-choſen pain
With ſoul-enchanting ſounds, your accents ſtrain
Unto thoſe tears inceſſantly which flow.
Sad treble weep, and you dull baſſes ſhew
Your maſter's ſorrow in a doleful ſtrain ;
Let never joyful hand upon you go,
Nor concert keep but when you do complain.
Fly Phœbus' rays, abhor the irkſome light ;
Woods' ſolitary ſhades for thee are beſt,
Or the black horrors of the blackeſt night,
When all the world ſave thou and I do reſt :
  Then ſound, ſad lute, and bear a mourning part,
  Thou hell canſt move, though not a woman's heart.

SONNET.

IN vain I haunt the cold and ſilver ſprings,
  To quench the fever burning in my veins,
In vain (love's pilgrim) mountains, dales and plains
I over-run, vain help long abſence brings.
In vain, my friends, your counſel me conſtrains
To fly, and place my thoughts on other things ;
Ah, like the bird that fir'd hath her wings,
The more I move the greater are my pains.

Deſire

Defire, (alas) defire, a Zeuxis new,
From th' orient borrowing gold, from weftern fkies
Heavenly cinnabar fets before my eyes
In every place, her hair, fweet look, and hue :
  That fly, run, reft I, all doth prove but vain,
  My life lies in thofe eyes which have me flain.

SONNET.

SLIDE foft, fair Forth, and make a cryftal plain,
  Cut your white locks, and on your foamy face
Let not a wrinkle be, when you embrace
The boat that earth's perfections doth contain.
Winds wonder, and through wond'ring hold your
        pace ;
Or if that ye your hearts cannot reftrain
From fending fighs, feeling a lover's cafe,
Sigh, and in her fair hair yourfelves enchain.
Or take thefe fighs which abfence makes arife
From my oppreffed breaft, and fill the fails,
Or fome fweet breath new brought from paradife :
The floods do fmile, love o'er the winds prevails,
  And yet huge waves arife ; the caufe is this,
  The ocean ftrives with Forth the boat to kifs.

SONNET.

TRUST not, fweet foul, thofe curled waves of gold
  With gentle tides that on your temples flow,
Nor temples fpread with flakes of virgin fnow,
Nor fnow of cheeks with Tyrian grain enroll'd ;

Truft

Truft not thofe fhining lights which wrought my wce,
When firft I did their azure rays behold,
Nor voice, whofe founds more ftrange effects do fhow
Than of the Thracian harper have been told :
Look to this dying lily, fading rofe,
Dark hyacinth, of late whofe blufhing beams
Made all the neighbouring herbs and grafs rejoice,
And think how little is 'twixt life's extremes;
 The cruel tyrant that did kill thofe flow'rs
 Shall once, ah me! not fpare that fpring of yours.

S O N N E T. *

IN Mind's pure glafs when I myfelf behold,
  And lively fee how my beft days are fpent,
What clouds of care above my head are roll'd,
What coming ill, which I cannot prevent ;
My courfe begun I wearied do repent,
And would embrace what reafon oft hath told,
But fcarce thus think I, when love hath controll'd
All the beft reafons reafon could invent.
Though fure I know my labour's end is grief,
The more I ftrive that I the more fhall pine,
That only death fhall be my laft relief :
Yet when I think upon that face divine,
 Like one with arrow fhot, in laughter's place,
 Maugre my heart, I joy in my difgrace.

SONNET.

SONNET.

D EAR chorifter, who from thofe fhadows fends,
 Ere that the blufhing morn dare fhew her light,
Such fad lamenting ftrains, that night attends
(Become all ear), ftars ftay to hear thy plight ;
If one whofe grief even reach of thought tranfcends,
Who ne'er (not in a dream) did tafte delight,
May thee importune who like cafe pretends,
And feems to joy in woe, in woe's defpite.;
Tell me (fo may thou fortune milder try,
And long long fing !) for what thou thus complains,
Since winter's gone, and fun in dappled fky
Enamour'd fmiles on woods and flow'ry plains?
 The bird, as if my queftions did her move,
 With trembling wings figh'd forth, I love, I love.

SONNET.

O CRUEL beauty, fweetnefs inhumane,
 That night and day contends with my defire,
And feeks my hope to kill, not quench my fire,
By death, not balm to eafe my pleafant pain !
Though ye my thoughts tread down which would
  afpire,
And bound my blifs, do not, alas! difdain
That I your matchlefs worth and grace admire,
And for their caufe thefe torments fharp fuftain.

D

Let

Let great Empedocles vaunt of his death
Found in the midſt of thoſe Sicilian flames,
And Phaeton that Heaven him reft of breath,
And Dædal's ſon who nam'd the Samian ſtreams :
　Their haps I not envy ; my praiſe ſhall be,
　That the moſt fair that lives mov'd me to die.

S O N N E T.

THE Hyperborean hills, Ceraunus' ſnow,
　Or Arimaſpus (cruel) firſt thee bred ;
The Caſpian tigers with their milk thee fed,
And Fauns did human blood on thee beſtow.
Fierce Orithyas' lover in thy bed
Thee lull'd aſleep, where he enrag'd doth blow ;
Thou didſt not drink the floods which here do flow,
But tears, or thoſe by icy Tanais' head.
Sith thou diſdains my love, neglects my grief,
Laughs at my groans, and ſtill affects my death :
Of thee nor Heaven I'll ſeek no more relief,
Nor longer entertain this loathſome breath ;
　But yield unto my ſtars, that thou may'ſt prove
　What loſs thou hadſt in loſing ſuch a love.

S O N G.

PHŒBUS, ariſe,
　And paint the ſable ſkies
With azure, white, and red :
Rouſe Memnon's mother from her Tython's bed,

　　　　　　　　　　　That

That she thy career may with roses spread,
The nightingales thy coming each where sing,
Make an eternal spring.
Give life to this dark world which lieth dead.
Spread forth thy golden hair
In larger locks than thou wast wont before,
And emperor-like decore
With diadem of pearl thy temples fair:
Chafe hence the ugly night,
Which serves but to make dear thy glorious light.
This is that happy morn,
That day, long-wished day,
Of all my life so dark,
(If cruel stars have not my ruin sworn,
And Fates my hopes betray)
Which (purely white) deserves
An everlasting diamond should it mark.
This is the morn should bring unto this grove
My love, to hear, and recompense my love.
Fair king, who all preserves,
But shew thy blushing beams,
And thou two sweeter eyes
Shalt see than those which by Peneus' streams
Did once thy heart surprise:
Nay, suns which shine as clear
As thou when two thou didst to Rome appear.
Now, Flora, deck thyself in fairest guise.
If that ye winds would hear
A voice surpassing far Amphion's lyre,

D 2

Your

Your furious chiding ſtay,
Let Zephyr only breathe,
And with her treſſes play,
Kiſſing ſometimes thoſe purple ports of death.
The winds all ſilent are,
And Phœbus in his chair ·
Enſaffroning ſea and air,
Makes vaniſh every ſtar :
Night like a drunkard reels
Beyond the hills, to ſhun his flaming wheels.
The fields with flow'rs are deck'd in every hue,
The clouds with orient gold ſpangle their blue :
   Here is the pleaſant place,
   And nothing wanting is, ſave ſhe, alas !

S O N N E T.

WHO hath not ſeen into her ſaffron bed
     The morning's goddeſs mildly her repoſe,
Or her of whoſe pure blood firſt ſprang the roſe
Lull'd in a ſlumber by a myrtle ſhade ?
Who hath not ſeen that ſleeping white and red
Makes Phœbe look ſo pale, which ſhe did cloſe
In that Ionian hill, to eaſe her woes,
Which only lives by her dear kiſſes fed ?
Come but and ſee my lady ſweetly ſleep,
The ſighing rubies of thoſe heavenly lips,
The Cupids which breaſts golden apples keep,
Thoſe eyes which ſhine in midſt of their eclipſe :
   And he them all ſhall ſee, perhaps and prove
   She waking but perſuades, now forceth love.
SONNET.

SONNET.

SEE Cytherea's birds, that milk-white pair
  On yonder leafy myrtle-tree which groan,
And waken with their kiffes in the air
Th'enamour'd zephyrs murmuring one by one ;
If thou but fenfe hadft like Pygmalion's ftone,
Or hadft not feen Medufa's fnaky hair,
Love's leffons thou might'ft learn ; and learn, fweet
     fair,
To fummer's heat ere that thy fpring be grown.
And if thofe kiffing lovers feem but cold,
Look how that elm this ivy doth embrace,
And binds and clafps with many a wanton fold,
And, courting fleep, o'erfhadows all the place ;
  Nay, feems to fay, Dear tree, we fhall not part,
  In fign whereof, lo, in each leaf a heart !

SONNET.

THE fun is fair when he with crimfon crown,
  And flaming rubies, leaves his eaftern bed ;
Fair is Thaumantias in her cryftal gown,
When clouds engemm'd fhew azure, green, and red.
To weftern worlds when wearied day goes down,
And from heaven's windows each ftar fhews her head,
Earth's filent daughter, Night, is fair though brown ;
Fair is the moon, though in love's livery clad.

D 3

The

The fpring is fair when it doth paint April,
Fair are the meads, the woods, the floods are fair ;
Fair looketh Ceres with her yellow hair,
And apple's-queen when rofe-cheek'd fhe doth fmile.
   That heaven, and earth, and feas are fair, is true,
   Yet true, that all not pleafe fo much as you.

MADRIGAL.

L IKE the Idalian queen
  Her hair about her eyne,
And neck, on breafts ripe apples to be feen,
At firft glance of the morn
In Cyprus' gardens gathering thofe fair flowers
Which of her blood were borne,
I faw, but fainting faw my paramours.
The Graces naked danc'd about the place,
The winds and trees amaz'd
With filence on her gaz'd,
The flowers did fmile like thofe upon her face ;
And as their afpin ftalks thofe fingers bind,
That fhe might read my cafe,
I wifh'd to be a hyacinth in her hand.

SONNET.

T HEN is fhe gone ? O fool and coward I !
  O good occafion loft, ne'er to be found !
What fatal chains have my dull fenfes bound,
When beft they might, that did not fortune try ?

                 Here

Here is the fainting grafs where fhe did lie,
With rofes here fhe ftellified the ground ;
She fix'd her eyes on this yet fmiling pond,
Nor time, nor place feem'd aught for to deny.
Too long, too long, Refpect I do embrace
Your counfel full of threats and fharp difdain.
Difdain in her fweet heart can have no place,
And though come there, muft ftraight retire again :
    Henceforth, Refpect, farewel! I've heard it told,
    Who lives in love can never be too bold.

S O N N E T.

WHAT cruel ftar into this world me brought ?
      What gloomy day did dawn to give me light ?
What unkind hand to nurfe me (orphan) fought,
And would not leave me in eternal night ?
What thing fo dear as I hath effence bought ?
The elements dry, humid, heavy, light,
The fmalleft living things which Nature wrought
Be freed of woe if they have fmall delight.
Ah only I abandon'd to defpair,
Nail'd to my torments in pale Horror's fhade,
Like wand'ring clouds fee all my comforts fled,
And ill on ill with hours my life impair:
    The Heavens and Fortune, which were wont to
      turn,
    Stay in one manfion fix'd to caufe me mourn.

SONNET.

DEAR eye, which deign'ft on this fad monument,
 The fable fcroll of my mifhaps to view,   •
Though it with mourning Mufes' tears be fpent,
And darkly drawn, which is not feign'd, but true ;
If thou not dazzled with a heavenly hue,
And comely feature, didft not yet lament,
But happy lives unto thyfelf content,
O let not Love thee to his laws fubdue ;
Look on the woeful fhipwreck of my youth,
And let my ruins thee for beacon ferve,
To fhun this rock Capharean of untruth,
And ferve no God which doth his churchmen ftarve :
 His kingdom's but of plaints, his guerdon tears ;
 What he gives more is jealoufies and fears.

MADRIGAL.

TO the delightful green
 Of you, fair radiant eine,   /
Let each black yield beneath the ftarry arch.
Eyes burnifh'd heavens of love,
Sinople lamps of Jove,
Save all thofe hearts which with your flames you
      parch
Two burning funs you prove ;   •
All other eyes, compar'd with you, dear lights,
Are hells, or if not hells, yet dumpifh nights.

                              The

The heavens (if we their glaſs
The ſea believe) are green, not perfeﬅ blue ;
They all make fair whatever fair yet was,
And they are fair becauſe they look like you.

S O N N E T.

NYMPHS, ſiſter nymphs which haunt this
cryſtal brook,
And happy in theſe floating bowers abide,
Where trembling roofs of trees from ſun you hide,
Which make Idæan woods in every crook ;
Whether ye garlands for your locks provide,
Or pearly letters ſeek in ſandy book,
Or count your loves when Thetis was a bride,
Lift up your golden heads and on me look.
Read in mine eyes my agonizing cares,
And what ye read, recount to her again :
Fair nymphs, ſay all theſe ſtreams are but my tears ;
And, if ſhe aſk you how they ſweet remain,
  Tell, that the bitt'reſt tears which eyes can pour,
  When ſhed for her, can be no longer four.

S O N N E T.

SHE whoſe fair flowers no autumn makes decay,
  Whoſe hue cœleſtial, earthly hues doth ſtain,
Into a pleaſant odoriferous plain
Did walk alone to brave the pride of May.

                                        And

And whilſt through flow'ry liſts ſhe made her way,
That proudly ſmil'd her ſight to entertain,
Lo, unawares where Love did hid remain
She ſpied, and ſought to make of him her prey :
For which of golden locks a faireſt hair
To bind the boy ſhe took, but he afraid
At her approach ſprang ſwiftly in the air,
And, mounting far from reach, look'd back and ſaid,
   Why ſhouldſt thou (ſweet) me ſeek in chains to
      bind,
   Sith in thy eyes I daily am confin'd?

MADRIGAL.

SWEET Roſe, whence is this hue
  Which doth all hues excel ?
Whence this moſt fragrant ſmell ?
And whence this form and gracing grace in you?
In fair Pæſtana's fields perhaps you grew,
Or Hybla's hills you bred,
Or odoriferous Enna's plains you fed,
Or Tmolus, or where boar young Adon ſlew ;
Or hath the queen of love you dyed of new
In that dear blood, which makes you look ſo red ?
  No, none of thoſe, but cauſe more high you bliſs'd,
  My lady's breaſt you bore, her lips you kiſs'd.

MADRIGAL.

MADRIGAL.

O N this cold world of ours,
  Flow'r of the feafons, feafon of the flow'rs,
Sun of the fun, fweet Spring,
Such hot and burning days why doft thou bring?
Is it becaufe thofe high eternal pow'rs
Flafh down that fire this world environing?
Or that now Phœbus keeps his fifter's fphere?
Or doth fome Phaeton
Enflame the fea and air?
Or rather, is't not ufher of the year,
Or that laft day among the flow'rs alone
Unmafk'd thou faw'ft my fair?
  And whilft thou on her gaz'd fhe did thee burn,
  And to thy brother Summer doth thee turn.

SONNET.

D EAR wood, and you fweet folitary place,
  Where I eftranged from the vulgar live,
Contented more with what your fhades me give,
Than if I had what Thetis doth embrace:
What fnaky eye, grown jealous of my pace,
Now from your filent horrors would me drive,
When fun advancing in his glorious race
Beyond the Twins, doth near our pole arrive?

What

What fweet delight a quiet life affords,
And what it is to be from bondage free,
Far from the madding worldling's hoarfe difcords,
Sweet flow'ry place, I firft did learn of thee.
    Ah! if I were mine own, your dear reforts
    I would not change with princes' ftatelieft courts.

SONNET.

AH! who can fee thofe fruits of paradife,
   Cœleftial cherries which fo fweetly fwell,
That fweetnefs' felf confin'd there feems to dwell,
And all thofe fweeteft parts about defpife?
Ah! who can fee, and feel no flame furprife
His harden'd heart? For me, alas, too well
I know their force, and how they do excel:
Now through defire I burn, and now I freeze;
I die (dear life) unlefs to me be given
As many kiffes as the fpring hath flow'rs,
Or there be filver drops in Iris' fhow'rs,
Or ftars there be in all-embracing heaven;
    And if difpleas'd ye of the match complain,
    Ye fhall have leave to take them back again.

SONNET.

IS'T not enough (ah me!) me thus to fee
   Like fome heaven-banifh'd ghoft ftill wailing go,
A fhadow which your rays do only fhew;
To vex me more, unlefs ye bid me die,

What

What could ye worfe allot unto your foe ?
But die will I, fo ye will not deny
That grace to me which mortal foes ev'n try,
To choofe what fort of death fhall end my woe.
Once did I find, that whiles you did me kifs,
Ye gave my panting foul fo fweet a touch,
That half I fwoon'd in midft of all my blifs ;
I do but crave my death's wound may be fuch :
    For though by grief I die not and annoy,
    Is't not enough to die through too much joy ?

MADRIGAL.

UNHAPPY light,
    Do not approach to bring the woeful day,
When I muft bid for aye
Farewel to her, and live in endlefs plight.
Fair moon with gentle beams,
The fight who never mars,
Clear long-heaven's fable vault, and you bright ftars,
Your golden locks long view in earth's pure ftreams ;
Let Phœbus never rife
To dim your watchful eyes.
Prolong, alas, prolong my fhort delight ;
And if ye can, make an eternal night.

SONNET.

SONNET.

WITH grief in heart, and tears in fwelling eyes,
　　When I to her had given a fad farewel,
Clofe fealed with a kifs, and dew which fell
On my elfe moiften'd face from beauty's fkies ;
So ftrange amazement did my mind furprife,
That at each pace I fainting turn'd again,
Like one whom a torpedo ftupefies,
Not feeling honour's bit, nor reafon's rein :
But when fierce ftars to part me did conftrain,
With back-caft looks, I both envy'd and blefs'd
The happy walls and place did her contain,
Until my eyes that flying object mifs'd :
　　So wailing parted Ganymede the fair,
　　When eagle's talons bore him through the air.

SEXTAIN.

SITH gone is my delight and only pleafure,
　　The laft of all my hopes, the cheerful fun
That clear'd my life's dark fphere, nature's fweet
　　　　treafure,
More dear to me than all beneath the moon ;
What refteth now, but that upon this mountain
I weep, till Heaven transform me to a fountain ?

Frefh.

Frefh, fair, delicious, cryftal, pearly fountain,
On whofe fmooth face to look fhe oft took pleafure,
Tell me (fo may thy ftreams long cheer this moun-
    tain,
So ferpent ne'er thee ftain, nor fcorch thee fun,
So may with wat'ry beams thee kifs the moon !)
Doft thou not mourn to want fo fair a treafure

While fhe here gaz'd on thee, rich Tagus' treafure
Thou needeft not envy, nor yet the fountain,
In which that hunter faw the naked moon ;
Abfence hath robb'd thee of thy wealth and pleafure,
And I remain, like marigold, of fun
Depriv'd, that dies by fhadow of fome mountain.

Nymphs of the forefts, nymphs who on this
    mountain
Are wont to dance, fhewing your beauty's treafure
To goat-feet fylvans, and the wond'ring fun,
When as you gather flow'rs about this fountain,
Bid her farewel who placed here her pleafure,
And fing her praifes to the ftars and moon.

Among the leffer lights as is the moon,
Blufhing through muffling clouds on Latmos' moun-
    tain ;
Or when fhe views her filver locks for pleafure
In Thetis' ftreams, proud of fo gay a treafure :
Such was my fair, when fhe fate by this fountain
With other nymphs, to fhun the amorous fun.

A₅

As is our earth in abfence of the fun,
Or when of fun deprived is the moon ;
As is without a verdant fhade a fountain,
Or, wanting grafs, a mead, a vale, a mountain ;
Such is my ftate, bereft of my dear treafure,
To know whofe only worth, was all my pleafure.

Ne'er think of pleafure, heart ; eyes, fhun the fun ;
Tears be your treafure, which the wand'ring moon
Shall fee you fhed by mountain, vale and fountain.

S O N N E T.

WINDOW fome time which ferved for a fphere
To that dear planet of my heart, whofe light .
Made often blufh the glorious queen of night,.
While fhe in thee more beauteous did appear ;
What mourning weeds, alas, doft thou now wear ?
How loathfome to my eyes is thy fad fight !
How poorly look'ft thou, with what heavy cheer,
Since fets that fun which made thee fhine fo bright ?
Unhappy now thee clofe ; for, as of late
To wond'ring eyes thou wert a paradife,
Bereft of her who made thee fortunate,
A gulph thou art, whence clouds of fighs arife :
     But unto none fo noifome as to me,
     Who hourly fees my murder'd joys in thee.

SONNET.

SONNET.

HOW many times night's filent queen her face
    Hath hid, how oft with ftars in filver mafk,
In heaven's great hall, fhe hath begun her tafk,
And cheer'd the waking eye in lower place ;
How oft the fun hath made, by heaven's fwift race,
The happy lover to forfake the breaft
Of his dear lady, wifhing in the weft
His golden coach to run had larger fpace ;
I ever count and tell, fince I, alas !
Did bid farewel to my heart's deareft gueft ;
The miles I number, and in mind I chafe,
The floods and mountains hold me from my reft.
    But wo is me, long count and count may I,
    Ere I fee her whofe abfence makes me die.

SONNET.

OF death fome tell, fome of the cruel pain
    Which that bad craftfman in his work did try,
When (a new monfter) flames once did conftrain
A human corpfe to yield a bellowing cry.
Some tell of thofe in burning beds who lie,
Becaufe they durft in the Phlegrean plain
The mighty Ruler of the fkies defy,
And fiege thofe cryftal tow'rs which all contain.

E

Another

Another counts of Phlegethon's hot floods,
The fouls which drink Ixion's endlefs fmart,
And his who feeds a vulture with his heart.
One tells of fpeétres in enchanted woods:
  Of all thofe pains th' extremeft who would prove,
  Let him be abfent and but burn in love.

S O N N E T.

HAIR, precious hair, which Midas' hand did
       ftrain,
Part of the wreath of gold that crowns thofe brows
Which winter's whiteft white in whitenefs ftain,
And lily by Eridan's bank that grows:
Hair (fatal prefent!) which firft caus'd my woes,
When loofe ye hang like Danae's golden rain,
Sweet nets which fweetly do all hearts enchain,
Strings, deadly ftrings, with which Love bends his
       bows:
How are ye hither come? Tell me, O hair!
Dear armelet, for what thus were ye given?
I know, a badge of bondage I you wear,
Yet, hair, for you O that I were a heaven!
  Like Berenice's locks, that ye might fhine
  (But brighter far) about this arm of mine.

S O N N E T.

ARE thefe the flow'ry banks? Is this the mead
Where fhe was wont to pafs the pleafant hours?
Was't here her eyes exhal'd mine eyes' falt fhow'rs,
And on her lap did lay my wearied head?
Is this the goodly elm did us o'erfpread,
Whofe tender rind, cut forth in curious flow'rs
By that white hand, contains thofe flames of ours?
Is this the murmuring fpring us mufick made?
Deflourifh'd mead, where is your heavenly hue?
And bank, that Arras did you late adorn?
How look'ft thou elm all wither'd and forlorn!
Only, fweet Spring, nought alter'd feems in you.
But while here chang'd each other thing appears,
To falt your ftreams take of mine eyes thefe tears.

S O N N E T.

ALEXIS, here fhe ftay'd, among thefe pines,
Sweet hermitrefs, fhe did all alone repair;
Here did fhe fpread the treafure of her hair,
More rich than that brought from the Colchian mines:
Here fate fhe by thefe mufked eglantines;
The happy flow'rs feem yet the print to bear;
Her voice did fweeten here thy fugar'd lines,
To which winds, trees, beafts, birds, did lend an ear.

She

She here me firſt perceiv'd, and here a morn
Of bright carnations did o'erſpread her face ;
Here did ſhe ſigh, here firſt my hopes were born,
Here firſt I got a pledge of promis'd grace :
    But ah ! what ſerves 't t' have been made happy ſo,
    Sith paſſed pleaſures double but new woe ?

SONNET.

PLACE me where angry Titan burns the Moor,
    And thirſty Africk fiery monſters brings,
Or where the new-born phœnix ſpreads her wings,
And troops of wond'ring birds her flight adore :
Place me by Gange or Inde's enamell'd ſhore,
Where ſmiling heavens on earth cauſe double ſprings ;
Place me where Neptune's choir of ſyrens ſings,
Or where made hoarſe through cold he leaves to roar :
Place me where Fortune doth her darlings crown,
A wonder or a ſpark in Envy's eye ;
Or you outrageous Fates upon me frown,
Till Pity wailing ſee diſaſter'd me ;
    Affection's print my mind ſo deep doth prove,
    I may forget myſelf—but not my love.

MADRIGAL.

THE ivory, coral, gold,
    Of breaſt, of lip, of hair,
So lively Sleep doth ſhew to inward ſight,
That 'wake I think I hold

No fhadow, but my fair:
Myfelf fo to deceive
With long-fhut eyes I fhun the irkfome light.
Such pleafure here I have
Delighting in falfe gleams,
If Death Sleep's brother be,
And fouls bereft of fenfe have fo fweet dreams,
How could I wifh thus ftill to dream and die !

S O N N E T.

FAME, who with golden wings abroad doth range
    Where Phœbus leaves the night or brings the
      day ;
Fame, in one place who reftlefs doft not ftay
Till thou haft flow'd from Atlas unto Gange :
Fame, euemy to Time, that ftill doth change,
And in his changing courfe would make decay
What here below he findeth in his way,
Even making virtue to herfelf look ftrange :
Daughter of heaven ! now all thy trumpets found,
Raife up thy head unto the higheft fky,
With wonder blaze the gifts in her are found ;
And when fhe from this mortal globe fhall fly,
    In thy wide mouth keep long, keep long her name ;
    So thou by her, fhe by thee live fhall Fame.

P O E M S.

THE SECOND PART.

S O N N E T.

OF mortal glory O foon darken'd ray !
   O winged joys of man, more fwift than wind !
O fond defires, which in our fancies ftray !
O trait'rous hopes, which do our judgments blind !
Lo, in a flaſh that light is gone away,
Which dazzle did each eye, delight each mind,
And with that fun, from whence it came, combin'd,
Now makes more radiant heaven's eternal day.
Let Beauty now bedew her cheeks with tears,
Let widow'd Mufick only roar and groan,
Poor Virtue get thee wings and mount the fpheres,
For dwelling place on earth for thee is none :
   Death hath thy temple raz'd, Love's empire foil'd,
   The world of honour, worth, and fweetnefs fpoil'd.

S O N N E T.

THOSE eyes, thofe fparkling fapphires of delight,
  Which thoufand thoufand hearts did fet on fire,
Of which that eye of heaven which brings the light
Oft jealous, ftaid amaz'd them to admire :
That living fnow, thofe crimfon rofes bright,
Thofe pearls, thofe rubies which enflam'd defire,
Thofe locks of gold, that purple fair of Tyre,
Are wrapt (ah me !) up in eternal night.
What haft thou more to vaunt of, wretched world,
Sith fhe who caufed all thy blifs is gone ?
Thy ever-burning lamps, rounds ever whorl'd,
Cannot unto thee model fuch a one :
  Or if they would fuch beauty bring on earth,
  They fhould be forc'd again to give her birth.

S O N N E T.

O FATE, conjur'd to pour your worft on me !
  O rigorous rigour which doth all confound !
With cruel hands ye have cut down the tree,
And fruit with leaves have fcatter'd on the ground.
A little fpace of earth my love doth bound ;
That beauty which did raife it to the fky,
Turn'd in difdained duft, now low doth lie,
Deaf to my plaints, and fenfelefs of my wound.

                                        Ah !

Ah! did I live for this ? Ah ! did I love ?
And was't for this (fierce powers) she did excel,
That ere she well the sweets of life did prove,
She should (too dear a guest) with darkness dwell ?
   Weak influence of Heaven ! what fair is wrought,
   Falls in the prime, and passeth like a thought.

S O N N E T.

O WOFUL life ! Life ? No, but living death,
    Frail boat of cryftal in a rocky sea,
A gem expos'd to fortune's stormy breath,
Which kept with pain, with terror doth decay :
The false delights, true woes thou dost bequeath
My all-appalled mind so do affray,
That I those envy who are laid in earth,
And pity those who run thy dreadful way.
When did mine·eyes behold one cheerful morn ?
When had my tossed soul one night of rest ?
When did not angry stars my designs scorn ?
O ! now I find what is for mortals best :
   Even, since our voyage shameful is, and short,
   Soon to strike sail, and perish in the port.

S O N N E T.

DISSOLVE, my eyes, your globes in briny
    streams,
And with a cloud of sorrow dim your sight,
The sun's bright sun is set, of late whose beams
Gave luftre to your day, day to your night.

My

My voice, now cleave the earth with anathems,
Roar forth a challenge in the world's defpite,.
Till that difguifed grief is her delight,
That life a flumber is of fearful dreams ;
And woful mind abhor to think of joy ;
My fenfes all from comforts all you hide,
Accept no object but of black annoy,
Tears, plaints, fighs, mourning weeds, graves gaping
              wide :
   I have nought left to wifh ; my hopes are dead,
   And all with her beneath a marble laid.

S O N N E T.

SWEET foul, which in the April of thy years,
   For to enrich the heaven mad'ft poor this round,
And now, with flaming rays of glory crown'd,
Moft bleft abides above the fphere of fpheres ;.
If heavenly laws, alas ! have not thee bound
From looking to this globe that all up-bears,
If ruth and pity there-above be found,
O deign to lend a look unto thefe tears :
Do not difdain (dear ghoft) this facrifice ;
And though I raife not pillars to thy praife,
My off'rings take, let this for me fuffice,
My heart a living pyramid I'll raife :
   And whilft kings' tombs with laurels flourifh green,
Thine fhall with myrtles and thefe flow'rs be feen.

SONNET.

SONNET.

SWEET Spring, thou com'ſt with all thy goodly
    train,
Thy head with flames, thy mantle bright with flow'rs,
The zephyrs curl the green locks of the plain,
The clouds for joy in pearls weep down their ſhow'rs.
Sweet Spring, thou com'ſt—but, ah! my pleaſant hours,
And happy days, with thee come not again ;
The ſad memorials only of my pain
Do with thee come, which turn my ſweets to ſours.
Thou art the ſame which ſtill thou wert before,
Delicious, luſty, amiable, fair ;
But ſhe whoſe breath embalm'd thy wholeſome air
Is gone ; nor gold, nor gems can her reſtore.
    Neglected virtue, ſeaſons go and come,
    When thine forgot lie cloſed in a tomb.

SONNET.

WHAT doth it ſerve to ſee the ſun's bright
    face,
And ſkies enamell'd with the Indian gold ?
Or the moon in a fierce chariot roll'd,
And all the glory of that ſtarry place ?
What doth it ſerve earth's beauty to behold,
The mountain's pride, the meadow's flow'ry grace,
The ſtately comelineſs of foreſts old,
The ſport of floods which would themſelves embrace ?
                        What

What doth it ferve to hear the fylvans' fongs,
The cheerful thrufh, the nightingale's fad ftrains,
Which in dark fhades feems to deplore my wrongs?
For what doth ferve all that this world contains,
   Since fhe, for whom thofe once to me were dear,
   Can have no part of them now with me here?

MADRIGAL.

THIS life, which feems fo fair,
   Is like a bubble blown up in the air,
By fporting children's breath,
Who chafe it every where,
And ftrive who can moft motion it bequeath.
And though it fometimes feem of its own might
Like to an eye of gold to be fix'd there,
And firm to hover in that empty height,
That only is becaufe it is fo light.
But in that pomp it doth not long appear;
For when 'tis moft admired, in a thought,
Becaufe it erft was nought, it turns to nought.

SONNET.

MY lute, be as thou wert when thou didft grow
   With thy green mother in fome fhady grove,
When immelodious winds but made thee move,
And birds their ramage did on thee beftow.
Since that dear voice which did thy founds approve,
Which wont in fuch harmonious ftrains to flow,
Is reft from earth to tune thofe fpheres above,
What art thou but a harbinger of woe?

                         Thy

Thy pleafing notes be pleafing notes no more,
But orphans' wailings to the fainting ear,
Each ftroke a figh, each found draws forth a tear,
For which be filent as in woods before :
   Or if that any hand to touch thee deign,
   Like widow'd turtle ftill her lofs complain.

S O N N E T.

AH! handkerchief, fad prefent of my dear,
   Gift miferable, which doth now remain
The only guerdon of my helplefs pain ;
When I thee got thou fhewd'ft my ftate too clear.
I never fince have ceafed to complain ;
I fince the badge of grief did ever wear ;
Joy in my face durft never fince appear ;
Care was the food which did me entertain.
But fince that thou art mine, O do not grieve,
That I this tribute pay thee for mine eine,
And that I (this fhort time I am to live)
Launder thy filken figures in this brine ;
   No, I muft yet ev'n beg of thee the grace,
   That in my grave thou deign to fhroud my face.

M A D R I G A L.

TREES happier far than I,
   Which have the grace to heave your heads fo
   high,

And

And overlook thofe plains ;
Grow till your branches kifs that lofty fky
Which her fweet felf contains.
There make her know my endlefs love, and pains,
And how thefe tears which from mine eyes do fall,
Help'd you to rife fo tall :
Tell her, as once I for her fake lov'd breath,
So for her fake I now court ling'ring death.

SONG.

SAD Damon being come
    To that for-ever lamentable tomb,
Which thofe eternal powers that all controul,
Unto his living foul
A melancholy prifon had prefcrib'd ;
Of colour, heat, and motion depriv'd,
In arms weak, fainting, cold,
A marble, he the marble did infold :
And having warm it made with many a fhow'r
Which dimmed eyes did pour,
When grief had given him leave, and fighs them
        ftaid,
Thus with a fad alas at laft he faid :
    Who would have thought to me
The place where thou didft lie could grievous be ?
And that (dear body) long thee having fought,
(O me!) who would have thought
Thee once to find it fhould my foul confound,
And give my heart than death a deeper wound ?

                                        Thou

Thou didſt diſdain my tears,
But grieve not that this ruthful ſtone them bears ;
Mine eyes for nothing ſerve, but thee to weep,
And let that courſe them keep;
Although thou never wouldſt them comfort ſhew,
Do not repine, they have part of thy woe.
 Ah wretch ! too late I find
How virtue's glorious titles prove but wind ;
For if that virtue could releaſe from death,
Thou yet enjoy'd hadſt breath :
For if ſhe ere appear'd to mortal eine,
It was in thy fair ſhape that ſhe was ſeen.
But O ! if I was made
For thee, with thee why too am I not dead ?
Why do outrageous Fates, which dimm'd thy ſight,
Let me ſee hateful light ?
They without me made Death thee ſurpriſe,
Tyrants (no doubt) that they might kill me twice.
 O grief ! And could one day
Have force ſuch excellence to take away ?
Could a ſwift-flying moment, ah ! deface
Thoſe matchleſs gifts, that grace,
Which art and nature had in thee combin'd
To make thy body paragon thy mind ?
Hath all paſs'd like a cloud,
And doth eternal ſilence now them ſhroud ?
Is that, ſo much admir'd, now nought but duſt,
Of which a ſtone hath truſt ?
O change ! O cruel change ! Thou to our ſight
Shew'ſt the Fates' rigour equal to their might !

When

When thou from earth didſt paſs,
Sweet nymph, perfection's mirror broken was,
And this of late ſo glorious world of ours,
Like the meadows without flowers,
Or ring of a rich gem which blind appear'd,
Or ſtarleſs night, or Cynthia nothing clear'd.
Love when he ſaw thee die
Entomb'd him in the lid of either eye,
And left his torch within thy ſacred urn,
There for a lamp to burn :
Worth, honour, pleaſure, with thy life expir'd,
Death, ſince grown ſweet, begins to be deſir'd.
   Whilſt thou to us wert given,
The earth her Venus had as well as heaven :
Nay, and her ſuns, which burnt as many hearts,
As he the eaſtern parts ;
Bright ſuns which, forc'd to leave theſe hemiſpheres,
Benighted ſet into a ſea of tears.
Ah ! Death, who ſhall thee flee,
Since the moſt mighty are o'erthrown by thee ?
Thou ſpar'ſt the crow, and nightingale doſt kill,
And triumph'ſt at thy will :
But give thou cannot ſuch another blow,
Becauſe earth cannot ſuch another ſhew.
   O bitter ſweets of love !
How better is't at all you not to prove,
Than when we do your pleaſures moſt poſſeſs
To find them thus made leſs !
O ! that the cauſe which doth conſume our joy
Would the remembrance of it too deſtroy !

What

What doth this life beſtow,
But flow'rs on thorns which grow?
Which though they ſometimes blandiſh ſoft delight,
Yet afterwards us ſmite:
And if the riſing ſun them fair doth ſee,
That planet ſetting doth behold them die.
   This world is made a hell,
Depriv'd of all that in it did excel.
O Pan! O Pan! winter is fall'n in May,
Turn'd is to night our day.
Forſake thy pipe, a ſceptre take to thee,
Thy locks diſgarland, thou black Jove ſhalt be.
The flocks do leave the meads,
And, loathing three-leav'd graſs, hold up their heads;
The ſtreams not glide now with a gentle roar,
Nor birds ſing as before;
Hills ſtand with clouds like mourners veil'd in black,
And owls upon our roofs foretel our wreck.
   That zephyr every year
So ſoon was heard to ſigh in foreſts here,
It was for her that, wrapt in gowns of green,
Meads were ſo early ſeen:
That in the ſaddeſt months oft ſang the mearls,
It was for her: for her trees dropt forth pearls.
That proud and ſtately courts
Did envy theſe our ſhades and calm reſorts,
It was for her: and ſhe is gone, O woe!
Woods cut again do grow,
Bud doth the roſe, and daiſy, winter done,
But we once dead do no more ſee the ſun.
                    F   Whoſe

Whofe name fhall now make ring
The echoes ? of whom fhall the nymphets fing ?
Whofe heavenly voice, whofe foul-invading ftrains,
Shall fill with joy the plains ?
What hair, what eyes, can make the morn in eaft
Weep that a fairer rifeth in the weft ?
Fair fun poft ftill away,
No mufick here is left thy courfe to ftay.
Sweet Hybla fwarms, with wormwood fill your bow'rs,
Gone is the flower of flow'rs :
Blufh no more rofe, nor lily pale remain,
Dead is that beauty which yours late did ftain.
　Ah me ! to wail my plight
Why have not I as many eyes as night ;
Or as that fhepherd which Jove's love did keep,
That I ftill, ftill may weep ?
But though I had, my tears unto my crofs
Were not yet equal, nor grief to my lofs.
Yet of you briny fhow'rs
Which I here pour, may fpring as many flow'rs,
As come of thofe which fell from Helen's eyes ;
And when ye do arife,
May every leaf in fable letters bear
The doleful caufe for which ye fpring up here.

MADRIGAL.

THE beauty and the life
　Of life's and beauty's faireft paragon,
O tears ! O grief ! hung at a feeble thread
To which pale Atropos had fet her knife.

The

The foul with many a groan
Had left each outward part,
And now did take his laſt leave of the heart ;
Nought elſe did want fave death for to be dead :
When the ſad company about her bed
Seeing death invade her lips, her cheeks, her eyes,
Cried ah ! and can death enter Paradiſe ?

SONNET.

O! It is not to me, bright lamp of day,
    That in the eaſt thou ſhew'ſt thy golden face ;
O! it is not to me thou leav'ſt that ſea,
And in thoſe azure liſts beginn'ſt thy race.
Thou ſhin'ſt not to the dead in any place ;
And I dead from this world am paſt away,
Or if I ſeem (a ſhadow) yet to ſtay,
It is a while but to bewail my caſe.
My mirth is loſt, my comforts are diſmay'd,
And unto ſad miſhaps their place do yield ;
My knowledge repreſents a bloody field,
Where I my hopes and helps ſee proſtrate laid.
    So plaintful is life's courſe which I have run,
    That I do wiſh it never had begun.

MADRIGAL.

DEAR night, the eaſe of care,
    Untroubled ſeat of peace,
Time's eldeſt child, which oft the blind do ſee,

On

On this our hemifphere
What makes thee now fo fadly dark to be ?
Com'ft thou in funeral pomp her grave to grace ?
Or do thofe ftars which fhould thy horror clear,
In Jove's high hall advife,
In what part of the fkies,
With them, or Cynthia fhe fhall appear ?
Or, ah, alas ! becaufe thofe matchlefs eyes,
Which fhone fo fair, below thou doft not find,
Striv'ft thou to make all others' eyes look blind ?

S O N N E T.

SINCE it hath pleas'd that firft and fupreme Fair
To take that beauty to himfelf again,
Which in this world of fenfe not to remain,
But to amaze was fent, and home repair ;
The love which to that beauty I did bear,
Made pure of mortal fpots which did it ftain,
And endlefs, which even death cannot impair,
I place on him who will it not difdain.
No fhining eyes, no locks of curling gold,
No blufhing rofes on a virgin face,
No outward fhow, no, nor no inward grace,
Shall power have my thoughts henceforth to hold :
    Love here on earth huge ftorms of care doth tofs,
    But plac'd above exempted is from lofs.

S O N G.

S O N G.

IT autumn was, and on our hemifphere
  Fair Ericine began bright to appear,
Night weftward did her gemmy world decline,
And hide her lights, that greater light might fhine :
The crefted bird had given alarum twice
To lazy mortals to unlock their eyes,
The owl had left to plain, and from each throne
The wing'd muficians did falute the Morn,
Who (while fhe drefs'd her locks in Ganges' ftreams)
Set open wide the cryftal port of dreams :
When I, whofe eyes no drowfy night could clofe,
In Sleep's foft arms did quietly repofe,
And, for that heavens to die did me deny,
Death's image kiffed, and as dead did lie.
I lay as dead, but fcarce charm'd were my cares,
And flaked fcarce my fighs, fcarce dried my tears,
Sleep fcarce the ugly figures of the day
Had with his fable pencil put away,
And left me in a ftill and calmy mood,
When by my bed methought a virgin ftood,
A virgin in the blooming of her prime,
If fuch rare beauty meafur'd be by time.
Her head a garland wore of opals bright,
About her flow'd a gown like pureft light ;
Pure amber locks gave umbrage to her face,
Where modefty high majefty did grace ;

F 3   Her

Her eyes fuch beams fent forth, that but with pain
My weaker fight their fparklings could fuftain.
No feigned deity which haunts the woods
Is like to her, nor fyren of the floods:
Such is the golden planet of the year,
When blufhing in the eaft he doth appear.
Her grace did beauty, voice yet grace did pafs,
Which thus through pearls and rubies broken was.
　　How long wilt thou (faid fhe), eftrang'd from joy,
Paint fhadows to thyfelf of falfe annoy ;
How long thy mind with horrid fhapes affright,
And in imaginary evils delight ;
Efteem that lofs which (well when view'd) is gain,
Or if a lofs, yet not a lofs too plain ?
O leave thy plaintful foul more to moleft,
And think that woe when fhorteft then is beft.
If fhe for whom thou thus doft deaf the fky
Be dead, what then ? was fhe not born to die ?
Was fhe not mortal born ? If thou doft grieve
'That times fhould be in which fhe fhould not live,
Ere e'er fhe was weep that day's wheel was roll'd,
Weep that fhe liv'd not in the age of gold.
For that fhe was not then thou may'ft deplore,
As well as that fhe now can be no more.
If only fhe had died, thou fure hadft caufe
To blame the Fates, and their too iron laws.
But look how many millions her advance,
What numbers with her enter in this dance,
With thofe which are to come: fhall Heavens them ftay,
And th' univerfe diffolve thee to obey ?

　　　　　　　　　　　　　　　As

As birth, death, which fo much thee doth appal,
'A piece is of the life of this great All.
Strong cities die, die do high palmy reigns,
And fondling thou thus to be us'd complains !
    If fhe be dead, then fhe of loathfome days
Hath pafs'd the line whofe length but lofs bewrays,
Then fhe hath left this filthy ftage of care,
Where pleafure feldom, woe doth ftill repair.
For all the pleafures which it doth contain
Not countervail the fmalleft minute's pain.
And tell me, thou who doft fo much admire
This little vapour, this poor fpark of fire,
Which life is call'd, what doth it thee bequeath
But fome few years which birth draws out to death ?
Which if thou parallel with luftres run,
Or thofe whofe courfes are but now begun,
In days' great numbers they fhall lefs appear,
Than with the fea when matched is a tear.
But why fhould'ft thou here longer wifh to be ?
One year doth ferve all Nature's pomp to fee.
Nay, even one day, and night : this moon, that fun,
Thofe leffer fires about this round which run,
Be but the fame which under Saturn's reign
Did the ferpenting feafons interchain.
How oft doth life grow lefs by living long !
And what excelleth but what dieth young ?
For age, which all abhor, yet would embrace,
Doth make the mind as wrinkled as the face.
Then leave laments, and think thou didft not live,
Laws to that firft eternal Caufe to give ;

But

But to obey thofe laws which he hath given,
And bow unto the juft decrees of Heaven,
Which cannot err, whatever foggy mifts
Do blind men in thefe fublunary lifts.
But what if fhe for whom thou fpend'ft thofe groans,
And waftes thy life's dear torch in ruthful moans,
She for whofe fake thou hat'ft the joyful light,
Courts folitary fhades and irkfome night,
Doth live ? Ah ! (if thou canft) through tears, a
      fpace,
Lift thy dimm'd lights, and look upon this face ;
Look if thofe eyes which, fool ! thou didft adore,
Shine not more bright than they were wont before.
Look if thofe rofes death could aught impair,
Thofe rofes which thou once faidft were fo fair ;
And if thefe locks have loft aught of that gold,
Which once they had when thou them didft behold.
I live, and happy live, but thou art dead,
And ftill fhalt be till thou be like me made.
Alas ! while we are wrapt in gowns of earth,
And, blind, here fuck the air of woe beneath ;
Each thing in fenfe's balances we weigh,
And but with toil and pain the truth defcry.
   Above this vaft and admirable frame,
This temple vifible, which world we name,
Within whofe walls fo many lamps do burn,
So many arches with crofs motions turn,
Where th' elemental brothers nurfe their ftrife,
And by inteftine wars maintain their life ;

                     There

There is a world, a world of perfect blifs,
Pure, immaterial, as brighter far from this,
As that high circle which the reft enfpheres
Is from this dull, ignoble vale of tears:
A world where all is found, that here is found,
But further difcrepant than heaven and ground :
It hath an earth, as hath this world of yours,
With creatures peopled, and adorn'd with flow'rs
It hath a fea, like fapphire girdle caft,
Which decks of the harmonious fhores the wafte ;
It hath pure fire, it hath delicious air,
Moon, fun, and ftars, heavens wonderfully fair :
Flow'rs never there do fade, trees grow not old,
No creature dieth there through heat or cold ;
Sea there not tofled is, nor air made black,
Fire doth not greedy feed on others' wrack :
There heavens be not conftrain'd about to range,
For this world hath no need of any change :
Minutes mount not to hours, nor hours to days,
Days make no months, but ever-blooming Mays.
    Here I remain, and hitherward do tend
All who their fpan of days in virtue fpend :
Whatever pleafant this low place contains,
Is but a glance of what above remains.
Thofe who (perchance) think there can nothing be
Beyond this wide expanfion which they fee,
And that nought elfe mounts ftars' circumference,
For that nought elfe is fubject to their fenfe,
Feel fuch a cafe, as one whom fome abifme
In the deep ocean kept had all his time :

Who

Who, born and nourifh'd there, cannot believe
That elfewhere aught without thofe waves can live :
Cannot believe that there be temples, tow'rs,
Which go beyond his caves and dampifh bow'rs :
Or there be other people, manners, laws,
Than what he finds within the churlifh waves :
That fweeter flow'rs do fpring than grow on rocks,
Or beafts there are excel the fkaly flocks :
That other elements are to be found,
Than is the water and this ball of ground.
But think that man from this abifme being brought,
Did fee what curious Nature here hath 'wrought,
Did view the meads, the tall and fhady woods,
And mark'd the hills, and the clear rolling floods ;
And all the beafts which Nature forth doth bring,
The feather'd troops that fly and fweetly fing :
Obferv'd the palaces, and cities fair,
Men's fafhion of life, the fire, the air,
The brightnefs of the fun that dims his fight,
The moon, and 'fplendors of the painted night :
What fudden rapture would his mind furprife !
How would he his late-dear refort defpife !
How would he mufe how foolifh he had been,
To think all nothing but what there was feen !
Why do we get this high and vaft defire,
Unto immortal things ftill to afpire ?
Why doth our mind extend it beyond time,
And to that higheft happinefs even climb ?
For we are more than what to fenfe we feem,
And more than duft us worldlings do efteem ;

We

We be not made for earth though here we come,
More than the embryo for the mother's womb :
It weeps to be made free, and we complain
To leave this loathsome gaol of care and pain.
    But thou who vulgar footsteps dost not trace,
Learn to rouse up thy mind to view this place,
And what earth-creeping mortals most affect,
If not at all to scorn, yet to neglect :
Seek not vain shadows, which when once obtain'd
Are better lost than with such travel gain'd.
Think that on earth what worldlings greatness call,
Is but a glorious title to live thrall :
That sceptres, diadems, and chairs of state,
Not in themselves, but to small minds are great :
That those who loftiest mount do hardest light,
And deepest falls be from the highest height :
That fame an echo is, and all renown
Like to a blasted rose, ere night falls down :
And though it something were, think how this round
Is but a little point which doth it bound.
O leave that love which reacheth but to dust,
And in that love eternal only trust,
And beauty, which when once it is possest
Can only fill the soul, and make it blest.
Pale envy, jealous emulations, fears,
Sighs, plaints, remorse, here have no place, nor tears :
False joys, vain hopes, here be not, hate nor wrath,
What ends all love here most augments it, Death.
If such force had the dim glance of an eye,
Which but some few days afterwards did die,

That

That it could make thee leave all other things,.
And like a taper-fly there burn thy wings;
And if a voice, of late which could but wail,
Such power had, as through ears thy foul to fteal;
If once thou on that poorly fair couldft gaze,
What flames of love would this within thee raife?'
In what a mufing maze would it thee bring,.
To hear but once that choir celeftial fing?
The faireft fhapes on which thy love did feize,.
Which erft did breed delight,. then would difpleafe ;.
But difcords hoarfe were earth's enticing founds,
All mufic but a noife, which feufe confounds.
This great and burning glafs which clears all eyes,.
And mufters with fuch glory in the fkies;
That filver ftar, which with her purer light
Makes day oft envy the eye-pleafing night ;
Thofe golden letters which fo brightly fhine
In heaven's great volume gorgeoufly divine ;
All wonders in the fea, the earth, the air,
Be but dark pictures of that fov'reign fair,
And tongues, which ftill thus cry into your ear
Could ye amidft world's cataracts them hear) :
From fading things, fond men, lift your defire,
And in our beauty, his us made admire :
If we feem fair, O think how fair is He,
Of whofe great fairnefs, fhadows, fteps we be.
No fhadow can compare unto the face,
No ftep with that dear foot which did it trace ;
Your fouls immortal are, then place them hence,.
And do not drown them in the mift of fenfe :.

Do

Do not, O do not by falfe pleafure's might
Deprive them of that true and fole delight.
That happinefs ye feek is not below,
Earth's fweeteft joy is but difguifed woe.
 Here did fhe paufe, and with a mild afpect
Did towards me thofe lamping twins direct.
The wonted rays I knew, and thrice effay'd
To anfwer make, thrice fault'ring tongue it ftay'd.
And while upon that face I fed my fight,
Methought fhe vanifh'd up to Titan's light ;
Who gilding with his rays each hill and plain,
Seem'd to have brought the golden world again.

U R A N I A.

TRIUMPHING chariots, ftatues, crowns of
 bays,
Sky-threat'ning arches, the rewards of worth,
Books heavenly-wife in fweet harmonious lays,
Which men divine unto the world fet forth :
States which ambitious minds, in blood, do raife,
From frozen Tanais unto fun-burnt Gange,
Gigantic frames held wonders rarely ftrange,
Like fpiders' webs, are made the fport of days.
Nothing is conftant but in conftant change,
What's done ftill is undone, and when undone
Into fome other fafhion doth it range ;
Thus goes the floating world beneath the moon :
 Wherefore my mind above time, motion, place,
 Rife up, and fteps unknown to nature trace.

TOO

TOO long I followed have my fond defire,
  And too long painted on the ocean ftreams,
Too long refrefhment fought amidft the fire,
Purfu'd thofe joys which to my foul are blames.
Ah when I had what moft I did admire,
And feen of life's delights the laft extremes,
I found all but a rofe hedg'd with a brier,
A nought, a thought, a mafquerade of dreams.
Henceforth on thee, my only good, I'll think,
For only thou canft grant what I do crave :
Thy nail my pen fhall be ; thy blood mine ink ;
Thy winding-fheet my paper ; ftudy, grave :
  And till my foul forth of this body fly,
  No hope I'll have, but only only thee.

TO fpread the azure canopy of heaven,
  And fpangle it all with fparks of burning gold,
To place this ponderous globe of earth fo even,
That it fhould all, and nought fhould it uphold ;
With motions ftrange t' indue the planets feven,
And Jove to make fo mild, and Mars fo bold ;
To temper what is moift, dry, hot, and cold,
Of all their jars that fweet accords are given ;—
                              Lord,

Lord, to thy wifdom's nought, nought to thy might :
But that thou fhould'ft, thy glory laid afide,
Come bafely in mortality to bide,
And die for thofe deferv'd an endlefs night ;
  A wonder is fo far above our wit,
  That angels ftand amaz'd to think on it.

WHAT haplefs hap had I for to be born
    In thefe unhappy times, and dying days
Of this now doting world, when good decays,
Love's quite extinct, and virtue's held a fcorn !
When fuch are only priz'd by wretched ways
Who with a golden fleece them can adorn !
When avarice and luft are counted praife,
And braveft minds live, orphan-like, forlorn !
Why was not I born in that golden age,
When gold yet was not known ? and thofe black arts
By which bafe worldlings vilely play their parts,
With horrid acts ftaining earth's ftately ftage ?
  To have been then, O heaven ! 't had been my
    blifs,
  But blefs me now, and take me foon from this.

ON THE PORTRAIT OF THE COUNTESS OF PERTH.

SONNET.

THE goddefs that in Amathus doth reign
  With filver trammels, and fapphire-colour'd eyes,
                    When

When naked from her mother's cryftal plain,
She firft appear'd unto the wond'ring fkies;
Or when the golden apple to obtain,
Her blufhing fnow amazed Ida's trees,
Did never look in half fo fair a guife,
As fhe here drawn all other ages ftain.
O God, what beauties to inflame the foul,
And hold the hardeft hearts in chains of gold!
Fair locks, fweet face, love's ftately capitol,
Pure neck, which doth that heavenly frame uphold!
    If virtue would to mortal eyes appear,
    To ravifh fenfe, fhe would your beauty wear.

SONNET.

IF heaven, the ftars, and nature did her grace
    With all perfections found the moon above,
And what excelleth in this lower place,
Found place in her to breed a world of love:
If angels' gleams fhine on her faireft face,
Which makes heaven's joy on earth the gazer prove,
And her bright eyes (the orbs which beauty move)
As Phœbus dazzle in his glorious race;
What pencil paint, what colour to the fight
So fweet a fhape can fhew? The blufhing Morn
The red muft lend, the Milky-way the white,
And Night, the ftars which her rich crown adorn;
    To draw her right then, and make all agree,
    The heaven the table, Zeuxis Jove muft be.

Fair foul, in this black age fo fhin'd thou bright,
And made all eyes with wonder thee behold,
Till ugly Death, depriving us of light,
In his grim mifty arms thee did enfold.
Who more fhall vaunt true beauty here to fee ?
What hope doth more in any heart remain,
That fuch perfections fhall his reafon rein,
If beauty with thee born, too died with thee?
 World plain no more of Love, nor count his harms ;
 With his pale trophies Death has hung his arms.

MADRIGAL.

MY thoughts hold mortal ftrife,
 I do deteft my life,
And with lamenting cries,
Peace to my foul to bring,
Oft call that prince which here doth monarchize :
But he grim grinning king,
Who caitiffs fcorns, and doth the bleft furprife,
 Late having deckt with beauty's rofe his tomb,
 Difdains to crop a weed, and will not come.

G

AN

E L E G Y

UPON THE

VICTORIOUS KING of SWEDEN,

GUSTAVUS ADOLPHUS.

L I K E a cold fatal fweat which ufhers death,
My thoughts hang on me; and by labouring
breath,
Stopt up with fighs, my fancy big with woes
Feels two twin mountains ftruggle in her throws,
Of boundlefs forrow th' one, th' other of fin ;
For lefs let no man call it, to begin
Where honour ends in great Guftavus' flame,
That ftill burnt out and wafted to a name,
Does barely live with us ; and when the ftuff
Which fed it fails, the taper turns to fnuff :
With this poor fnuff, this airy fhadow, we
Of fame and honour muft contented be,
Since from the vain grafp of our wifhes fled
Their glorious fubftances, now he is dead.
Speak it again, and louder, louder yet,
Elfe whilft we hear the found, we fhall forget

What

What it delivers; let hoarfe Rumour cry
Till fhe fo many echoes multiply,
That may like numerous witneffes confute
Our unbelieving fouls, that would difpute
And doubt this truth for ever, this one way
Is left our incredulity to fway,
T' awaken our deaf fenfe, and make our ears
As open and dilated as our tears ;
That we may feel the blow, and feeling grieve
At what we would not fain, but muft believe,
And in that horrid faith behold the world
From her proud height of expectation hurl'd ;
Stooping with him, as if fhe ftrove to have
No lower center now, than Sweden's grave.

　　O! could not all the purchas'd victories
Like to thy fame thy flefh immortalize ?
Were not thy virtue nor thy valour charms
To guard thy body from thofe outward harms
Which could not reach thy foul ? Could not thy fpirit
Lend fomewhat which thy frailty could inherit,
From thy diviner part that death nor heat,
Nor envy's bullets e'er could penetrate ?
Could not thy early trophies in ftern fight
Turn from the Pole, the Dane, the Mufcovite ?
Which were thy triumphs, feeds as pledges fown,
That, when thy honour's harveft was ripe grown,
With full plum'd wing thou faulcon-like could fly,
And cuff the eagle in the German fky,
Forcing his iron beak, and feathers feel
They were not proof 'gainft thy victorious fteel.

Could not all thefe protect thee, or prevail
To fright that coward Death, who oft grew pale
To look thee and thy battles in the face ?
Alas ! they could not ; Deftiny gives place
To none : nor is it feen that princes' lives
Can faved be by their prerogatives :
No more was thine ; who clos'd in thy cold lead
Doft from thyfelf a mournful lecture read
Of man's fhort-dated glory. Learn you kings,
You are like him but penetrable things ;
Though you from demi-gods derive your birth,
You are at beft but honourable earth :
And howe'er fifted from that coarfer bran
Which doth compound, and knead the common man ;
Nothing immortal, or from earth refin'd
About you, but your office and your mind.
Hear then, break your falfe glaffes, which prefent
You greater than your Maker ever meant.
Make truth your mirror now, fince you find all
That flatter you, confuted by his fall.
    Yet fince it was decreed thy life's bright fun
Muft be eclips'd ere thy full courfe was run,
Be proud thou didft in thy black obfequies
With greater glory fet than others rife :
For in thy death, as life, thou holdeft one
Moft juft and regular proportion.
Look how the circles drawn by compafs meet
Indivifibly, joined head to feet ;
And by continued points which them unite
Grow at once circular, and infinite :

                                                    So

So did thy fate and honour both contend
To match thy brave beginning with thine end.
Therefore thou hadſt, inſtead of paſſing-bells,
The drums and cannons thunder for thy knells;
And in the field thou didſt triumphing die,
Cloſing thy eyelids with a victory;
That ſo by thouſands that there loſt their breath,
King-like thou might'ſt be waited on in death.

Liv'd Plutarch now, and would of Cæſar tell,
He could make none but thee his parallel,
Whoſe tide of glory, ſwelling to the brim,
Needs borrow no addition from him:
When did great Julius in any clime
Achieve ſo much, and in ſo ſhort a time?
Or if he did, yet ſhalt thou in that land
Single for him, and unexampled ſtand.
When o'er the Germans firſt his eagle tow'r'd,
What ſaw the legions which on them he pour'd,
But maſſy bodies made their ſwords to try,
Subjects, not for his fight, but ſlavery?
In that ſo vaſt expanded piece of ground
(Now Sweden's theatre and ſcorn) he found
Nothing worth Cæſar's valour, or his fear,
No conqu'ring army, nor a Tilly there,
Whoſe ſtrength nor wiles, nor practice in the war
Might the fierce torrent of his triumphs bar;
But that thy winged ſword twice made him yield,
Both from his trenches beat, and from the field.
Beſides, the Roman thought he had done much,
Did he the banks of Rhenus only touch:

G 3   But

But though his march was bounded by the Rhine,
Not Oder nor the Danube thee confine.
And but thy frailty did thy fame prevent,
Thou hadſt thy conqueſt ſtretch'd to ſuch extent
Thou might'ſt Vienna reach, and after Spain ;
From Mulda to the Baltic ocean.
 But death hath ſpann'd thee, nor muſt we divine
What here thou hadſt to finiſh thy deſign ;
Or who ſhall thee ſucceed as champion
For liberty, and for religion.
Thy taſk is done : as in a watch the ſpring,
Wound to the height, relaxes with the ſtring ;
So thy ſteel nerves of conqueſt, from their ſteep
Aſcent declin'd, lie ſlackt in thy laſt ſleep.
Reſt then, triumphant ſoul, for ever reſt,
And, like the phœnix in her ſpicy neſt,
Embalm'd with thine own merit, upward fly,
Borne in a cloud of perfume to the ſky ;
Whilſt, as in deathleſs urns, each noble mind
Treaſures thine aſhes which are left behind.
And if perhaps no Caſſiopeian ſpark
(Which in the North did thy firſt riſing mark)
Shine o'er thy hearſe, the breath of our juſt praiſe
Shall to the firmament thy virtues raiſe ;
There fix and kindle them into a ſtar,
Whoſe influence may crown thy glorious war.

TEARS

T E A R S

ON THE

D E A T H

OF

M Œ L I A D E S.*

O HEAVENS ! then is it true that thou art gone,
And left this woful ifle her lofs to moan ;
Mœliades, bright day-ftar of the weft,
A comet blazing terror to the eaft ;
And neither that thy fpirit fo heavenly wife,
Nor body (though of earth), more pure than fkies,
Nor royal ftem, nor thy fweet tender age,
Of cruel deftinies could quench the rage ?
O fading hopes ! O fhort-while lafting joy
Of earth-born man, that one hour can deftroy !
Then even of virtue's fpoils death trophies rears,
As if he gloried moft in many tears.
Forc'd by hard fates, do heavens neglect our cries?
Are ftars fet only to act tragedies ?

* The name which in thefe verfes is given unto prince Henry,
is that which he himfelf, in the challenges of his martial fports
and mafquerades, was wont to ufe ; MœLIADES, Prince of the
Ifles, which in anagram maketh a word moft worthy of fuch a
knight as he was, a knight (if time had fuffered his actions to
anfwer the world's expectation), only worthy of fuch a word,
Miles à Deo.

Then let them do their worſt, ſince thou art gone,
Raiſe whom thou liſt to thrones, enthron'd dethrone ;
Stain princely bow'rs with blood, and even to Gange,
In cypreſs ſad, glad Hymen's torches change.
Ah! thou haſt left to live; and in the time
When ſcarce thou bloſſom'dſt in thy pleaſant prime :
So falls by northern blaſt a virgin roſe,
At half that doth her baſhful boſom cloſe ;
So a ſweet flower languiſhing decays,
That late did bluſh when kiſs'd by Phœbus' rays ;
So Phœbus mounting the meridian's height,
Choak'd by pale Phœbe, faints unto our ſight ;
Aſtoniſh'd nature ſullen ſtands to ſee
The life of all this all ſo chang'd to be ;
In gloomy gowns the ſtars this loſs deplore,
The ſea with murmuring mountains beats the ſhore,
Black darkneſs reels o'er all, in thouſand ſhow'rs
The weeping air on earth her ſorrow pours,
That, in a palſy, quakes to ſee ſo ſoon
Her lover ſet, and night burſt forth ere noon.
    If heaven, alas! ordain'd thee young to die,
Why was't not where thou might'ſt thy valour try ;
And to the wond'ring world at leaſt ſet forth
Some little ſpark of thy expected worth?
Mœliades, O that by Iſter's ſtreams,
'Mong ſounding trumpets, fiery twinkling gleams
Of warm vermilion ſwords, and cannons' roar,
Balls thick as rain pour'd on the Caſpian ſhore,
'Mongſt broken ſpears, 'mongſt ringing helms and
        ſhields,
Huge heaps of ſlaughter'd bodies 'long the fields,
2   In

In Turkiſh blood made red like Mars's ſtar,
Thou endedſt had thy life, and chriſtian war ;
Or as brave Bourbon, thou hadſt made old Rome,
Queen of the world, thy triumph, and thy tomb !
So heaven's fair face, to th' unborn world, which
     reads,
A book had been of thy illuſtrious deeds :
So to their nephews, aged ſires had told
The high exploits perform'd by thee of old ;
Towns ras'd, and rais'd, victorious, vanquiſh'd bands,
Fierce tyrants flying, foil'd, kill'd by thy hands :
And in rich arras virgins fair had wrought
The bays and trophics to thy country brought :
While ſome new Homer, imping wings to Fame,
Deaf Nilus' dwellers had made hear thy name.
That thou didſt not attain theſe honour's ſpheres,
Through want of worth it was not, but of years.
A youth more brave, pale Troy with trembling walls
Did never ſee, nor ſhe whoſe name appals
Both Titan's golden bow'rs, in bloody fights,
Muſt'ring on Mars his field, ſuch Mars-like knights.
The heavens had brought thee to the higheſt height
Of wit and courage, ſhewing all their might
When they thee fram'd.   Ah me ! that what is brave
On earth, they as their own ſo ſoon ſhould crave !
Mœliades ſweet courtly nymphs deplore,
From Thule to Hydaſpes' pearly ſhore.
     When Forth, thy nurſe, Forth where thou firſt
          didſt paſs
Thy tender days (who ſmil'd oft on her glaſs,

                                   To

To fee thee gaze), meand'ring with her ftreams,
Heard thou hadft left this round, from Phœbus' beams
She fought to fly, but forced to return
By neighbouring brooks, fhe fet herfelf to mourn :
And as fhe rufh'd her Cyclades among,
She feem'd to plain that heaven had done her
  wrong.
With a hoarfe plaint, Clyde down her fteepy rocks,
And Tweed through her green mountains clad with
  flocks,
Did wound the ocean murmuring thy death ;
The ocean it roar'd about the earth,
And to the Mauritanian Atlas told,
Who fhrunk through grief, and down his white hairs
  roll'd
Huge ftreams of tears, which changed were to floods,
Wherewith he drown'd the neighbour plains and
  woods.
The leffer brooks, as they did bubbling go,
Did keep a confort to the public woe.
The fhepherds left their flocks with downcaft eyes,
'Sdaining to look up to the angry fkies :
Some brake their pipes, and fome in fweet-fad lays
Made fenfelefs things amazed at thy praife.
His reed Alexis hung upon a tree,
And with his tears made Doven great to be.
Mœliades fweet courtly nymphs deplore,
From Thule to Hydafpes' pearly fhore.
  Chafte maids which haunt fair Aganippe's well,
And you in Tempe's facred fhade who dwell,
         Let

Let fall your harps, ceafe tunes of joy to fing,
Difhevelled make all Parnaffus ring
With anthems fad ; thy mufick Phœbus turn
To doleful plaints, whilft joy itfelf doth mourn.
Dead is thy darling who adorn'd thy bays,
Who oft was wont to cherifh thy fweet lays,
And to a trumpet raife thy amorous ftyle,
That floating Delos envy might this ifle.
You Acidalian archers break your bows,
Your torches quench, with tears blot beauty's fnows,
And bid your weeping mother yet again
A fecond Adon's death, nay Mars his plain.
His eyes once were your darts ; nay, even his name,
Wherever heard, did every heart inflame.
Tagus did court his love with golden ftreams,
Rhine with his towns, fair Seine with all fhe claims.
But ah ! (poor lovers) death did them betray,
And, not fufpected, made their hopes his prey !
Tagus bewails his lofs in golden ftreams,
Rhine with his towns, fair Seine with all fhe claims.
Mœliades fweet courtly nymphs deplore,
From Thule to Hydafpes' pearly fhore.
    Eye-pleafing   meads, whofe   painted plain forth
        brings
White, golden, azure flow'rs, which once were kings,
To mourning black their fhining colours dye,
Bow down their heads, while fighing zephyrs fly.
Queen of the fields, whofe blufh makes blufh the
        morn,
Sweet rofe, a prince's death in purple mourn ;
                                    O hya-

O hyacinths, for aye your AI keep ſtill,
Nay, with more marks of woe your leaves now fill ?
And you, O flow'r, of Helen's tears that's born,
Into theſe liquid pearls again you turn :
Your green locks, foreſts, cut ; to weeping myrrhs,
To deadly cypreſs, and ink-dropping firs,
Your palms and myrtles change ; from ſhadows dark
Wing'd ſyrens wail, and you ſad echoes mark
The lamentable accents of their moan,
And plain that brave Mœliades is gone.
Stay, ſky, thy turning courſe, and now become
A ſtately arch, unto the earth his tomb :
And over it ſtill wat'ry Iris keep,
And ſad Electra's ſiſters, who ſtill weep :
Mœliades ſweet courtly nymphs deplore,
From Thules to Hydaſpes' pearly ſhore.

Dear ghoſt, forgive theſe our untimely tears,
By which our loving mind, though weak, appears :
Our loſs, not thine (when we complain), we weep,
For thee the gliſtering walls of heaven do keep,
Beyond the planet's wheels, 'bove higheſt ſource
Of ſpheres, that turns the lower in his courſe :
Where ſun doth never ſet, nor ugly night
Ever appears in mourning garments dight :
Where Boreas' ſtormy trumpet doth not ſound,
Nor clouds, in lightnings burſting, minds aſtound.
From cares, cold climates far, and hot deſire,
Where time's exil'd, and ages ne'er expire ;
'Mong pureſt ſpirits environed with beams,
Thou think'ſt all things below t' have been but dreams ;

And

And joy'ft to look down to the azur'd bars
Of heaven powder'd with troops of ftreaming ftars ;
And in their turning temples to behold,
In filver robe the moon, the fun in gold ;
Like young eye-fpeaking lovers in a dance,
With majefty by turns retire, advance :
Thou wonder'ft earth to fee hang like a ball,
Clos'd in the mighty cloifter of this all ;
And that poor men fhould prove fo madly fond,
To tofs themfelves for a fmall fpot of ground :
Nay, that they ev'n dare brave the powers above,
From this bafe ftage of change that cannot move.
All worldly pomp and pride thou feeft arife,
Like fmoak that's fcatter'd in the empty fkies.
Other high hills and forefts, other tow'rs,
Amaz'd thou find'ft excelling our poor bow'rs ;
Courts void of flattery, of malice minds,
Pleafure which lafts, not fuch as reafon blinds.
Thou fweeter fongs doft hear, and carollings,
Whilft heavens do dance, and choirs of angels fings,
Than muddy minds could feign ; even our annoy
(If it approach that place) is chang'd to joy.
    Reft, bleffed foul, reft fatiate with the fight
Of him whofe beams (though dazzling) do delight ;
Life of all lives, caufe of each other caufe ;
The fphere and centre where the mind doth paufe ;
Narciffus of himfelf, himfelf the well,
Lover, and beauty that doth all excel.   :
Reft, happy foul, and wonder in that glafs,
Where feen is all that fhall be, is, or was,
                                          While

While fhall be, is, or was, do pafs away,
And nothing be, but an eternal day.
For ever reft ; thy praife Fame will enrol
In golden annals, while about the pole
The flow Boötes turns, or fun doth rife
With fcarlet fcarf to cheer the mourning fkies.
The virgins to thy tomb will garlands bear
Of flow'rs, and with each flow'r let fall a tear.
Mœliades fweet courtly nymphs deplore,
From Thule to Hydafpes' pearly fhore.

OF jet,
Or porphyry,
Or that white ftone
Paros affords alone,
Or thefe in azure dye,
Which feem to fcorn the fky ;
Here Memphis' wonders do not fet,
Nor Artemifia's huge frame,
That keeps fo long her lover's name,
Make no great marble Atlas ftoop with gold,
To pleafe the vulgar eye fhall it behold.
The Mufes, Phœbus, Love, have raifed of their tears
A cryftal tomb to him, through which his worth
appears.

E P I T A P H.

STAY, paffenger, fee where enclofed lies
    The paragon of princes, faireft frame,
Time, nature, place, could fhew to mortal eyes,
In worth, wit, virtue, miracle of fame :

At

At leaft that part the earth of him could claim
This marble holds (hard like the deftinies) :
For as to his brave fpirit, and glorious name,
The one the world, the other fills the fkies.
Th' immortal amaranthus, princely rofe,
Sad violet, and that fweet flow'r that bears
In fanguine fpots the tenor of our woes,
Spread on this ftone, and wafh it with your tears ;
   Then go and tell from Gades unto Inde,
   You faw where earth's perfections were confin'd.

ANOTHER.

A PASSING glance, a lightning long the fkies,
   Which, ufhering thunder, dies ftraight to our
     fight ;
A fpark that doth from jarring mixtures rife,
Thus drown'd is in th' huge depths of day and night :
Is this fmall trifle, life, held in fuch price
Of blinded wights, who ne'er judge aught aright ?
Of Parthian fhaft fo fwift is not the flight,
As life, that waftes itfelf, and living dies.
Ah ! what is human greatnefs, valour, wit ?
What fading beauty, riches, honour, praife ?
To what doth ferve in golden thrones to fit,
Thrall earth's vaft round, triumphal arches raife ?
   That all's a dream, learn in this prince's fall,
   In whom, fave death, nought mortal was at all.

A TRANS-

A

TRANSLATION

OF

SIR JOHN SCOT'S VERSES,

BEGINNING

Quod vitæ sectabor iter?

WHAT courſe of life ſhould wretched mortals
    take?
In books hard queſtions large contention make.
Care dwells in houſes, labour in the field;
Tumultuous ſeas affrighting dangers yield.
In foreign lands thou never canſt be bleſt:
If rich, thou art in fear; if poor, diſtreſs'd.
In wedlock frequent diſcontentments ſwell;
Unmarried perſons as in deſarts dwell.
How many troubles are with children born!
Yet he that wants them counts himſelf forlorn.
Young men are wanton, and of wiſdom void;
Grey hairs are cold, unfit to be employ'd.
Who would not one of theſe two offers try,
Not to be born; or, being born, to die?

MADRIGALS

MADRIGALS

AND

EPIGRAMS.

H

MADRIGALS

AND

EPIGRAMS.

THE

STATUE OF MEDUSA.

OF that Medusa strange,
    Who those that did her see in rocks did change,
No image carv'd is this;
Medusa's self it is :
For while at heat of day
To quench her thirst she by this spring did stay,
Her hideous head beholding in this glass,
Her senses fail'd, and thus transform'd she was.

THE

PORTRAIT of MARS and VENUS.

FAIR Paphos' wanton queen
    (Not drawn in white and red)
Is truly here, as when in Vulcan's bed
She was of all heaven's laughing fenate feen.
Gaze on her hair, and eine,
Her brows, the bows of Love,
Her back with lilies fpread :
Ye alfo might perceive her turn and move,
But that fhe neither fo will do, nor dare,
For fear to wake the angry god of war.

NARCISSUS.

FLOODS cannot quench my flames, ah ! in this
    well
I burn, not drown, for what I cannot tell.

DAMETA's DREAM.

DAMETA dream'd he faw his wife at fport,
    And found that fight was through the horny
    port.

CHERRIES.

MY wanton, weep no more
    The lofing of your cherries;
Thofe, and far fweeter berries,
Your fifter, in good ftore,

Hath

Hath in her lips and face;
Be glad, kifs her with me, and hold your peace.

ICARUS.

WHILE with audacious wings
    I cleav'd thofe airy ways,
And fill'd (a monfter new) with dread and fears,
The feather'd people and their eagle kings:
Dazzled with Phœbus' rays,
And charm'd with the mufick of the fpheres,
When quills could move no more, and force did fail,
Though down I fell from heaven's high azure
       bounds;
Yet doth renown my loffes countervail,
For ftill the fhore my brave attempt refounds.
A fea, an element doth bear my name;
What mortal's tomb's fo great in place or fame?

ON HIS LADY BEHOLDING HERSELF IN A MARBIE.

WORLD wonder not, that I
    Keep in my breaft engraven
That angel's face hath me of reft bereaven.
See dead and fenfelefs things cannot deny
To lodge fo dear a gueft:
Ev'n this hard marble ftone
Receives the fame, and loves, but cannot groan.

H 3.   TO

TO SLEEP.

HOW comes it, Sleep, that thou
    Even kiffes me affords
Of her, dear her, fo far who's abfent now ?
How did I hear thofe words,
Which rocks might move, and move the pines to bow ?
Ah me ! before half day
Why didft thou fteal away ?
Return, I thine for ever will remain,
If thou wilt bring with thee that gueft again.

A PLEASANT DECEIT.

OVER a cryftal fource
    Iolas laid his face,
Of purling ftreams to fee the reftlefs courfe.
But fcarce he had o'erfhadowed the place,
When in the water he a child efpies,
So like himfelf in ftature, face and eyes,
That glad he rofe, and cried,
Dear mates approach, fee whom I have defcried,
The boy of whom ftrange ftories fhepherds tell,
Oft called Hylas, dwelleth in this well.

THE CANNON.

WHEN firft the cannon from her gaping throat
    Againft the heaven her roaring fulphur fhot,
Jove, waken'd with the noife, did afk with wonder,
What mortal wight had ftol'n from him his thunder :

His

His cryſtal tow'rs he fear'd, but fire and air
So high ḍid ſtay the ball from mounting there.

THAIS' METAMORPHOSIS.

INTO Briareus huge
   Thais wiſh'd ſhe might change
Her man, and pray'd him not thereat to grudge,
Nor fondly think it ſtrange;
For if, ſaid ſhe, I might the parts diſpoſe,
I wiſh you not a hundred arms nor hands,
But hundred things like thoſe
With which Priapus in our garden ſtands.

THE QUALITY OF A KISS.

THE kiſs with ſo much ſtrife
   Which I late got, ſweet heart,
Was it a ſign of death, or was it life?
Of life it could not be,
For I by it did ſigh my ſoul in thee:
Nor was it death, death doth no joy impart.
Thou ſilent ſtand'ſt, ah! what didſt thou bequeath,
A dying life to me, or living death?

HIS LADY's DOG.

WHEN her dear boſom clips
   That little cur which fawns to touch her
     lips,

O·

Or when it is his hap
To lie lapp'd in her lap,
O it grows noon with me ;
With hotter-pointed beams
I burn, than thofe are which the fun forth ftreams,
When piercing lightning his rays call'd may be ;
And as I mufe how I to thofe extremes
Am brought, I find no caufe, except that fhe
In Love's bright zodiack having trac'd each room,
To the hot dog-ftar now at laft is come.

AN ALMANACK.

THIS ftrange eclipfe one fays
   Strange wonders doth foretel ;
But you whofe wives excel,
And love to count their praife,
Shut all your gates, your hedges plant with thorns,
The fun did threat the world this time with horns.

The SILK - WORM of LOVE.

A DÆDALE of my death
   Now I refemble that fly worm on earth,
Which prone to its own harm doth take no reft :
For day and night oppreft,
I feed on fading leaves
Of hope, which me deceives,
And thoufand webs do warp within my breaft :
And thus in end unto myfelf I weave
A faft-fhut prifon, or a clofer grave.

DEEP

Deep Impression of Love to his Mistress.

WHOM a mad dog doth bite,
    He doth in water ftill
That mad dog's image fee :
Love, mad, perhaps, when he my heart did fmite,
More to diffemble his ill,
Transform'd himfelf to thee :
For thou art prefent ever fince to me.
No fpring there is, no flood, nor other place
Where I, alas ! not fee thy heavenly face.

A CHAIN of GOLD.

ARE not thofe locks of gold
    Sufficient chains the wildeft hearts to hold?
Is not that ivory hand
A diamantine band,
Moft fure to keep the moft untamed mind,
But ye muft others find ?
O yes ! why is that golden one then worn ?
Thus free in chains, perhaps, love's chains to fcorn.

On the DEATH of a LINNET.

IF cruel Death had ears,
    Or could be pleas'd by fongs,
This wing'd mufician had liv'd many years,
And Nifa mine had never wept thefe wrongs :

For

For when it firſt took breath,
The heavens their notes did unto it bequeath :
And if that Samian's ſentences be true,
Amphion in this body liv'd anew.
But Death, who nothing ſpares, and nothing hears,
As he doth kings, kill'd it, O grief ! O tears!

LILLA's PRAYER.

L OVE, if thou wilt once more
     That I to thee return,
Sweet god ! make me not burn
For quivering age, that doth ſpent days deplore.
Nor do thou wound my heart
For ſome inconſtant boy
Who joys to love, yet makes of love a toy.
But, ah ! if I muſt prove thy golden dart,
Of grace, O let me find
A ſweet young lover with an aged mind.
Thus Lillá pray'd, and Idas did reply,
(Who heard) Dear, have thy wiſh, for ſuch am I.

ARMELIN's EPITAPH.

N EAR to this eglantine
     Encloſed lies the milk-white Armeline ;
Once Cloris' only joy,
Now only her annoy ;
Who envied was of the moſt happy ſwains
That keep their flocks in mountains, dales, or plains :

For

For oft she bore the wanton in her arm,
And oft her bed and bosom did he warm ;
Now when unkinder Fates did him destroy,
Blest dog, he had the grace,
That Cloris for him wet with tears her face.

EPITAPH.

THE bawd of justice, he who laws controll'd,
    And made them fawn and frown as he got gold,
That Proteus of our state, whose heart and mouth
Were farther distant than is north from south,
That cormorant who made himself so grofs
On people's ruin, and the prince's lofs,
Is gone to hell ; and though he here did evil,
He there perchance may prove an honest devil.

A TRANSLATION.

FIERCE robbers were of old
    Exil'd the champaign ground,
From hamlets chas'd, in cities kill'd, or bound,
And only woods, caves, mountains, did them hold :
But now, when all is fold,
Woods, mountains, caves, to good men be refuge,
And do the guiltlefs lodge,
And clad in purple gowns
The greatest thieves command within the towns.

EPITAPH.

EPITAPH.

THEN Death thee hath beguil'd,
 Alecto's firft born child;
Then thou who thrall'd all laws,
Now againft worms cannot maintain thy caufe :
Yet worms (more juft than thou) now do no wrong,
Since all do wonder they thee fpar'd fo long ;
For though from life thou didft but lately pafs,
Twelve fprings are gone fince thou corrupted was.

Come, citizens, erect to Death an altar,
Who keeps you from axe, fuel, timber, halter.

A JEST.

IN a moft holy church, a holy man,
 Unto a holy faint with vifage wan,
And eyes like fountains, mumbled forth a prayer,
And with ftrange words and fighs made black the air.
And having long fo ftay'd, and long long pray'd,
A thoufand croffes on himfelf he laid ;
And with fome facred beads hung on his arm,
His eyes, his mouth, his temples, breaft did charm.
Thus not content (ftrange worfhip hath no end)
To kifs the earth at laft he did pretend,
And bowing down befought, with humble grace,
An aged woman near to give fome place :
 She turn'd, and turning up her hole beneath,
 Said, Sir, kifs here, for it is all but earth.

PROTEUS

PROTEUS of MARBLE.

THIS is no work of ſtone,
  Though it ſeems breathleſs, cold, and ſenſe
hath none,
But that falſe god which keeps
The monſtrous people of the raging deeps :
Now that he doth not change his ſhape this while,
It is thus conſtant more you to beguile.

PAMPHILUS.

SOME Ladies wed, ſome love, and ſome adore
  them,
I like their wanton ſport, then care not for them.

APELLES ENAMOURED OF CAMPASPE, ALEXANDER'S MISTRESS.

POOR painter, while I ſought
  To counterfeit by art
The faireſt frame which Nature ever wrought,
And having limn'd each part,
Except her matchleſs eyes :
Scarce on thoſe ſuns I gaz'd,
As lightning falls from ſkies,
When ſtraight my hand grew weak, my mind amaz'd,
And ere that pencil half them had expreſs'd,
Love had them drawn, no, grav'd them in my breaſt.

CAMPASPE.

CAMPASPE.

ON ſtars ſhall I exclaim,
    Which thus my fortune change,
Or ſhall I elſe revenge
Upon myſelf this ſhame,
Inconſtant monarch, or ſhall I thee blame
Who lets Apelles prove
The ſweet delights of Alexander's love ?
No, ſtars, myſelf, and thee, I all forgive,
And joy that thus I live ;
Of thee, blind king, ˒my beauty was deſpis'd,
Thou didſt not know it, now being known 'tis priz'd.

CORNUCOPIA.

IF for one only horn,
    Which Nature to him gave,
So famous is the noble unicorn ;
What praiſe ſhould that man have,
Whoſe head a lady brave
Doth with a goodly pair at once adorn ?

LOVE SUFFERS NO PARASOL.

THOSE eyes, dear eyes, be ſpheres
    Where two bright ſuns are roll'd,
That fair hand to behold,
Of whiteſt ſnow appears :

Then

Then while ye coyly ſtand
To hide from me thoſe eyes,
Sweet, I would you adviſe
To chooſe ſome other fan than that white hand:
For if ye do, for truth moſt true this know,
Thoſe ſuns ere long muſt needs conſume warm ſnow.

UNPLEASANT MUSICK.

IN fields Ribaldo ſtray'd,
   May's tapeſtry to ſee,
And hearing on a tree
A cuckow ſing, ſigh'd to himſelf, and ſaid,
Lo! how, alas! even birds ſit mocking me!

SLEEPING BEAUTY.

O SIGHT, too dearly bought!
   She ſleeps, and though thoſe eyes,
Which lighten Cupid's ſkiés,
Be clos'd, yet ſuch a grace
Environeth that place,
That I, through wonder, to grow faint am brought:
Suns, if eclips'd you have ſuch power divine,
What power have I t'endure you when you ſhine?

ALCON's KISS.

WHAT others at their ear,
   Two pearls, Camilla at her noſe did wear,
                                          Which

Which Alcon, who nought faw,
(For Love is blind) robb'd with a pretty kifs ;
But having known his mifs,
And felt what ore he from that mine did draw,
When fhe to come again did him defire,
He fled, and faid, foul water quenched fire.

THE

STATUE of VENUS SLEEPING.

PASSENGER, vex not thy mind,
  To make me mine eyes unfold ;
For if thou fhouldeft them behold,
Thine, perhaps, they will make blind.

LAURA to PETRARCH.

I RATHER love a youth, and childifh rhyme,
  Than thee, whofe verfe and head are wife through
    time.

THE ROSE.

FLOW'R, which of Adon's blood
  Sprang, when of that clear flood,
Which Venus wept, another white was borne,
The fweet Cynarean youth thou lively fhews ;
But this fharp-pointed thorn,
So proud about thy crimfon fold that grows,

                                                    What

What doth it reprefent?
Boar's teeth, perhaps, his milk-white flank which
    rent.
O fhew, in one of unefteemed worth,
That both the kill'd and killer fetteth forth!

A LOVER's PRAYER.

NEAR to a cryftal fpring,
    With thirft and heat oppreft,
Narciffa fair doth reft,
Trees, pleafant trees, which thofe green plains forth
      bring,
Now interlace your trembling tops above,
And make a canopy unto my love;
So in heaven's higheft houfe, when fun appears,
Aurora may you cherifh with her tears.

IOLAS' EPITAPH.

HERE dear Iolas lies,
    Who whilft he liv'd in beauty did furpafs
That boy, whofe heavenly eyes
Brought Cypris from above,
Or him to death who look'd in wat'ry glafs,
Even judge the god of love.
And if the nymph, once held of him fo dear,
Dorine the fair, would here but fhed one tear,
Thou fhould'ft, in nature's fcorn,
A purple flow'r fee of this marble born.

        I   THE

THE TROJAN HORSE.

A HORSE I am, who bit,
  Rein, rod, fpur, do not fear ;
When I my riders bear,
Within my womb, not on my back they fit.
No ftreams I drink, nor care for grafs or corn ;
Art me a monfter wrought,
All nature's works to fcorn ;
A mother I was without mother born,
In end all arm'd my father I forth brought :
What thoufand fhips and champions of renown
Could not do free, captiv'd I raz'd Troy's town.

FOR DORUS.

W HY, Nais, ftand ye nice,
  Like to a well-wrought ftone,
When Dorus would you kifs ?
Deny him not that blifs,
He's but a child (old men be children twice),
And even a toothlefs one :
And when his lips yours touch in that delight,
Ye need not fear he will thofe cherries bite.

LOVE VAGABONDING.

S WEET nymphs, if as ye ftray
  Ye find the froth-born goddefs of the fea,

All

All blubber'd, pale, undone,
Who feeks her giddy fon,
That little god of love,
Whofe golden fhafts your chafteft bofoms prove ;
Who leaving all the heavens hath run away :
If aught to him that finds him fhe'll impart,
Tell her he nightly lodgeth in my heart.

TO A RIVER.

SITH fhe will not that I
  Shew to the world my joy,
Thou, who oft mine annoy
Haft heard, dear flood, tell Thetis if thou can
That not a happier man
Doth breathe beneath the fky.
More fweet, more white, more fair,
Lips, hands, and amber hair,
Tell none did ever touch ;
A fmaller, daintier waift
Tell never was embrac'd ;
But peace, fince fhe forbids thee tell too much.

LIDA.

SUCH Lida is, that who her fees,
  Through envy, or through love, ftraight dies.

PHRÆNE.

PHRÆNE.

AONIAN fifters, help my Phræne's praife to
tell,
Phræne, heart of my heart, with whom the Graces
dwell ;
For I furcharged am fo fore that I not know
What firft to praife of her, her breaft, or neck of
fnow,
Her cheeks with rofes fpread, or her two fun-like
eyes,
Her teeth of brighteft pearl, her lips where fweetnefs
lies :
But thofe fo praife themfelves, being to all eyes fet
forth,
That, Mufes, ye need not to fay aught of their worth ;
Then her white fwelling paps effay for to make
known,
But her white fwelling paps through fmalleft veil
are fhewn ;
Yet fhe hath fomething elfe, more worthy than the
reft,
Not feen ; go fing of that which lies beneath her breaft,
And mounts like fair Parnaffe, where Pegafe well
doth run——
Here Phræne ftay'd my mufe ere fhe had well begun.

KISSES

KISSES DESIRED.

THOUGH I with ftrange defire
    To kifs thofe rofy lips am fet on fire,
Yet will I ceafe to crave
Sweet kiffes in fuch ftore,
As he who long before
In thoufands them from Lefbia did receive :
Sweetheart, but once me kifs,
And I by that fweet blifs
Even fwear to ceafe you to importune more ;
Poor one no number is ;
Another word of me ye fhall not hear
After one kifs, but ftill one kifs, my dear.

DESIRED DEATH.

DEAR life, while I do touch
    Thefe coral ports of blifs,
Which ftill themfelves do kifs,
And fweetly me invite to do as much,
All panting in my lips,
My heart my life doth leave,
No fenfe my fenfes have,
And inward powers do find a ftrange eclipfe :
This death fo heavenly well
Doth fo me pleafe, that I
Would never longer feek in fenfe to dwell,
If that even thus I only could but die.

I 3   PHŒBE.

PHŒBÉ.

IF for to be alone, and all the night to wander,
Maids can prove chafte, then chafte is Phœbe
without flander.

ANSWER.

FOOL, ftill to be alone, all night in heaven to
wander,
Would make the wanton chafte, then fhe's chafte
without flander.

THE CRUELTY OF RORA.

WHILST fighing forth his wrongs,
In fweet, though doleful fongs,
Alexis fought to charm his Rora's ears,
The hills were heard to moan,
To figh each fpring appear'd,
Trees, hardeft trees, through rine diftill'd their tears,
And foft grew every ftone :
But tears, nor fighs, nor fongs could Rora move,
For fhe rejoiced at his plaint and love.

A KISS.

A KISS.

HARK, happy lovers, hark,
    This firſt and laſt of joys,
This ſweet'ner of annoys,
This nectar of the gods,
You call a kiſs, is with itſelf at odds ;
And half ſo ſweet is not
In equal meaſure got,
At light of ſun, as it is in the dark ;
Hark, happy lovers, hark.

KALA's COMPLAINT.

KALA, old Mopſus' wife,
    Kala with faireſt face,
For whom the neighbour ſwains oft were at ſtrife,
As ſhe to milk her ſnowy flock did tend,
Sigh'd with a heavy grace,
And ſaid, What wretch like me doth lead her life ?
I ſee not how my taſk ſhall have an end ;
All day I draw theſe ſtreaming dugs in fold,
All night mine empty huſband's ſoft and cold.

PHILLIS.

IN petticoat of green,
    Her hair about her eine,
        I 4   Phillis,

Phillis, beneath an oak,
Sat milking her fair flock :
'Mongſt that ſweet-ſtrained moiſture (rare delight)
Her hand ſeem'd milk, in milk it was ſo white.

A WISH.

TO forge to mighty Jove
    The thunderbolts above,
Nor on this round below
Rich Midas' ſkill to know,
And make all gold I touch,
Do I deſire ; it is for me too much :
Of all the arts practis'd beneath the ſky,
I would but Phillis' lapidary be.

NISA.

NISA, Palemon's wife, him weeping told
    He kept not grammar rules, now being old ;
For why, quoth ſhe, poſition falſe make ye,
Putting a ſhort thing where a long ſhould be.

A LOVER's HEAVEN.

THOSE ſtars, nay ſuns, which turn
    So ſtately in their ſpheres,
And dazzling do not burn,
The beauty of the morn
Which on theſe cheeks appears,

The harmony which to that voice is given,
Makes me think you are heaven.
If heaven you be, O ! that by powerful charms
I Atlas were, infolded in your arms !

EPITAPH.

THIS dear, though not refpected earth doth
    hold
One, for his worth, whofe tomb fhould be of gold.

BEAUTY's IDEA.

WHO would perfection's fair idea fee,
    On pretty Cloris let him look with me ;
White is her hair, her teeth white, white her fkin,
Black be her eyes, her eye-brows Cupid's inn :
Her locks, her body, hands do long appear,
But teeth fhort, fhort her womb, and either ear,
The fpace 'twixt fhoulders ; eyes are wide, brow wide,
Strait waift, the mouth ftrait, and her virgin pride.
Thick are her lips, thighs, with banks fwelling there,
Her nofe is fmall, fmall fingers, and her hair :
Her fugar'd mouth, her cheeks, her nails be red,
Little her foot, breaft little, and her head.
    Such Venus was, fuch was that flame of Troy,
    Such Cloris is, mine hope, and only joy.

LALUS' DEATH.

A MIDST the waves profound,
   Far, far from all relief,
The honeſt fiſher Lalus, ah! is drown'd,
   Shut in this little ſkiff;
The boards of which did ſerve him for a bier,
So that when he to the black world came near,
Of him no ſilver greedy Charon got;
   For he in his own boat
Did paſs that flood, by which the gods do ſwear.

FLOWERS

FLOWERS of SION:

OR,

SPIRITUAL POEMS.

TRIUMPHANT arches, ftatues crown'd with
    bays,
Proud obelifks, tombs of the vafteft frame,
Brazen Coloffes, Atlafes of fame,
And temples builded to vain deities' praife ;
States which unfatiate minds in blood do raife,
From fouthern pole unto the arctic team,
And even what we write to keep our name,
Like fpiders' cauls, are made the fport of days ;
All only conftant is in conftant change ;
What done is, is undone, and when undone,
Into fome other figure doth it range ;
Thus rolls the reftlefs world beneath the moon :
    Wherefore, my mind, above time, motion, place,
    Afpire, and fteps, not reach'd by nature, trace.

A GOOD that never fatisfies the mind,
    A beauty fading like the April flow'rs,
A fweet with floods of gall that runs combin'd,
A pleafure paffing ere in thought made ours,
                  A honour

A honour that more fickle is than wind,
A glory at opinion's frown that low'rs,
A treafury which bankrupt time devours,
A knowledge than grave ignorance more blind,
A vain delight our equals to command,
A ftyle of greatnefs, in effect a dream,.
A fwelling thought of holding fea and land,
A fervile lot, deck'd with a pompous name;
  Are the ftrange ends we toil for here below,.
  Till wifeft death make us our errors know.

L IFE a right fhadow is;
     For if it long appear,
Then is it fpent, and death's long night draws near;
Shadows are moving, light,
And is there aught fo moving as is this?
When it is moft in fight,
It fteals away, and none knows how or where,
So near our cradles to our coffins are.

L OOK as the flow'r, which ling'ringly doth fade,
     The morning's darling late, the fummer's queen,
Spoil'd of that juice which kept it frefh and green,
As high as it did raife, bows low the head:
Juft fo the pleafures of my life being dead,
Or in their contraries but only feen,
With fwifter fpeed declines than erft it fpread,
And, blafted, fcarce now fhews what it hath been..
                                        Therefore,

Therefore, as doth the pilgrim, whom the night
Haftes darkly to imprifon on his way,
Think on thy home, my foul, and think aright
Of what's yet left thee of life's wafting day :
  Thy fun pofts weftward, paffed is thy morn,
  And twice it is not given thee to be born. ˙

———————

THE weary mariner fo far not flies
  An howling tempeft, harbour to attain ;
Nor fhepherd haftes, when frays of wolves arife,
So faft to fold to fave his bleating train,
As I (wing'd with contempt and juft difdain)
Now fly the world, and what it moft doth prize,
And fanctuary feek, free to remain
From wounds of abject times, and Envy's eyes :
To me this world did once feem fweet and fair,
While fenfe's light mind's perfpective kept blind ;
Now like imagin'd landfcape in the air,
And weeping rainbows her beft joys I find :
  Or if aught here is had that praife fhould have,
  It is an obfcure life and filent grave.

———————

OF this fair volume which we world do name,
  If we the fheets and leaves could turn with
      care,
Of him who it corrects, and did it frame,
We clear might read the art and wifdom rare,

                        Find

Find out his power which wildeft powers doth tame,
His providence extending every where,
His juftice, which proud rebels doth not fpare,
In every page, no period of the fame :
But filly we, like foolifh children, reft
Well pleas'd with colour'd vellum, leaves of gold,
Fair dangling ribbands, leaving what is beft,
On the great writer's fenfe ne'er taking hold ;
   Or if by chance we ftay our minds on aught,
   It is fome picture on the margin wrought.

THE grief was common, common were the cries,
    Tears, fobs, and groans of that afflicted train,
Which of God's chofen did the fum contain,
And earth rebounded with them, pierc'd were fkies;
All good had left the world, each vice did reign
In the moft monftrous forts hell could devife,
And all degrees and each eftate did ftain,
Nor further had to go whom to furprife ;
The world beneath, the prince of darknefs lay,
And in each temple had himfelf inftall'd,
Was facrific'd unto, by prayers call'd,
Refponfes gave, which, fools, they did obey;
   When, pitying man, God of a virgin's womb
   Was born, and thofe falfe deities ftruck dumb.

RUN.

R UN, fhepherds, run, where Bethlem bleft ap-
      pears;
We bring the beft of news, be not difmay'd,
A Saviour there is born, more old than years,
Amidft the rolling heaven this earth who ftay'd;
In a poor cottage inn'd, a virgin maid
A weakling did him bear who all upbears;
There he in clothes is wrapp'd, in manger laid,
To whom too narrow fwadlings are our fpheres.
Run, fhepherds, run, and folemnize his birth;
This is that night, no day, grown great with blifs,
In which the power of Satan broken is;
In heaven be glory; peace unto the earth:
   Thus finging through the air the angels fwam,
   And all the ftars re-echoed the fame.

O THAN the faireft day, thrice fairer night,
    Night to beft days, in which a fun doth rife,
Of which the golden eye which clears the fkies
Is but a fparkling ray, a fhadow light;
And bleffed ye, in filly paftors' fight,
Mild creatures, in whofe warm crib now lies
That heaven-fent youngling, holy-maid-born wight,
'Midft, end, beginning of our prophecies:
Bleft cottage, that hath flow'rs in winter fpread;
'Though wither'd bleffed grafs, that hath the grace
To deck and be a carpet to that place.
                     Thus

Thus finging to the founds of oaten reed,
Before the babe the fhepherds bow'd their knees,
And fprings ran nectar, honey dropp'd from trees.

———————

THE laft and greateft herald of heaven's king,
    Girt with rough fkins, hies to the defarts wild,
Among that favage brood the woods forth bring,
Which he more harmlefs found than man, and mild.
His food was locufts, and what there doth fpring,
With honey that from virgin hives diftill'd :
Parch'd body, hollow eyes, fome uncouth thing
Made him appear, long fince from earth exil'd.
There burft he forth. All ye whofe hopes rely
On God, with me amidft thefe defarts mourn,
Repent, repent, and from old errors turn.

Who liften'd to his voice, obey'd his cry?
Only the Echoes, which he made relent,
Rung from their flinty caves, Repent, repent.

———————

THESE eyes, dear Lord, once tapers of defire,
    Frail fcouts betraying what they had to keep,
Which their own heart, then others fet on fire,
Their trait'rous black before thee here out-weep ;
Thefe locks of blufhing deeds, the gilt attire,
Waves curling, wreckful fhelves to fhadow deep,
Rings, wedding fouls to fin's lethargic fleep,
To touch thy facred feet do now afpire.

In feas of care behold a finking bark,
By winds of fharp remorfe unto thee driven :
O let me not be ruin's aim'd-at mark ;
My faults confefs'd, Lord, fay they are forgiven.
  Thus figh'd to Jefus the Bethanian fair,
  His tear-wet feet ftill drying with her hair.

I Changed countries new delights to find,
  But, ah ! for pleafure I did find new pain ;
Enchanting pleafure fo did reafon blind,
That father's love and words I fcorn'd as vain.
For tables rich, for bed, for following train
Of careful fervants to obferve my mind ;
Thefe herds I keep my fellows are affign'd,
My bed's a rock, and herbs my life fuftain.
Now while I famine feel, fear worfer harms,
Father and Lord, I turn, thy love, yet great,
My faults will pardon, pity mine eftate.

This, where an aged oak had fpread its arms,
Thought the loft child, while as the herds he led,   .
And pin'd with hunger on wild acorns fed.

K   IF

———————————

IF that the world doth in amaze remain,
   To hear in what a fad, deploring mood,
The pelican pours from her breaft her blood,
To bring to life her younglings back again ;
How fhould we wonder at that fovereign good,
Who from that ferpent's fting that had us flain,
To fave our lives, fhed his life's purple flood,
And turn'd to endlefs joy our endlefs pain !
Ungrateful foul, that charm'd with falfe delight,
Haft long, long wander'd in fin's flow'ry path,
And didft not think at all, or thought'ft not right
On this thy Pelican's great love and death.
   Here paufe, and let (though earth it fcorn) heaven
      fee
   Thee pour forth tears to him pour'd blood for thee.

———————————

IF in the eaft when you do there behold
   Forth from his cryftal bed the fun to rife,
With rofy robes and crown of flaming gold;
If gazing on that emprefs of the fkies
   That takes fo many forms, and thofe fair brands
   Which blaze in heaven's high vault, night's watch-
      ful eyes ;
If feeing how the fea's tumultuous bands

                                             Of

Of bellowing billows have their courſe confin'd ;
How unſuſtain'd the earth ſtill ſtedfaſt ſtands ;
Poor mortal wights, you e'er found in your mind
. A thought that ſome great king did ſit above,
Who had ſuch laws and rites to them aſſign'd ;
A king who fix'd the poles, made ſpheres to move,
All wiſdom, pureneſs, excellency, might,
All goodneſs, greatneſs, juſtice, beauty, love ;—
With fear and wonder hither turn your ſight,
 See, ſee, alas ! him now, not in that ſtate
Thought could forecaſt him into reaſon's light.
Now eyes with tears, now hearts with grief make
   great,
Bemoan this cruel death and ruthful caſe,
If ever plaints juſt woe could aggravate :
From ſin and hell to ſave us human race,
See this great king nail'd to an abjeЄt tree,
An objeЄt of reproach and ſad diſgrace.
O unheard pity ! love in ſtrange degree !
He his own life doth give, his blood doth ſhed,
For wormlings baſe ſuch worthineſs to ſee.
Poor wights ! behold his viſage pale as lead,
His head bow'd to his breaſt, locks ſadly rent,
Like a cropp'd roſe, that languiſhing doth fade.
Weak nature, weep ! aſtoniſh'd world, lament !
 Lament, you winds ! you heaven, that all con-
   tains !
And thou, my ſoul, let nought thy griefs relent
Thoſe hands, thoſe ſacred hands, which hold the reins

Of this great all, and kept from mutual wars
The elements, bare rent for thee their veins:
Thofe feet, which once muft tread on golden ftars,
  For thee with nails would be pierc'd through and
    torn;
,For thee, heaven's king, from heaven himfelf de-
    bars:
This great heart-quaking dolour wail and mourn,
  Ye that long fince him faw by might of faith,
  Ye now that are, and ye yet to be born.
Not to behold his great Creator's death,
  - The fun from finful eyes hath veil'd his light,
  And faintly journies up heaven's fapphire path;
And cutting from her prows her treffes bright
  The moon doth keep her Lord's fad obfequies,
  Impearling with her tears her robe of night;
All ftaggering and lazy lour the fkies;
  The earth and elemental ftages quake;
  The long-fince dead from burfted graves arife.
And can things, wanting fenfe, yet forrow take,
  And bear a part with him who all them wrought,
  And man (though born with cries) fhall pity lack?
Think what had been your ftate, had he not brought
  To thefe fharp pangs himfelf, and priz'd fo high
  Your fouls, that with his life them life he bought!
What woes do you attend, if ftill ye lie,
  Plung'd in your wonted ordures! Wretched brood!
  Shall for your fake again God ever die?
O leave deluding fhews, embrace true good,

                                          He

He on you calls, forego fin's shameful trade;
With prayers now seek heaven, and not with blood.
Let not the lambs more from their dams be had,
  Nor altars blush for fin; live every thing;
  That long time long'd-for sacrifice is made.
All that is from you crav'd by this great king
  Is to believe: a pure heart incense is.
  What gift, alas! can we him meaner bring?
Haste, fin-fick fouls! this feafon do not mifs,
  Now while remorfelefs time doth grant you fpace,
  And God invites you to your only blifs:
He who you calls will not deny you grace,
  But low-deep bury faults, fo ye repent;
  His arms, lo! ftretched are, you to embrace.
When days are done, and life's fmall fpark is fpent,
  So you accept what freely here is given,
  Like brood of angels deathlefs, all-content,
Ye fhall for ever live with him in heaven.

COME forth, come forth, ye bleft triumphing
    bands,
Fair citizens of that immortal town;
Come fee that king which all this all commands,
Now, overcharg'd with love, die for his own:
Look on thofe nails which pierce his feet and hands;
What a fharp diadem his brows doth crown!
Behold his pallid face, his heavy frown,
And what a throng of thieves him mocking ftands!

Come forth ye empyrean troops, come forth,
Preferve this facred blood that earth adorns,
Gather thofe liquid rofes off his thorns;
O! to be loft they be of too much worth:
For ftreams, juice, balm, they are, which quench,
       kills, charms,
Of God, death, hell, the wrath, the life, the harms.

SOUL, whom hell did once inthral,
  He, he for thine offence
Did fuffer death, who could not die at all.
O fovereign excellence!
O life of all that lives!
Eternal bounty which each good thing gives!
How could Death mount fo high?
No wit this point can reach,
Faith only doth us teach,
He died for us at all who could not die.

LIFE, to give life, deprived is of life,
  And Death difplay'd hath enfign againft death;
So violent the rigour was of Death,
That nought could daunt it but the Life of life:
No power had power to thrall Life's pow'rs to death,
But willingly Life down hath laid his life.

                           Love

Love gave the wound which wrought this work of
  Death ;
His bow and fhafts were of the tree of life.
Now quakes the author of eternal death,
To find that they whom late he reft of life,
Shall fill his room above the lifts of death ;
Now all rejoice in death who hope for life.
  Dead Jefus lives, who Death hath kill'd by death;
  No tomb his tomb is, but new fource of life.

———

R ISE from thofe fragrant climes, thee now em-
    brace ;
Unto this world of ours O hafte thy race,
Fair fun, and though contrary ways all year
Thou hold thy courfe, now with the higheft fhare,
Join thy blue wheels to haften time that low'rs,
And lazy minutes turn to perfect hours ;
The Night and Death too long a league have made,
To ftow the world in horror's ugly fhade.
Shake from thy locks a day with faffron rays
So fair, that it outfhine all other days ;
And yet do not prefume, great Eye of Light,
To be that which this day muft make fo bright.
See an Eternal Sun haftes to arife ;
Not from the eaftern blufhing feas or fkies,
Or any ftranger worlds heaven's concaves have,
But from the darknefs of an hollow grave.

And

And this is that all-powerful Sun above,
That crown'd thy brows with rays, firſt made thee
    move.
Light's trumpeters, ye need not from your bow'rs
Proclaim this day ; this the angelick powr's
Have done for you : but now an opal hue
Bepaints heaven's cryſtal to the longing view :
Earth's late-hid colours ſhine, light doth adorn
The world, and, weeping joy, forth comes the Morn ;
And with her, as from a lethargic trance
The breath return'd, that bodies doth advance,
Which two ſad nights in rock lay coffin'd dead,
And with an iron guard environed :
Life out of death, light out of darkneſs ſprings,
From a baſe gaol forth comes the King of Kings ;
What late was mortal, thrall'd to every woe
That lackeys life, or upon ſenſe doth grow,
Immortal is, of an eternal ſtamp,
Far brighter beaming than the morning lamp.
So from a black eclipſe out-peers the ſun :
Such (when her courſe of days have on her run,
In a far foreſt in the pearly eaſt,
And ſhe herſelf hath burnt, and ſpicy neſt,)
The lovely bird, with youthful pens and comb,
Doth ſoar from out her cradle and her tomb :
So a ſmall ſeed that in the earth lies hid,
And dies, reviving burſts her cloddy ſide,
Adorn'd with yellow locks anew is born,
And doth become a mother great with corn ;

    4   Of

Of grains brings hundreds with it, which when old
Enrich the furrows, which do float with gold.
    Hail, holy Victor! greateſt Victor, hail!
That hell doth ranſack, againſt death prevail:
 O! how thou long'd for com'ſt! With joyful cries,
The all-triumphing palatines of ſkies
Salute thy riſing; earth would joys no more
Bear, if thou riſing didſt them not reſtore.
A ſilly tomb ſhould not his fleſh encloſe,
Who did heaven's trembling terraſſes diſpoſe;
.No monument ſhould ſuch a jewel hold,
No rock, though ruby, diamond, and gold.
Thou didſt lament and pity human race,
Beſtowing on us of thy free-given grace
More than we forfeited and loſed firſt,
In Eden rebels when we were accurſt.
Then earth our portion was, earth's joys but given,
Earth, and earth's bliſs, thou haſt exchang'd with
       heaven.
O! what a height of good upon us ſtreams
From the great ſplendour of thy bounty's beams!
When we deſerv'd ſhame, horror, flames of wrath,
Thou bled'ſt our wounds, and ſuffer didſt our death:
But Father's juſtice pleas'd, Hell, Death, o'ercome,
In triumph now thou riſeſt from thy tomb,
With glories, which paſt ſorrows countervail;
Hail, holy Victor! greateſt Victor, hail!
    Hence, humble ſenſe, and hence ye guides of ſenſe!
We now reach heaven; your weak intelligence
                 And

And fearching pow'rs were in a flafh made dim,
To learn from all eternity, that him
The Father bred, then that he here did come
(His bearer's parent) in a virgin's womb :
But then when fold, betray'd, crown'd, fcourg'd with
       thorn,
Nail'd to a tree, all breathlefs, bloodlefs, torn,
Entomb'd, him rifen from a grave to find,
Confounds your cunning, turns, like moles, you blind.
Death, thou that heretofore ftill barren waft,
Nay, didft each other birth eat up and wafte,
Imperious, hateful, pitilefs, unjuft,
Unpartial equaller of all with duft,
Stern executioner of heavenly doom,
Made fruitful, now Life's mother art become ;
A fweet relief of cares the foul moleft ;
An harbinger to glory, peace and reft :
Put off thy mourning weeds, yield all thy gall
To daily finning life, proud of thy fall ;
Affemble all thy captives, hafte to rife,
And every corfe, in earthquakes where it lies,
Sound from each flowry grave and rocky gaol :
Hail, holy Victor ! greateft Victor, hail !
, The world, that wanning late and faint did lie,
Applauding to our joys, thy victory,
To a young prime effays to turn again,
And as ere foil'd with fin yet to remain ;
Her chilling agues fhe begins to mifs ;
All blifs returning with the Lord of blifs..

                             With

With greater light, heaven's temples opened 'shine;
Morns smiling rise, evens blushing do decline,
Clouds dappled glister, boist'rous winds are calm,
Soft zephyrs do the fields with sighs embalm,
In silent calms the sea hath hush'd his roars,
And with enamour'd curls doth kiss the shores;
All-bearing Earth, like a new-married queen,
Her beauties heightens, in a gown of green
Perfumes the air, her meads are wrought with flow'rs,
In colours various, figures, smelling, pow'rs;
Trees wanton in the groves with leavy locks,
Here hills enamell'd stand, the vales, the rocks,
Ring peals of joy, here floods and prattling brooks,
(Stars' liquid mirrors) with serpenting crooks,
And whispering murmurs, sound unto the main,
The golden age returned is again.
The honey people leave their golden bow'rs,
And innocently prey on budding flow'rs;
In gloomy shades perch'd on the tender sprays,
The painted singers fill the air with lays:
Seas, floods, earth, air, all diversely do sound,
Yet all their diverse notes hath but one ground,
Re-echo'd here down from heaven's azure vail;
Hail, holy Victor! greatest Victor, hail!
     O day, on which Death's adamantine chain
The Lord did break, did ransack Satan's reign,
And in triumphing pomp his trophies rear'd,
Be thou blest ever, henceforth still endear'd
With name of his own day, the law to grace,
Types to their substance yield, to thee give place

                                          The

The old new-moons, with all feftival days;
And, what above the reft deferveth praife,
The reverend fabbath : What could elfe they be
Than golden heralds, telling what by thee
We fhould enjoy ? Shades paft, now fhine thou clear,
And henceforth be thou emprefs of the year,
This glory of thy fifter's fex to win,
From work on thee, as other days from fin,
That mankind fhall forbear, in every place
The prince of planets warmeth in his race,
And far beyond his paths in frozen climes :
And may thou be fo bleft to out-date times,
That when heaven's choir fhall blaze in accents loud
The many mercies of their fovereign good,
How he on thee did fin, death, hell deftroy,
It may be ftill the burthen of their joy.

BENEATH a fable veil, and fhadows deep,
     Of inacceffible and dimming light,
In filence ebon clouds more black than night,
The world's great Mind his fecrets hid doth keep :
Through thofe thick mifts when any mortal wight
Afpires, with halting pace, and eyes that weep
To pry, and in his myfteries to creep,
With thunders he and lightnings blafts their fight.
O Sun invifible, that doft abide
Within thy bright abyfmes, moft fair, moft dark,
Where with thy proper rays thou doft thee hide,
O ever-fhining, never full-feen mark,

                                        To

To guide me in life's night, thy light me fhew;
The more I fearch of thee the lefs I know.

I F with fuch paffing beauty, choice delights,
 The Architect of this great round did frame
This palace vifible, fhort lifts of fame,
And filly manfion but of dying wights ;
How many wonders, what amazing lights
Muft that triumphing feat of glory claim,
That doth tranfcend all this all's vafty heights,
Of whofe bright fun, ours here is but a beam !
O bleft abode ! O happy dwelling-place !
Where vifibly th' Invifible doth reign ;
Bleft people, which do fee true Beauty's face,
With whofe far fhadows fcarce he earth doth deign :
 All joy is but annoy, all concord ftrife,
 Match'd with your endlefs blifs and happy life.

L OVE which is here a care,
 That wit and will doth mar,
Uncertain truce, and a moft certain war ;
A fhrill tempeftuous wind,
Which doth difturb the mind,
And like wild waves all our defigns commove ;
Among thofe powers above,

 Which

Which fee their maker's face,
It a contentment is, a quiet peace,
A pleafure void of grief, a conftant reft,
Eternal joy, which nothing can moleft.

———————

THAT fpace where curled waves do now divide
    From the great continent our happy ifle,
Was fometime land; and now where fhips do glide,
Once with laborious art the plough did toil:
Once thofe fair bounds ftretch'd out fo far and wide,
Where towns, no fhires enwall'd, endear each mile,
Were all ignoble fea and marifh vile,
Where Proteus' flocks danc'd meafures to the tide:
So age transforming all, ftill forward runs;
No wonder though the earth doth change her face,
New manners, pleafures new, turn with new funs,
Locks now like gold grow to an hoary grace;
    Nay, mind's rare fhape doth change, that lies
        defpis'd
Which was fo dear of late, and highly priz'd.

———————

THIS world a hunting is,
    The prey, poor man; the Nimrod fierce, is
        Death;
His fpeedy greyhounds are,
Luft, Sicknefs, Envy, Care;

                                        Strife

Strife that ne'er falls amifs,
With all thofe ills which haunt us while we breathe.
Now, if by chance we fly
Of thefe the eager chace,
Old Age with ftealing pace
Cafts on his nets, and there we panting die.

———————

WHY, worldlings, do ye truft frail honour's
dreams,
And lean to gilded glories which decay?
Why do ye toil to regiftrate your names
On icy pillars, which foon melt away?
True honour is not here, that place it claims
Where black-brow'd night doth not exile the day,
Nor no far-fhining lamp dives in the fea,
But an eternal fun fpreads lafting beams;
There it attendeth you, where fpotlefs bands
Of fp'rits ftand gazing on their fovereign blifs,
Where years not hold it in their cank'ring hands,
But who once noble, ever noble is.
    Look home, left he your weaken'd wit make thrall,
    Who Eden's foolifh gard'ner erft made fall.

———————

AS are thofe apples, pleafant to the eye,
    But full of fmoke within, which ufe to grow
Near that ftrange lake where God pour'd from the fky
Huge fhow'rs of flames, worfe flames to overthrow:
                                        Such

Such are their works that with a glaring fhow
Of humble holinefs in virtue's dye
Would colour mifchief, while within they glow
With coals of fin, though none the fmoke defcry.
Bad is that angel that erft fell from heaven;
But not fo bad as he, nor in worfe cafe,
Who hides a trait'rous mind with fmiling face,
And with a dove's white feathers clothes a raven.
   Each fin fome colour hath it to adorn,
 Hypocrify Almighty God doth fcorn.

———————

NEW doth the fun appear,
    The mountains fnows decay,
Crown'd with frail flow'rs forth comes the infant
      year;
My foe, time pofts away,
And thou, yet in that froft
Which flow'r and fruit hath loft,
As if all here immortal were, doft ftay:
For fhame! thy powers awake,
Look to that heaven which never night makes black,
And there at that immortal fun's bright rays,
Deck thee with flow'rs, which fear not rage of days.

———————

THRICE happy he who by fome fhady grove,
    Far from the clamorous world, doth live his own,
Though folitary, who is not alone,
But doth converfe with that eternal love.
                O how

O how more fweet is bird's harmonious moan,
Or the hoarfe fobbings of the widow'd dove,
Than thofe fmooth whifp'rings near a prince's throne,
Which good make doubtful, do the evil approve!
O! how more fweet is zephyrs' wholefome breath,
And fighs embalm'd, which new-born flow'rs unfold,
Than that applaufe vain honour doth bequeath!
How fweet are ftreams to poifon drank in gold!
   The world is full of horrors, troubles, flights:
   Woods' harmlefs fhades have only true delights.

SWEET bird, that fing'ft away the early hours
  Of winters paft, or coming, void of care,
Well pleafed with delights which prefent are,
Fair feafons, budding fprays, fweet-fmelling flow'rs:
To rocks, to fprings, to rills, from leavy bow'rs
Thou thy Creator's goodnefs doft declare,
And what dear gifts on thee he did not fpare,
A ftain to human fenfe in fin that low'rs.
What foul can be fo fick, which by thy fongs
(Attir'd in fweetnefs) fweetly is not driven
Quite to forget earth's turmoils, fpites, and wrongs,
And lift a reverend eye and thought to heaven?
   Sweet, artlefs fongfter, thou my mind doft raife
   To airs of fpheres, yes, and to angels' lays.

L   AS

———————

A S when it happeneth that fome lovely town
    Unto a barbarous befieger falls,
Who both by fword and flame himfelf inftals,
And fhamelefs it in tears and blood doth drown ;
Her beauty fpoil'd, her citizens made thralls,
His fpite yet cannot fo her all throw down,
But that fome ftatue, pillar of renown,
Yet lurks unmaim'd within her weeping walls :
So after all the fpoil, difgrace and wreck,
That time, the world, and death, could bring com-
      bin'd,
Amidft that mafs of ruins they did make,
Safe and all fcarlefs yet remains my mind :
   From this fo high tranfcendent rapture fprings,
   That I, all elfe defac'd, not envy kings.

———————

L ET us each day inure ourfelves to die,
    If this, and not our fears, be truly death,
Above the circles both of hope and faith
With fair immortal pinions to fly ;
If this be death, our beft part to untie,
By ruining the gaol, from luft and wrath,
And every drowfy languor here beneath,
To be made deniz'd citizen of fky ;

                      To

To have more knowledge than all books contain,
All pleasures even surmounting wishing pow'r,
The fellowship of God's immortal train,
And these that time nor force shall e'er devour:
  If this be death, what joy, what golden care
  Of life, can with death's uglinefs compare?

———

Amidst the azure clear
    Of Jordan's sacred streams,
Jordan, of Lebanon the offspring dear,
  When zephyrs flow'rs unclofe,
  And fun shines with new beams,
  With grave and stately grace a nymph arofe.
Upon her head she wear
  Of amaranths a crown;
  Her left hand palms, her right a torch did bear;
  Unveil'd skin's whitenefs lay,
  Gold hairs in curls hung down,
  Eyes sparkled joy, more bright than star of day.
The flood a throne her rear'd
  Of waves, moft like that heaven
  Where beaming stars in glory turn enfpher'd:
  The air stood calm and clear,
  No figh by winds was given,
  Birds left to fing, herds feed, her voice to hear.
World-wand'ring forry wights,
  Whom nothing can content
  Within thefe varying lifts of days and nights,

L. 2   Whose

Whofe life, ere known amifs,
In glitt'ring griefs is fpent,
Come learn, faid fhe, what is your choiceft blifs :
From toil and preffing cares
How ye may refpite find,
A fanctuary from foul-thralling fnares ;
A port to harbour fure,
In fpite of waves and wind,
Which fhall when time's fwift glafs is run endure.
Not happy is that life
Which you as happy hold,   ●
No, but a fea of fears, a field of ftrife,
Charg'd on a throne to fit
With diadems of gold,
Preferv'd by force, and ftill obferv'd by wit.
Huge treafures to enjoy,
Of all her gems fpoil Inde,
All Seres' filk in garments to employ,
Delicioufly to feed,
The phœnix' plumes to find
To reft upon, or deck your purple bed.
Frail beauty to abufe,
And, wanton Sybarites,
On paft or prefent touch of fenfe to mufe ;
Never to hear of noife
But what the ear delights,
Sweet mufick's charms, or charming flatterer's voice.
Nor can it blifs you bring,
Hid nature's depths to know,
Why matter changeth, whence each form doth
      fpring.

Nor

Nor that your fame fhould range,
And after-worlds it blow
From Tanais to Nile, from Nile to Gange:
All thefe have not the pow'r
To free the mind from fears,
Nor hideous horror can allay one hour,
When Death in ftealth doth glance,
In ficknefs lurks or years,.
And wakes the foul from out her mortal trance..
No, but bleft life is this,
With chafte and pure defire
To turn unto the load-ftar of all blifs,
On God the mind to reft,.
Burnt up with facred fire,
Poffeffing him to be by him poffeft :
When to the balmy eaft
Sun doth his light impart,
Or when he diveth in the lowly weft,
And ravifheth the day,.
With fpotlefs hand and heart,
Him cheerfully to praife, and to him pray :
To heed each action fo
As ever in his fight,
More fearing doing ill than paffive woe;
Not to feem other thing
Than what ye are aright ;
Never to do what may repentance bring :
Not to be blown with pride,
Nor mov'd at glory's breath,
Which fhadow-like on wings of time doth glide ;.

L 3   So

So malice to difarm,
  And conquer hafty wrath,
  As to do good to thofe that work your harm :
To hatch no bafe defires,
  Or gold or land to gain,
  Well pleas'd with that which virtue fair acquires ;·
To have the wit and will
  Conforting in one ftrain,
  Than what is good to have no higher fkill :
Never on neighbour's goods,
  With cockatrice's eye
  To look, nor make another's heaven your hell ;
  Nor to be beauty's thrall ;
  All fruitlefs love to fly,
  Yet loving ftill a love tranfcendent all ;
A love, which while it burns
  The foul with faireft beams,
  To that increated fun the foul it turns,
  And makes fuch beauty prove,
  That, if fenfe faw her gleams,
  All lookers on would pine and die for love.
Who fuch a life doth live
  You happy even may call,
  Ere ruthlefs Death a wifhed end him give ;
  And after then when given,
  More happy by his fall,
  For humanes, earth, enjoying angels, heaven.
Swift is your mortal race,
  And glaffy is the field ;
  Vaft are defires not limited by grace :

                                              Life

Life a weak taper is ;
Then while it light doth yield,
Leave flying joys, embrace this lasting blifs.
This when the nymph had said,
   She div'd within the flood,
   Whose face with smiling curls long after staid ;
   Then sighs did zephyrs prefs,
   Birds sang from every wood,
And echoes rang, This was true happiness.

A N

HYMN on the FAIREST FAIR.

I FEEL my bosom glow with wontless fires,
   Rais'd from the vulgar prefs my mind aspires,
Wing'd with high thoughts, unto his praise to climb,
From deep eternity, who call'd forth time ;
That Essence which, not mov'd, makes each thing
      move,
Uncreate beauty all-creating love :
But by so great an object, radiant light,
My heart apall'd, enfeebled refts my fight,
Thick clouds benight my labouring engine,
And at my high attempts my wits repine.
If thou in me this sacred heat hast wrought,
My knowledge sharpen, farcels lend my thought :
Grant me, Time's Father, world-containing King,
A pow'r of thee in pow'rful lays to sing ;
That as thy beauty in earth lives, heaven shines,
It dawning may or shadow in my lines.

L 4   A³

As far beyond the ftarry walls of heaven,
As is the loftieft of the planets feven,
Sequefter'd from this earth in pureft light,
Out-fhining ours, as ours doth fable night,
Thou All-fufficient, Omnipotent,
Thou Ever Glorious, Moft Excellent,
God various in names, in effence one,
High art inftalled on a golden throne,
Out-ftretching heaven's wide befpangled vault,
Tranfcending all the circles of our thought ;
With diamantine fceptre in thy hand,
There thou giv'ft laws, and doft this world command,
This world of concords rais'd unlikely fweet,
Which like a ball lies proftrate at thy feet.
  If fo we may well fay (and what we fay
Here wrapp'd in flefh, led by dim Reafon's ray,
To fhew, by earthly beauties which we fee,
That fpiritual excellence that fhines in thee,
Good Lord forgive), not far from thy right fide,
With curled locks Youth ever doth abide ;
Rofe-cheeked Youth, who garlanded with flow'rs,
Still blooming, ceafelefsly unto thee pours
Immortal nectar in a cup of gold,
That by no darts of ages thou grow old ;
And as ends and beginnings thee not claim,
Succeffionlefs that thou be ftill the fame.
  Near to thy other fide refiftlefs Might,
From head to foot in burnifh'd armour dight,
That rings about him, with a waving brand,
And watchful eye, great centinel doth ftand ;

4   That

That neither time nor force in aught impair
Thy workmanſhip, nor harm thine empire fair;
Soon to give death to all again that would
Stern Diſcord raiſe, which thou deſtroy'd of old;
Diſcord, that foe to order, nurſe of war,
By which the nobleſt things demoliſh'd are:
But, caitiff! ſhe no treaſon doth deviſe,
When Might to nought doth bring her enterprize:
Thy all-upholding Might her malice reins,
And her to hell throws, bound in iron chains.

With locks in waves of gold, that ebb and flow
On ivory neck, in robes more white than ſnow,
Truth ſtedfaſtly before thee holds a glaſs,
Indent with gems, where ſhineth all that was,
That is, or ſhall be, here ere aught was wrought.
Thou knew all that thy pow'r with time forth brought,
And more, things numberleſs which thou couldſt make,
That actually ſhall never being take;
Here thou behold'ſt thyſelf, and, ſtrange! doſt prove
At once the beauty, lover, and the love.

With faces two, like ſiſters, ſweetly fair,
Whoſe bloſſoms no rough autumn can impair,
Stands Providence, and doth her looks diſperſe
Through every corner of this univerſe;
Thy Providence, at once which general things
And ſingular doth rule, as empires kings;
Without whoſe care this world loſt would remain,
As ſhip without a maſter in the main,
As chariot alone, as bodies prove
Depriv'd of ſouls, whereby they be, live, move.

But

But who are they which fhine thy throne fo near,
With facred countenance and look fevere ?
This in one hand a pond'rous fword doth hold,
Her left ftays charg'd with balances of gold ;
That, with brows girt with bays, fweet-fmiling face,
Doth bear a brandon with a babifh grace :
Two milk-white wings him eafily do move ;
O! fhe thy Juftice is, and this thy Love !
By this thou brought'ft this engine great to light ;
By that it fram'd in number, meafure, weight,
That deftine doth reward to ill and good :
But fway of Juftice is by Love withftood,
Which did it not relent, and mildly ftay,
This world ere now had found its funeral day.

What bands, enclufter'd, near to thefe abide,
Which into vaft infinity them hide !
Infinity that neither doth admit
Place, time, nor number to encroach on it.
Here bounty fparkleth, here doth beauty fhine,
Simplicity, more white than gelfomine,
Mercy with open wings, aye-varied blifs,
Glory, and joy, that blifs's darling is.

Ineffable, all-pow'rful God, all free,
Thou only liv'ft, and each thing lives by thee ;
No joy, no, nor perfection to thee came
By the contriving of this world's great frame :
Ere fun, moon, ftars began their reftlefs race,
Ere painted was with light heaven's pure face,
Ere air had clouds, ere clouds wept down their fhow'rs,
Ere fea embraced earth, ere earth bare flow'rs,

Thou

Thou happy liv'dſt ; world nought to thee ſupply'd,
All in thyſelf, thyſelf thou ſatisfy'd :
Of good no ſlender ſhadow doth appear,
No age-worn track, whîch ſhin'd in thee not clear, .
Perfection's ſum, prime cauſe of every cauſe,
Midſt, end, beginning where all good doth pauſe :
Hence of thy ſubſtance, differing in nought,
Thou in eternity thy ſon forth brought ;
The only birth of thy unchanging mind,
Thine image, pattern-like that ever ſhin'd ;
Light out of light, begotten not by will,
But nature, all and that ſame eſſence ſtill
Which thou thyſelf, for thou doſt nought poſſeſs
Which he hath not, in aught nor is he leſs
Than thee his great begetter ; of this light,
Eternal, double-kindled was thy ſpright
Eternally, who is with thee the ſame,
All-holy Gift, Ambaſſador, Knot, Flame :
Moſt ſacred Triad, O moſt holy One !
Unprocreate Father, ever procreate Son,
Ghoſt breath'd from both, you were, are ſtill, ſhall be,
(Moſt bleſſed) Three in One, and One in Three,
Incomprehenſible by reachleſs height,
And unperceived by exceſſive light.
So in our ſouls three and yet one are ſtill,
The underſtanding, memory, and will ;
So (though unlike) the planet of the days,
So ſoon as he was made, begat his rays,
Which are his offspring, and from both was hurl'd
The roſy light which conſolates the world,

And ..

And none forewent another : so the spring,
The well-head, and the stream which they forth bring,
Are but one self-same essence, nor in aught
Do differ, save in order ; and our thought
No chime of time discerns in them to fall,
But three distinctly 'bide one essence all.
But these express not thee : who can declare
Thy being ? Men and angels dazzled are.
Who would this Eden force with wit or sense,
A cherubin shall find to bar him thence.

   Great Architect, Lord of this universe,
That light is blinded would thy greatness pierce.
Ah ! as a pilgrim who the Alps doth pass,
Or Atlas' temples crown'd with winter glass,
The airy Caucasus, the Apennine,
Pyrenees' clifts where sun doth never shine,
When he some craggy hills hath overwent,
Begins to think on rest, his journey spent,
Till mounting some tall mountain, he do find
More heights before him than he left behind :
With halting pace so while I would me raise
To the unbounded limits of thy praise,
Some part of way I thought to have o'er-run,
But now I see how scarce I have begun ;
With wonders new my spirits range possest,
And wandering wayless in a maze them rest.

   In these vast fields of light, ethereal plains,
Thou art attended by immortal trains
Of intellectual pow'rs, which thou brought'st forth
To praise thy goodness, and admire thy worth,

In numbers paffing other creatures far,
Since creatures moft noble manyeft are,
Which do in knowledge us not lefs outrun
Than moon in light doth ftars, or moon the fun;
Unlike, in orders rang'd and many a band,
(If beauty in difparity doth ftand)
Archangels, angels, cherubs, feraphines,
And what with name of thrones amongft them fhines,
Large-ruling princes, dominations, pow'rs,
All-acting virtues of thofe flaming tow'rs:
Thefe freed of umbrage, thefe of labour free,
Reft ravifhed with ftill beholding thee;
Inflam'd with beams which fparkle from thy face,
They can no more defire, far lefs embrace.
    Low under them, with flow and ftaggering pace
Thy hand-maid Nature thy great fteps doth trace,
The fource of fecond caufe's golden chain
That links this frame as thou it doth ordain.
Nature gaz'd on with fuch a curious eye,
That earthlings oft her deem'd a deity.
By Nature led, thofe bodies fair and great,
Which faint not in their courfe, nor change their ftate,
Unintermix'd, which no diforder prove,
Though aye and contrary they always move,
The organs of thy providence divine,
Books ever open, figns that clearly fhine;
Time's purpled mafkers then do them advance,
As by fweet mufick in a meafur'd dance;
Stars, hoft of heaven, ye firmaments, bright flow'rs,
Clear lamps which overhang this ftage of ours,

                                              Ye

Ye turn not there to deck the weeds of night,
Nor, pageant like, to pleafe the vulgar fight:
Great caufes, fure ye muft bring great effects;
But who can defcant right your grave afpects?
He only who you made decypher can
Your notes; heaven's eyes, ye blind the eyes of man.
   Amidft thefe fapphire far-extending heights,
The never-twinkling, ever wand'ring lights
Their fixed motions keep; one dry and cold,
Deep-leaden colour'd, flowly there is roll'd,
With rule and line for time's fteps meting even,
In twice three luftres he but turns his heaven.
With temperate qualities and countenance fair,
Still mildly fmiling, fweetly debonnaire,
Another cheers the world, and way doth make
In twice fix autumns through the zodiack.
But hot and dry with flaming locks and brows
Enrag'd, this in his red pavilion glows:
Together running with like fpeed, if fpace,
Two equally in hands atchieve their race;
With blufhing face this oft doth bring the day,
And ufhers oft to ftately ftars the way;
That various in virtue, changing, light,
With his fmall flame impearls the vail of night.
Prince of this court, the fun in triumph rides,
With the year fnake-like in herfelf that glides,
Time's difpenfator, fair life-giving fource,
Through fkies twelve pofts as he doth run his courfe;
Heart of this all, of what is known to fenfe,
The likeft to his Maker's excellence;

                                        In.

In whofe diurnal motion doth appear
A fhadow, no true portrait of the year.
The moon moves loweft, filver fun of night,
Difperfing through the world her borrow'd light;
Who in three forms her head abroad doth range,
And only conftant is in conftant change.
   Sad queen of filence, I ne'er fee thy face
To wax, or wane, or fhine with a full grace,
But ftraight, amaz'd, on man I think, each day
His ftate who changeth, or if he find ftay,
It is in doleful anguifh, cares, and pains,
And of his labours death is all the gains.
Immortal Monarch, can fo fond a thought
Lodge in my breaft, as to truft thou firft brought
Here in earth's fhady cloifter, wretched man,
To fuck the air of woe, to fpend life's fpan
'Midft fighs and plaints, a ftranger unto mirth,
To give himfelf his death rebucking birth?
By fenfe and wit of creatures made king,
By fenfe and wit to live their underling?
And what is worft, have eaglets eyes to fee
His own difgrace, and know an high degree
Of blifs, the place, if he might thereto climb,
And not live thralled to imperious time?
Or, dotard! fhall I fo from reafon fwerve,
To dim thofe lights, which to our ufe do ferve,
For thou doft not them need, more nobly fram'd
Than us, that know their courfe, and have them
    nam'd?

                    No,

No, I ne'er think but we did them furpafs
As far as they do afterifms of glafs.
When thou us made, by treafon high defil'd,
Thruft from our firft eftate, we live exil'd,
Wand'ring this earth, which is of Death the lot,
Where he doth ufe the power which he hath got,
Indifferent umpire unto clowns and kings,
The fupreme monarch of all mortal things.
When firft this flow'ry orb was to us given,
It but a place difvalu'd was to heaven:
Thefe creatures which now our fovereigns are,
And as to rebels do denounce us war,
Then were our vaffals; no tumultuous ftorm,
No thunders, earthquakes, did her form deform;
The feas in tumbling mountains did not roar,
But like moift cryftal whifper'd on the fhore;
No fnake did trace her meads, nor ambufh'd low'r
In azure curls beneath the fweet fpring flow'r;
The nightfhade, henbane, napel, aconite,
Her bowels then not bear, with death to fmite
Her guiltlefs brood: thy meffengers of grace,
As their high rounds, did haunt this lower place.
O joy of joys! with our firft parents thou
To commune then didft deign, as friends do now;
Againft thee we rebell'd, and juftly thus
Each creature rebelled againft us;
Earth, reft of what did chief in her excel,
To all became a gaol, to moft a hell:
In time's full term, until thy Son was given,
Who man with thee, earth reconcil'd with Heaven.

                                        Whole

Whole and entire, all in thyfelf thou art;
All-where diffus'd, yet of this all no part:
For infinite, in making this fair frame,
Great without quantity, in all thou came;
And filling all, how can thy ftate admit,
Or place or fubftance to be void of it?
Were worlds as many as the rays which ftream
From day's bright lamp, or madding wits do dream,
They would not reel in aught, nor wand'ring ftray,
But draw to thee, who could their centres ftay;
Were but one hour this world disjoin'd from thee,
It in one hour to nought reduc'd fhould be.
For it thy fhadow is; and can they laft,
If fever'd from the fubftances them caft?
O! only blefs'd, and Author of all blifs!
No, Blifs itfelf, that all-where wifhed is;
Efficient, exemplary, final Good,
Of thine own felf but only underftood:
Light is thy curtain: thou art Light of light;
An ever-waking eye ftill fhining bright.
In-looking all, exempt of paffive pow'r,
And change, in change fince Death's pale fhade doth
         low'r:
All times to thee are one; that which hath run,
And that which is not brought yet by the fun,
To thee are prefent, who doft always fee
In prefent act, what paft is, or to be.
Day-livers, we rememberance do lofe
Of ages worn, fo miferies us tofs,

M   {Blind

(Blind and lethargick of thy heavenly grace,   -
Which fin in our firſt parents did deface ;
And even while embrions curſt by juſteſt doom)
That we negleƈt what gone is, or to come ;
But thou in thy great archives ſcrolled haſt,
In parts and whole, whatever yet hath paſt,
Since firſt the marble wheels of time were roll'd,
As ever living, never waxing old,
Still is the ſame thy day and yeſterday,
An undivided now, a conſtant aye.

   O ! King, whoſe greatneſs none can comprehend,
Whoſe boundleſs goodneſs doth to all extend ;
Light of all beauty, Ocean without ground,
That ſtanding, floweſt ; giving, doſt abound ;
Rich Palace, and In-dweller, ever bleſt,
Never not working, ever yet in reſt :
What wit cannot conceive, words ſay of thee,
Here where we as but in a mirror ſee,
Shadows of ſhadows, atoms of thy might,
Still owly-eyed when ſtaring on thy light ;
Grant, that, releaſed from this earthly jail,
And freed from clouds, which here our knowledge
     veil,
In heaven's high temples where thy praiſes ring,
In ſweeter notes I may hear angels ſing.

GREAT

GREAT God, whom we with humbled thoughts
    adore,
Eternal, infinite, almighty King,
Whofe dwellings heaven tranfcend, whofe throne before
Archangels ferve, and feraphim do fing ;
Of nought who wrought all that with wond'ring eyes
We do behold within this various round ;
Who makes the rocks to rock, to ftand the fkies ;
At whofe command clouds peals of thunder found :
Ah ! fpare us worms, weigh not how we, alas !
Evil to ourfelves, againft thy laws rebel ;
Wafh off thofe fpots, which ftill in confcience' glafs,
Though we be loath to look, we fee too well.
Deferv'd revenge, Oh ! do not, do not take :
If thou revenge, who fhall abide thy blow ?
Pafs fhall this world, this world which thou didft
    make,
Which fhould not perifh till thy trumpet blow.
What foul is found whofe parent's crime not ftains ?
Or what with its own fins defil'd is not ?
'Though Juftice rigour threaten, yet her reins
Let Mercy guide, and never be forgot.
    Lefs are our faults, far, far than is thy love :
O ! what can better feem thy grace divine,
Than they, who plagues deferve, thy bounty prove ?
And where thou fhow'r may'ft vengeance, there to
    fhine !

                    Then

Then look and pity; pitying, forgive
Us guilty flaves, or fervants now in thrall;
Slaves, if, alas! thou look how we do live,
Or doing ill, or doing nought at all;
Of an ungrateful mind the foul effect.
But if thy gifts, which largely heretofore
Thou haft upon us pour'd, thou doft refpect,
We are thy fervants, nay, than fervants more,
Thy children; yes, and children dearly bought:
But what ftrange chance us of this lot bereaves?
Poor, worthlefs wights, how lowly are we brought!
Whom grace once children made, fin hath made flaves.
Sin hath made flaves, but let thofe bands grace break,
That in our wrongs thy mercies may appear:
Thy wifdom not fo mean is, pow'r fo weak,
But thoufand ways they can make worlds thee fear.
    O wifdom boundlefs! O miraculous grace!
Grace, wifdom which make wink dim Reafon's eye!
And could heaven's King bring from his placelefs
        place,
On this ignoble ftage of care to die;
To die our death, and with the facred ftream
Of blood and water gufhing from his fide,
To make us clean of that contagious blame,
Firft on us brought by our firft parent's pride!
Thus thy great love and pity, heavenly King!
Love, pity, which fo well our lofs prevent,
Of evil itfelf, lo! could all goodnefs bring,
And fad beginning cheer with glad event.
                            O love

O love and pity! ill known of thefe times!
O love and pity! careful of our need!
O bounties! which our horrid acts and crimes,
Grown numberlefs, contend near to exceed.
Make this exceffive ardour of thy love.
So warm our coldnefs, fo our lives renew,
That we from fin, fin may from us remove,
Wifdom our will, faith may our wit fubdue.
Let thy pure love burn up all worldly luft,
Hell's candid poifon killing our beft part,
Which makes us joy in toys, adore frail duft
Inftead of thee, in temple of our heart.

Grant, when at laft our fouls thefe bodies leave,
Their loathfome fhops of fin and manfions blind,
And doom before thy royal feat receive,
A Saviour more than Judge they thee may find.

THE

WANDERING MUSES:

OR, THE

RIVER of FORTH FEASTING.

BEING

A PANEGYRICK

TO THE

HIGH and MIGHTY PRINCE JAMES,

King of *Great Britain*, *France* and *Ireland*.

M 4

HIS SACRED MAJESTY.

IF in this ftorm of joy and pompous throng,
 This nymph, great King, doth come to thee fo
  near,
That thy harmonious ears her accents hear,
Give pardon to her hoarfe and lowly fong.
Fain would fhe trophies to thy virtues rear:
But for this ftately tafk fhe is not ftrong,
And her defects her high attempts do wrong:
Yet as fhe could fhe makes thy worth appear.
So in a map is fhewn this flow'ry place;
So wrought in arras by a virgin's hand,
With heaven and blazing ftars doth Atlas ftand;
So drawn by charcoal is Narciffus' face:
 She like the morn may be to fome bright fun,
 The day to perfect that's by her begun.

RIVER of FORTH FEASTING.

WHAT bluft'ring noife now interrupts my fleeps?
What echoing fhouts thus cleave my cryftal
deeps?
And feem to call me from my watr'ry court?
What melody, what founds of joy and fport,
Are convey'd hither from each night-born fpring?
With what loud rumours do the mountains ring,
Which in unufual pomp on tip-toes ftand,
And, full of wonder, overlook the land?
Whence come thefe glitt'ring throngs, thefe meteors
bright,
This golden people glancing in my fight?
Whence doth this praife, applaufe, and love arife?
What load-ftar eaftward draweth thus all eyes?
Am I awake? Or have fome dreams confpir'd
To mock my fenfe with what I moft defir'd?

View

View I that living face, fee I thofe looks,
Which with delight were wont t' amaze my brooks?
Do I behold that worth, that man divine,.
This age's glory, by thefe banks of mine ?
Then find I true what long I wifh'd in vain ;
My much-beloved prince is come again.
So unto them whofe zenith is the pole,
When fix black months are paft, the fun doth roll :-
So after tempeft to fea-toffed wights,
Fair Helen's brothers fhew their clearing lights :
So comes Arabia's wonder from her woods,
And far, far off is feen by Memphis' floods ;
The feather'd fylvans, cloud-like, by her fly,
And with triumphing plaudits beat the fky ;
Nile marvels, Serap's priefts entranced rave,
And in Mygdonian ftone her fhape engrave ;
In lafting cedars they do mark the time
In which Apollo's bird came to their clime.
    Let mother Earth now deck'd with flow'rs be feen,
And fweet-breath'd zephyrs curl the meadows green :
Let heaven weep rubies in a crimfon fhow'r,
Such as on India's fhores they ufe to pour :
Or with that golden ftorm the fields adorn,
Which Jove rain'd when his blue-eyed maid was born.:
May never Hours the web of day out-weave,
May never Night rife from her fable cave !
Swell proud, my billows, faint not to declare
Your joys as ample as their caufes are :
For murmurs hoarfe found like Arion's harp,
Now delicately flat, now fweetly fharp.

                                        And.

And you, my nymphs, rife from your moift repair,
Strew all your fprings and grots with lilies fair :
Some fwifteft-footed, get them hence, and pray
Our floods and lakes come keep this holiday ;
Whate'er beneath Albania's hills do run,
Which fee the rifing, or the fetting fun,
Which drink ftern Grampus' mifts, or Ochel's fnows:
Stone-rolling Tay, Tine tortoife-like that flows,
The pearly Don, the Deas, the fertile Spay,
Wild Neverné, which doth fee our longeft day ;
Neffe fmoaking fulphur, Leave with mountains
    crown'd,
Strange Loumond for his floating ifles renown'd ;
The Irifh Rian, Ken, the filver Aire,
The fnaky Dun, the Ore with rufhy hair,
The cryftal-ftreaming Nid, loud-bellowing Clyde,
Tweed, which no more our kingdoms fhall divide ;
Rank-fwelling Annan, Lid with curled ftreams,
The Efkes, the Solway where they lofe their names ;
To every one proclaim our joys and feafts,
Our triumphs ; bid all come and be our guefts :
And as they meet in Neptune's azure hall,
Bid them bid fea-gods keep this feftival ;
This day fhall by our currents be renown'd ;
Our hills about fhall ftill this day refound :
Nay, that our love more to this day appear,
Let us with it henceforth begin our year.

    To virgins, flow'rs, to fun-burnt earth, the rain,
To mariners, fair winds amidft the main ;
Cool fhades to pilgrims, which hot glances burn,
Are not fo pleafing as thy bleft return.

                                    That

That day, dear prince, which robb'd us of thy fight
(Day? No, but darkneſs and a duſky night)
Did fill our breaſts with fighs, our eyes with tears,
Turn'd minutes to ſad months, ſad months to years:
Trees left to flouriſh, meadows to bear flow'rs,
Brooks hid their heads within their ſedgy bow'rs;
Fair Ceres curs'd our trees with barren froſt,
As if again ſhe had her daughter loſt:
The Muſes left our groves, and for ſweet ſongs
Sate ſadly ſilent, or did weep their wrongs:
You know it, meads; you murmuring woods it know,
Hills, dales, and caves, copartners of their woe;
And you it know, my ſtreams, which from their éine
Oft on your glaſs receiv'd their pearly brine:
O Naiads dear! ſaid they, Napæas fair!
O nymphs of trees! nymphs which on hills repair;
Gone are thoſe maiden glories, gone that ſtate,
Which made all eyes admire our bliſs of late.
As looks the heaven when never ſtar appears,
But flow and weary ſhroud them in their ſpheres,
While Tithon's wife emboſom'd by him lies,
And world doth languiſh in a mournful guiſé:
As looks a garden of its beauty ſpoil'd,
As woods in winter by rough Boreas foil'd,
As portraits ras'd of colours us'd to be;
So look'd theſe abject bounds depriv'd of thee.

While as my rills enjoy'd thy royal gleams,
They did not envy Tiber's haughty ſtreams,
Nor wealthy Tagus with his golden ore,
Nor clear Hydaſpes which on pearls doth roar,

Nor

Nor golden Gange that fees the fun new born,
Nor Achelous with his flow'ry horn,
Nor floods which near Elyfian fields do fall:
For why? Thy fight did ferve to them for all.
No place there is fo defert, fo alone,
Even from the frozen to the torrid zone;
From flaming Hecla to great Quincey's lake,
Which thy abode could not moft happy make:
All thofe perfections which by bounteous Heaven
To divers worlds in divers times were given,
The ftarry fenate pour'd at once on thee,
That thou exemplar might'ft to others be.
  Thy life was kept till the three fifters fpun
Their threads of gold, and then it was begun.
With chequer'd clouds when fkies do look moft fair,
And no diforder'd blafts difturb the air;
When lilies do them deck in azure gowns,
And new-born rofes blufh with golden crowns;
To prove how calm we under thee fhould live,
What halcyonean days thy reign fhould give;
And to two flow'ry diadems, thy right,
The heavens thee made a partner of the light.
Scarce waft thou born, when join'd in friendly bands
Two mortal foes with other clafped hands;
With Virtue Fortune ftrove, which moft fhould grace
Thy place for thee, thee for fo high a place:
One vow'd thy facred breaft not to forfake,
The other, on thee not to turn her back;
And that thou more her love's effects might'ft feel,
For thee fhe left her globe, and broke her wheel.

When

When years thee vigour gave, O then, how clear
Did ſmother'd ſparkles in bright flames appear!
Amongſt the woods to force the flying hart,
To pierce the mountain-wolf with feather'd dart;
See falcons climb the clouds, the fox enſnare,
Out-run the wind-out-running Dædale hare;
To breathe thy fiery ſteed on every plain,
And in meand'ring gyres him bring again;
The preſe thee making place, and vulgar things,
In admiration's air, on glory's wings:
O! Thou far from the common pitch didſt riſe,
With thy deſigns to dazzle Envy's eyes:
Thou ſought'ſt to know this all's eternal ſource,
Of ever-turning heavens the reſtleſs courſe;
Their fixed lamps, their lights, which wand'ring run,
Whence moon her ſilver hath, his gold the ſun;
If fate there be or no, if planets can,
By fierce aſpects, force the free will of man:
The light aſpiring fire, the liquid air,
The flaming dragons, comets with red hair,
Heaven's tilting lances, artillery, and bow,
Loud-ſounding trumpets, darts of hail and ſnow,
The roaring element, with people dumb,
The earth with what conceiv'd is in her womb,
What on her moves, were ſet unto thy ſight,
Till thou didſt find their cauſes, eſſence, might:
But unto nought thou ſo thy mind didſt ſtrain,
As to be read in man, and learn to reign;
To know the weight and Atlas of a crown,
To ſpare the humble, proud ones tumble down.

When

When from those piercing cares which thrones inveſt,
As thorns the roſe, thou wearied would'ſt thee reſt,
With lute in hand, full of celeſtial fire,
To the Pierian groves thou didſt retire :
There, garlanded with all Urania's flow'rs,
In ſweeter lays than builded Thebes' tow'rs ;
Or them which charm'd the dolphins in the main,
Or which did call Eurydice again ;
Thou ſung'ſt away the hours, till from their ſphere
Stars ſeem'd to ſhoot, thy melody to hear.
The god with golden hair, the ſiſter maids,
Did leave their Helicon and Tempe's ſhades,
To ſee thine iſle ; here loſt their native tongue,
And in thy world-divided language ſung.

   Who of thine after-age can count the deeds,
With all that Fame in Time's huge annals reads ;
How by example, more than any law,
This people fierce thou didſt to goodneſs draw ;
How while the neighbour worlds, toſs'd by the Fates,
So many Phactons had in their ſtates,
Which turn'd to heedleſs flames their burniſh'd thrones,
Thou, as enſpher'd, kept'ſt temperate thy zones ;
In Afric ſhores, the ſands that ebb and flow,
The ſhady leaves on Arden's trees that grow,
He ſure may count, with all the waves that meet
To waſh the Mauritanian Atlas' feet.
Though crown'd thou wert not, nor a king by birth,
Thy worth deſerves the richeſt crown on earth.
Search this half-ſphere, and the Antarctic ground,
Where are ſuch wit and bounty to be found ?

                   N   As

As into filent night, when near the Bear
The virgin huntrefs fhines at full moft clear,
And ftrives to match her brother's golden light,
The hoft of ftars doth vanifh in her fight ;
Arcturus dies ; cool'd is the Lion's ire,
Po burns no more with Phaetontal fire ;
Orion faints to fee his arms grow black,
And that his flaming fword he now doth lack :
So Europe's lights, all bright in their degree,
Lofe all their luftre, parallel'd with thee.
By juft defcent thou from more kings doft fhine,
Than many can name men in all their line :
What moft they toil to find, and finding hold,
Thou fcorneft, orient gems, and flatt'ring gold ;
Efteeming treafure furer in men's breafts,
Than when immur'd with marble, clos'd in chefts :
No ftormy paffions do difturb thy mind,
No mifts of greatnefs ever could thee blind :
Who yet hath been fo meek ? Thou life didft give
To them who did repine to fee thee live :
What prince by goodnefs hath fuch kingdoms gain'd ?
Who hath fo long his people's peace maintain'd ?
Their fwords are turn'd to fcythes, to coulters fpears,
Some giant poft their antique armour bears :
Now, where the wounded knight his life did bleed,
The wanton fwain fits piping on a reed ;
And where the cannon did Jove's thunder fcorn,
The gaudy huntfman winds his fhrill-tun'd horn :
Her green locks Ceres doth to yellow dye ;
The pilgrim fafely in the fhade doth lie ;

Both

Both Pan and Pales carelefs keep their flocks;
Seas have no dangers, fave the winds and rocks:
Thou art this Ifle's palladium; neither can
(Whiles thou doft live !) it be o'erthrown by man.
    Let others boaft of blood and fpoils of foes,
Fierce rapines, murders, iliads of woes;
Of hated pomp, and trophies reared fair,
Gore-fpangled enfigns ftreaming in the air;
Count how they make the Scythian them adore,
The Gaditan, and foldier of Aurore :
Unhappy boafting ! to enlarge their bounds,
That charge themfelves with cares, their friends
      with wounds;
Who have no law to their ambitious will,
But, man-plagues ! born are human blood to fpill :
Thou a true victor art, fent from above
What others ftrain by force to gain by love ;
World-wand'ring Fame this praife to thee imparts,
To be the only monarch of all hearts.
They many fear, who are of many fear'd,
And kingdoms got by wrongs, by wrongs are tear'd;
Such thrones as blood doth raife, blood throweth
      down ;
No guard fo fure as love unto a crown.
    Eye of our weftern world ! Mars-daunting king !
With whofe renown the earth's feven climates ring,
Thy deeds not only claim thefe diadems,
To which Thame, Litty, Tay, fubject their ftreams :
But to thy virtues rare, and gifts, is due
All that the planet of the year doth view ;
N 2

Sure,

Sure, if the world above did want a prince,
The world above to it would take thee hence.
  That Murder, Rapine, Luft, are fled to hell,
And in their rooms with us the Graces dwell;
That honour more than riches men refpeft,
That worthinefs than gold doth more effeft;
That Piety unmafked fhews her face,
That Innocency keeps with power her place;
That long-exil'd Aftrea leaves the heaven,
And turneth right her fword, her weights holds even;
That the Saturnian world is come again,
Are wifh'd effefts of thy moft happy reign.
That daily peace, love, truth, delights increafe,
And difcord, hate, fraud, with incumbers, ceafe;
That men ufe ftrength, not to fhed others blood,
But ufe their ftrength, now to do others good;
That fury is enchain'd, difarmed wrath,
That, fave by Nature's hand, there is no death;
That late grim foes, like brothers, other love,
That vultures prey not on the harmlefs dove;
That wolves with lambs do friendfhip entertain,
Are wifh'd effefts of thy moft happy reign.
That towns increafe, that ruin'd temples rife,
That their wind-moving vanes do kifs the fkies;
That ignorance and floth hence run away,
That bury'd arts now roufe them to the day;
That Hyperion far beyond his bed
Doth fee our lions ramp, our rofes fpread;
That Iber courts us, Tiber not us charms,
That Rhein with hence-brought beams his bofom
    warms;

4   That

That ill doth fear, and good doth us maintain,
Are wifh'd effects of thy moft happy reign.
 O virtue's pattern! glory of our times!
Sent of paft days to expiate the crimes;
Great king, but better far than thou art great,
Whom ftate not honours, but who honours ftate;
By wonder borne, by wonder firft inftall'd,
By wonder after to new kingdoms call'd;
Young, kept by wonder from home-bred alarms,
Old, fav'd by wonder from pale traitors' harms;
To be for this thy reign, which wonders brings,
A king of wonder, wonder unto kings.
If Pict, Dane, Norman, thy fmooth yoke had feen,
Pict, Dane, and Norman, had thy fubjects been:
If Brutus knew the blifs thy rule doth give,
Ev'n Brutus joy would under thee to live:
For thou thy people doft fo dearly love,
That they a father, more than prince, thee prove.
O days to be defir'd! age happy thrice!
If you your heaven-fent good could duly prize;
But we, half-palfy-fick, think never right
Of what we hold, till it be from our fight;
Prize only fummer's fweet and mufked breath,
When armed winters threaten us with death;
In pallid ficknefs do efteem of health,
And by fad poverty difcern of wealth:
I fee an age, when after fome few years,
And revolutions of the flow-pac'd fpheres,
Thefe days fhall be 'bove other far efteem'd,
And like Auguftus' palmy reign be deem'd.

N 3   The

The names of Arthur, fabulous Paladines,
Grav'n in Time's furly brow in wrinkled lines;
Of Henries, Edwards, famous for their fights,
Their neighbour conquefts, orders new of knights,
Shall, by this prince's name, be paft as far
As meteors are by the Idalian ftar.
If grey-hair'd Proteus' fongs the truth not mifs,
There is a land, hence diftant many miles,
Out-reaching fiction and Atlantic ifles;
Which (homelings) from this little world we name,
That fhall emblazon with ftrange rites his fame;
Shall rear him ftatues all of pureft gold,
Such as men gave unto the gods of old;
Name by him temples, palaces, and towns,
With fome great river, which their fields renowns.
This is that king, who fhould make right each wrong,
Of whom the bards and myftic fybils fung;
The man long promis'd, by whofe glorious reign
This Ifle fhould yet her ancient name regain,
And more of Fortunate deferve the ftyle,
Than thofe where heavens with double fummers fmile.
    Run on, great Prince! thy courfe in glory's way,
The end the life, the evening crowns the day;
Heap worth on worth, and ftrongly foar above
Thofe heights, which made the world thee firft to
        love;
Surmount thyfelf, and make thine actions paft
Be but as gleams or lightnings of thy laft;
Let them exceed thofe of thy younger time,
As far as autumn doth the flow'ry prime.
                                    Through

Through this thy empire range, like world's bright
    eye,
That once each year furveys all earth and fky;
Now glances on the flow and refty Bears,
Then turns to dry the weeping Aufter's tears;
Hurries to both the poles, and moveth even
In the infigur'd circle of the heaven.
O! long, long haunt thefe bounds, which by thy
    fight
Have now regain'd their former heat and light.
Here grow green woods, here filver brooks do glide,
Here meadows ftretch them out with painted pride;
Embroid'ring all the banks, here hills afpire
To crown their heads with the ethereal fire;
Hills, bulwarks of our freedom, giant walls,
Which never friends did flight, nor fword made
    thralls:
Each circling flood to Thetis tribute pays,
Men here, in health, outlive old Neftor's days:
Grim Saturn yet amongft our rocks remains,
Bound in our caves, with many metal'd chains:
Bulls haunt our fhades, like Leda's lover, white,
Which yet might breed Pafiphae delight;
Our flocks fair fleeces bear, with which, for fport,
Endymion of old the moon did court;
High-palmed harts amidft our forefts run,
And, not impell'd, the deep-mouth'd hounds do fhun;
The rough-foot hare fafe in our bufhes fhrouds,
And long-wing'd hawks do perch amidft our clouds.
The wanton wood-nymphs of the verdant fpring,
Blue, golden, purple flow'rs fhall to thee bring;

        Pomona's

Pomona's fruits the Panifks, Thetis' gyrles
Thy Thule's amber, with the ocean pearls;
The Tritons, herdfmen of the glaffy field,
Shall give thee what far-diftant fhores can yield;
The Serean fleeces, Erythrean gems,
Wafte Plata's filver, gold of Peru ftreams,
Antarctic parrots, Æthiopian plumes,
Sabæan odours, myrrh, and fweet perfumes:
And I myfelf, wrapt in a watchet gown
Of reeds and lilies, on mine head a crown,
Shall incenfe to thee burn, green altars. raife,
And yearly fing due Pæans to thy praife.
    Ah! why fhould Ifis only fee thee fhine?
Is not thy Forth, as well as Ifis, thine?
Though Ifis vaunt fhe hath more wealth in ftore,
Let it fuffice thy Forth doth love thee more:
Though fhe for beauty may compare with Seine,
For fwans and fea-nymphs with imperial Rheine;
Yet, for the title may be claim'd in thee,
Nor fhe, nor all the world, can match with me.
Now, when, by honour drawn, thou fhalt away
To her, already jealous of thy ftay;
When in her amorous arms fhe doth thee fold,
And dries thy dewy hairs with hers of gold,
Much afking of thy fare, much of thy fport,
Much of thine abfence, long, howe'er fo fhort,
And chides, perhaps, thy coming to the North,
Loath not to think on thy much-loving Forth:
O! love thefe bounds, where, of thy royal ftem,
More than an hundred wore a diadem.

So

So ever gold and bays thy brows adorn,
So never time may fee thy race out-worn ;
So of thine own ftill may'ft thou be defir'd,
Of ftrangers fear'd, redoubted, and admir'd;
So memory thee praife, fo precious hours
May charaćter thy name in ftarry flow'rs ;
So may thy high exploits at laft make even
With earth thy empire, glory with the heaven !

SPEECHES

S P E E C H E S

TO THE

HIGH ᴀɴᴅ EXCELLENT PRINCE

C H A R L E S,

KING OF GREAT BRITAIN, FRANCE, AND IRELAND,

At his entering his CITY of EDINBURGH.

———————

Delivered from the Pageants the 15th of June, 1633.

S P E E C H

AT THE WEST GATE.

S I R,

IF Nature could fuffer rocks to move, and abandon their natural places, this Town, founded on the ftrength of rocks (now, by the all-cheering rays of your Majefty's prefence, taking not only motion, but life), had, with her caftle, temples, and houfes, moved toward you, and befought you to acknowledge her yours, and her inhabitants your moft humble and affectionate fubjects; and to believe, how many fouls are within her circuits, fo many lives are devoted to your facred perfon and crown. And here, Sir, fhe offers, by me, to the altar of your glory, whole heca-tombs of moft happy defires, praying all things may prove profperous unto you; that every virtue and he-roic grace, which make a prince eminent, may, with a long and bleffed government, attend you; your kingdoms flourifhing abroad with bays, at home with olives; prefenting you, Sir (who are the ftrong key

of

of this little world of Great Britain), with thefe keys, which caft up the gates of her affection, and defign you power to open all the fprings of the hearts of thefe her moft loyal citizens. Yet this is almoft not neceffary; for as the rofe at the far appearing of the morning fun difplayeth and fpreadeth her purples, fo at the very report of your happy return to this your native country, their hearts (as might be apparent, if they could have fhined through their breafts) were with joy and fair hopes made fpacious; nor did they ever, in all parts, feel a more comfortable heat, than the glory of your prefence at this time darteth upon them.

The old forget their age, and look frefh and young at the fight of fo gracious a prince : the young bear a part in your welcome, defiring many years of life, that they may ferve you long ; all have more joys than tongues; for, as the words of other nations far go beyond and furpafs the affection of their hearts ; fo in this nation, the affection of their hearts is far above all they can exprefs by words. Deign then, Sir, from the higheft of majefty to look down on their lownefs, and embrace it ; accept the homage of their humble minds, accept their grateful zeal ; and, for deeds, accept that great good-will which they have ever carried to the high deferts of your anceftors, and fhall ever, to your own, and your royal race, whilft thefe rocks fhall be overfhadowed with build-ings, thefe buildings inhabited by men, and while men fhall be endued either with counfel or courage, or en-joy any piece of reafon, fenfe, or life.

THE

THE

SPEECH OF CALEDONIA,

REPRESENTING THE KINGDOM.

THE Heavens have heard our vows, our juſt de-
      ſires
Obtained are ; no higher now aſpires
Our wiſhing thought, ſince to his native clime,
The flower of princes, honour of his time,
Encheering all our dales, hills, foreſts, ſtreams,
(As Phœbus doth the ſummer with his beams)
Is come, and radiant to us, in his train,
The golden age and virtues brings again !
Prince ſo much longed for ! how thou becalm'ſt
Minds eaſeleſs anguiſh, every care embalm'ſt
With the ſweet odours of thy preſence ! Now,
In ſwelling tides, joys every where do flow
By thine approach ; and that the world may ſee
What unthought wonders do attend on thee,
This kingdom's angel I, who ſince that day
That ruthleſs Fate thy parent reft away,
And made a ſtar, appear'd not any where
To gratulate thy coming, come am here.
   Hail ! princes' phœnix, monarch of all hearts,
Sovereign of love and juſtice, who imparts
More than thou canſt receive ! To thee this crown
Is due by birth : but more, it is thine own

By

By juſt deſert ; and ere another brow
Than thine ſhould reach the ſame, my floods ſhould
   - flow   .
With hot vermilion gore, and every plain
Level the hills with carcaſes of ſlain,
This iſle become a Red Sea. Now how ſweet
Is it to me, when love and laws thus meet
To girt thy temples with this diadem,
My nurſelings ſacred fear, and deareſt gem,
Nor Roman, Saxon, Pict, by ſad alarms
Could thus acquire and keep ; the heavens in arms
From us repel all perils ; nor by wars
Aught here was won, ſave gaping wounds and ſcars :
Our Lion's climacteric now is paſt,
And crown'd with bays he rampeth free at laſt.
   Here are no Serean fleeces, Peru gold,
Aurora's gems, nor wares by Tyrians ſold ;
Towns ſwell not here with Babylonian walls,
Nor Nero's ſky-reſembling gold-ceil'd halls ;
Nor Memphis' ſpires, nor Quinzaye's arched frames,
Captiving ſeas, and giving lands their names :
Faith, milk-white Faith ! of old belov'd ſo well,
Yet in this corner of the world doth dwell
With her pure ſiſters, Truth, Simplicity ;
Here baniſh'd Honour bears them company :
A Mars-adoring brood is here, their wealth,
Sound minds, and bodies of as ſound a health ;
Walls here are men, who fence their cities more
Than Neptune, when he doth in mountains roar,
Doth guard this iſle, or all thoſe forts and tow'rs
Amphion's harp rais'd about Thebes' bow'rs.
                        Heaven's

Heaven's arch is oft their roof, the pleafant fhed
Of oak and plain oft ferves them for a bed.
To fuffer want, oft pleafure to defpife,
Run over panting mountains crown'd with ice,
Rivers o'ercome, the wafteft lakes appal,
(Being to themfelves, oars, fteerers, fhip and all)
Is their renown : a brave all-daring race,
Courageous, prudent, doth this climate grace;
Yet the firm bafe on which their glory ftands,
In peace, true hearts; in wars, is valiant hands,
Which here, great King! they offer up to thee,
Thy worth refpecting as thy pedigree.
Though it be much to come of princely ftem,
More is it to deferve a diadem.
      Vouchfafe, bleft people, ravifh'd here with me,
To think my thoughts, and fee what I do fee.
A prince all-gracious, affable, divine,
Meek, wife, juft, valiant, whofe radiant fhine
Of virtues, like the ftars about the Pole
Gilding the night, enlight'neth every foul,
Your fceptre fways; a prince, born in this age
To guard the innocent from tyrants' rage;
To make peace profper, juftice to reflow'r,
In defert hamlet, as in lordly bow'r;
A prince that, though of none he ftands in awe,
Yet firft fubjects himfelf to his own law;
Who joys in good, and ftill, as right directs,
His greatnefs meafures by his good effects;
His people's pedeftal, who rifing high,
To grace this throne, makes Scotland's name to fly

O   On

On halcyon's wings (her glory which reſtores)
Beyond the ocean to Columbus' ſhores :
God's ſacred picture in this man adore,
Honour his valour, zeal, his piety more ;
High value what you hold, him deep engrave
In your heart's heart, from whom all good ye have :
For as moon's ſplendor from her brother ſprings,
The people's welfare ſtreameth from their kings.
Since your love's object doth immortal prove,
O ! love this prince with an eternal love.

Pray that thoſe crowns his anceſtors did wear,
His temples long, more orient, may bear ;
That good he reach by ſweetneſs of his ſway,
That ev'n his ſhadow may the bad affray ;
That Heaven on him what he deſires beſtow,
That ſtill the glory of his greatneſs grow ;
That your begun felicities may laſt,
That no Orion do with ſtorms them blaſt ;
That victory his brave exploits attend,
Eaſt, weſt, or ſouth, where he his force ſhall bend,
Till his great deeds all former deeds ſurmount,
And quell the Nimrod of the Helleſpont ;
That when his well-ſpent care all care becalms,
He may in peace ſleep in a ſhade of palms ;
And rearing up fair trophies, that Heaven may
. Extend his life to world's extremeſt day.

THE

SONG of the MUSES at PARNASSUS.

AT length we fee thofe eyes,
    Which cheer both earth and fkies;
Now, ancient Caledon,
Thy beauties heighten, richeft robes put on,   . .
And let young joys to all thy parts arife.

Here, could thy Prince ftill ftay,
Each month fhould turn to May;
We need nor ftar, nor fun,
Save him, to lengthen days, and joys begun :
Sorrow and Night to far climes hafte away.

Now majefty and love
  Combin'd are from above;   .
Prince never fceptre fway'd,   .
Lov'd fubjects more, of fubjects more obey'd,
Which may endure whilft heaven's great orbs do
      move.

Joys, did you always laft,
Life's fpark you foon would wafte;
Grief follows fweet delight,
As day is fhadowed by fable night,
Yet fhall remembrance keep you ftill, when paft.

THE

SPEECHES

AT THE

HOROSCOPAL PAGEANT,

BY THE PLANETS.

———

ENDYMION.

ROUS'D from the Latmian cave, where many
years
That emprefs of the loweft of the fpheres,
Who. cheers the night, did keep me hid, apart
From mortal wights, to eafe her love-fick heart,
As young as when fhe did me firft inclofe,
As frefh in beauty as the morning rofe,
Endymion, that whilom kept my flocks
Upon Ionia's flow'ry hills and rocks,
And fweet lays warbling to my Cynthia's beams,
Out-fang the cygnets of Meander's ftreams:
To whom, for guerdon, fh heaven's fecret bars
Made open, taught the paths and pow'rs of ftars:

By

By this dear Lady's ſtrict commandement,
To celebrate this day I here am ſent.
But whether is this heaven, which ſtars do crown,
Or are heaven's flaming ſplendours here come down
To beautify this nether world with me ?
Such ſtate and glory did e'er ſhepherd ſee ?
My wits my ſenſe miſtruſt, and ſtay amaz'd ;
No eye on fairer objects ever gaz'd.
Sure this is heaven ; for ev'ry wand'ring ſtar,
Forſaking thoſe great orbs where whirl'd they are,
All diſmal, ſad aſpects abandoning,
Are here met to ſalute ſome gracious king.
Nor is it ſtrange if they heaven's height neglect ;
It of undoubted worth is the effect :
Then this it is, thy preſence, royal youth,
Hath brought them here within an azimuth,
To tell by me, their herald, coming things,
And what each Fate to her ſtern diſtaff ſings :
Heaven's volume to unclaſp, vaſt pages ſpread,
Myſterious golden cyphers clear to read.
Hear then the augur of thy future days,
And what the ſtarry ſenate of thee ſays ;
For, what is firm decreed in heaven above,
In vain on earth ſtrive mortals to improve.

O 3   SATURN.

SATURN.

TO fair hopes to give reins now is it time,
  And foar as high as juft defires may climb ;.
O halcyonian, clear, and happy day !
From forry wights let forrow fly away,.
And vex Antarctic climes ; great Britain's woes
Vanifh, for joy now in her zenith glows.
The old Lucadian fcythe-bearing fire,.
Though cold, for thee feels flames of fweet defire ;.
And many luftres at a perfect height
Shall keep thy fceptre's majefty as bright,
And ftrong in power and glory, every way,
As when thy peerlefs parent did it fway ;.
Ne'er turning wrinkled in Time's endlefs length,.
But one in her firft beauty, youthful ftrength,.
Like thy rare mind, which ftedfaft as the Pole
Still fixed ftands, however fpheres do roll.
More to enhance with favours this thy reign,
His age of gold he fhall reftore again ;
Love, Juftice, Honour, Innocence renew,
Men's fprights with white fimplicity indue ;·
Make all to live in plenty's ceafelefs ftore
With equal fhares, none wifhing to have more.
No more fhall cold the ploughmen's hopes beguile,
Skies fhall on earth with lovely glances fmile ;
Which fhall, untill'd, each flower and herb bring forth,
And lands to gardens turn, of equal worth ;
Life (long) fhall not be thrall'd to mortal dates :
Thus Heavens decree, fo have ordain'd the Fates.
                    JOVE.

JOVE.

DELIGHT of Heaven! fole honour of the Earth!
Jove (courting thine afcendant) at thy birth
Proclaimed thee a King, and made it true,
That to thy worth great monarchies are due:
He gave thee what was good, and what was great,
What did belong to love, and what to ftate;
Rare gifts, whofe ardours burn the hearts of all;
Like tinder, when flint's atoms on it fall.
The Tramontane, which thy fair courfe directs,
Thy counfels fhall approve by their effects;
Juftice, kept low by giants, wrongs, and jars,
Thou fhalt relieve, and crown with gliftering ftars;
Whom nought, fave law of force, could keep in awe,
Thou fhalt turn clients to the force of law;
Thou arms fhalt brandifh for thine own defence,
Wrongs to repel, and guard weak innocence,
Which to thy laft effort thou fhalt uphold,
As oak the ivy which it doth enfold.
All overcome, at laft thyfelf o'ercome,
Thou fhalt make Paffion yield to Reafon's doom;
For fmiles of Fortune fhall not raife thy mind,
Nor fhall difafters make it e'er declin'd:
True Honour fhall refide within thy court,
Sobriety and Truth there ftill refort;
Keep promis'd faith, thou fhalt all treacheries
Deteft, and fawning parafites defpife;
Thou, others to make rich, fhalt not make poor
Thyfelf, but give, that thou may'ft ftill give more

O 4

Thou

Thou fhalt no paranymph raife to high place,
For frizzled locks, quaint pace, or painted face :.
On gorgeous raiments, womanizing toys,
The works of worms, and what a moth deftroys,
The maze of fools, thou fhalt no treafure fpend,
Thy charge to immortality fhall tend ;.
Raife palaces, and temples vaulted high ;
Rivers o'erarch ; of hofpitality
And fciences the ruin'd inns reftore ;
With walls and ports encircle Neptune's fhore ;.
To new-found worlds thy fleets make hold their courfe,.
And find of Canada the unknown fource ;
People thofe lands which pafs Arabian fields
In fragrant woods, and mufk which zephyr yields.
Thou, fear'd of none, fhalt not thy people fear,
Thy people's love thy greatnefs fhall up-rear :.
Still rigour fhall not fhine, and mercy lower ;.
What love can do, thou fhalt not do by power ;.
New and vaft taxes thou fhalt not extort,
Load heavy thofe thy bounty fhould fupport.
Thou fhalt not ftrike the hinge nor mafter-beam;
Of thine eftate ; but errors in the fame,
By harmlefs juftice, gracioufly reform.
Delighting more in calm than roaring ftorm,.
Thou fhalt govern in peace, as did thy fire ;
Keep, fave thine own, and kingdoms new acquire
Beyond Alcides' pillars, and thofe bounds
Where Alexander gain'd the eaftern crowns,
Till thou the greateft be among the Greats :
Thus Heavens ordain, fo have decreed the Fates.

MARS.

MARS.

SON of the Lion! thou of loathfome bands
  Shalt free the earth, and whate'er thee withftands.
Thy noble paws fhall tear; the God of Thrace
Shall be thy fecond; and before thy face,
To Truth and Juftice whilft thou trophies rears,
Armies fhall fall difmay'd with panic fears.
As when Aurora in fky's azure lifts
Makes fhadows vanifh, doth difperfe the mifts,
And in a twinkling with her opal light
Night's horrors checketh, putting ftars to flight:
More to inflame thee to this noble tafk,
To thee he here refigns his fword and cafque.
A wall of flying caftles, armed pines,
Shall bridge thy fea; like heaven. with fteel that
    fhines
To aid Earth's tenants by foul yokes oppreft,
And fill with fears the great King of the Weft:
To thee already Victory difplays
Her garlands twin'd with olive, oak, and bays;
Thy triumphs finifh fhall all old debates:
Thus Heavens decree, fo have ordain'd the Fates.

SUN.

S U N.

WEALTH, wifdom, glory, pleafure, ftouteft
hearts,
Religion, laws, Hyperion imparts
To thy juft reign, which fhall far, far furpafs
Of emperors, kings, the beft that ever was :
Look how he dims the ftars ; thy glories' rays ,
So darken fhall the luftre of thefe days :
For in fair Virtue's zodiac thou fhalt run,
And in the heaven of worthies be the fun.
No more contemn'd fhall haplefs Learning lie ;
The maids of Pindus fhall be raifed high ;
For bay and ivy which their brows enroll'd,
Thou fhalt 'em deck with gems and fhining gold ;
Thou open fhalt Parnaffus' cryftal gates ;
Thus Heavens ordain, fo do decree the Fates.

V E N U S.

THE Acidalian Queen amidft thy bays
Shall twine her myrtles, grant thee pleafant days ;
She did make clear thy houfe, and, with her light,
Of churlifh ftars put back the difmal fpight ;
The hymenean bed fair brood fhall grace,
Which on the earth continue fhall their race ;
While Flora's treafure fhall the meads endear ;
While fweet Pomona rofe-cheek'd fruits fhall bear ;
While Phœbus' beams her brother's emulates :
Thus Heavens decree, fo have ordain'd the Fates.

MERCURY.

MERCURY.

GREAT Atlas' nephew shall the works of peace,
   The springs of plenty, tillage, trade, increase;
And arts, in time's gulphs lost, again restore
To their perfection; nay, find many more,
More perfect artists: Cyclops in their forge
Shall mould those brazen Typhons, which disgorge
From their hard bowels metal, flame, and smoke,
Muffling the air up in a sable cloke.
Geryons, harpies, dragons, sphinges strange
Wheel, where in spacious gires the fume doth range;
The sea shrinks at the blow, shake doth the ground,
The world's vast chambers doth the sound rebound;
The Stygian porter leaveth off to bark,
Black Jove, appall'd, doth shroud him in the dark;
Many a Typhis, in adventures toss'd,
By new-found skill shall many a maiden coast
With thy sail-winged Argoses find out,
Which, like the sun, shall run the earth about;
And far beyond his paths score wavy ways,
To Cathay's lands by Hyperborean seas;
He shall endue thee, both in peace and war,
With wisdom, which than strength is better far;
Wealth, honour, arms, and arts shall grace thy states:
Thus Heavens ordain, so do decree the Fates.

THE

THE MOON.

O HOW the fair Queen with the golden maids,
   The fun of night, thy happy fortunes aids!
Though turban'd princes for a badge her wear,
To them fhe wains, to thee would full appear;
Her hand-maid Thetis daily walks the round
About thy Delos, that no force it wound;
Then when thou left'ft it, and abroad didft ftray,
Dear pilgrim, fhe did ftrew with flowers thy way;
And, turning foreign force and counfel vain,
Thy guard and guide return'd thee home again;
To thee fhe kingdoms, years, blifs did divine,
Quailing Medufa's grim fnakes with her fhine.
Beneath thy reign Difcord (fell mifchief's forge,
The bane of people, ftate and kingdom's fcourge),
Pale Envy (with the cockatrice's eye,
Which feeing kills, but feen doth forthwith die),
Malice, Deceit, Rebellion, Impudence,
Beyond the Garamants fhall pack them hence,
With every monfter that thy glory hates:
Thus Heavens decree, fo have ordain'd the Fates.

ENDYMION.

ENDYMION.

THAT heretofore to thy heroic mind
  Hopes did not anfwer as they were defign'd,
'O do not think it ftrange : times were not come,
And thefe fair ftars had not pronounc'd their doom
The Deftinies did on that day attend,
When to this northern region thou fhouldft lend
Thy cheerful prefence, and, charg'd with renown,
Set on thy brows the Caledonian crown.
Thy virtues now thy juft defire fhall grace,
Stern chance fhall change, and to defert give place.
Let this be known to all the Fates, admit
To their grave counfel, and to every wit
That courts Heaven's infide : this let Sybils know,
And thofe mad Corybants who dance and glow
On Dindimus' high tops with frantic fire :
Let this be known to all Apollo's choir,
And People : let it not be hid from you,
What mountains' noife and floods proclaim as true;
'Wherever Fame abroad his praife fhall ring,
All fhall obferve, and ferve this bleffed King.

The End of King CHARLES's Entertainment
at *Edinburgh*, 1633.

A PAS-

A
PASTORAL ELEGY

ON THE

D   E   A   T   H

OF

S. W. A.

IN fweeteft prime and blooming of his age,
   Dear Alcon, ravifh'd from this mortal ftage,
The fhepherds mourn'd, as they him lov'd before.
Among the rout, him Idmon did deplore;
Idmon, who, whether fun in eaft did rife,
Or dive in weft, pour'd torrents from his eyes
Of liquid cryftal; under hawthorn fhade,
At laft to trees and flocks this plaint he made:
Alcon! delight of Heaven, defire of Earth,
Off-fpring of Phœbus, and the Mufes' birth,
The Graces' darling, Adon of our plains,
Flame of the faireft nymphs the earth fuftains!
What pow'r of thee hath us bereft? what Fate,
By thy untimely fall, would ruinate

7

Our hopes? O Death! what treafure in one hour
Haft thou difperfed! how doft thou devour
What we on earth hold deareft! All things good,
Too envious Heavens, how blaft ye in the bud!
The corn the greedy reapers cut not down
Before the fields with golden ears it crown ;
Nor doth the verdant fruits the gardener pull ;
But thou art cropt before thy years were full.
   With thee, fweet youth! the glories of our fields
Vanifh away, and what contentments yields.
The lakes their filver look, the woods their fhades,
The fprings their cryftal want, their verdure meads,
The years their early feafons, cheerful days ;
Hills gloomy ftand, now defolate of rays :
Their amorous whifpers zephyrs not us bring,
Nor do air's chorifters falute the fpring ;
The freezing winds our gardens do deflow'r.
Ah Deftinies, and you whom fkies embow'r,
To his fair fpoils his fpright again yet give,
And, like another phœnix, make him live!
The herbs, though cut, fprout fragrant from their
      ftems,
And make with crimfon blufh our anadems :
The fun, when in the weft he doth decline,
Heaven's brighteft tapers at his funerals fhine ;
His face, when wafh'd in the Atlantic feas,
Revives, and cheers the welkin with new rays :
Why fhould not he, fince of more pure a frame,
Return to us again, and be the fame ?
                                        But,

But, wretch! what wifh I ? To the winds I fend
Thefe plaints and pray'rs : Deftinies cannot lend
Thee more of time, nor Heavens confent will thus
Thou leave their ftarry world to dwell with us ;
Yet fhall they not thee keep amidft their fpheres
Without thefe lamentations and tears.

    Thou waft all virtue, courtefy, and worth ;
And, as fun's light is in the moon fet forth,
World's fupreme excellence in thee did fhine :
Nor, though eclipfed now, fhalt thou decline,
But in our memories live, while dolphins ftreams,
Shall haunt, whilft eaglets ftare on Titan's beams,
Whilft fwans upon their cryftal tombs fhall fing,
Whilft violets with purple paint the fpring.
A gentler fhepherd flocks did never feed
On Albion's hills, nor fing to oaten reed.
While what fhe found in thee my mufe would blaze,
Grief doth diftract her, and cut fhort thy praife.

    How oft have we, environ'd by the throng
Of tedious fwains, the cooler fhades among,
Contemn'd Earth's glow-worm Greatnefs, and the
    chace
Of Fortune fcorn'd, deeming it difgrace
To court inconftancy ! How oft have we
Some Chloris' name grav'n in each virgin tree ;
And, finding favours fading, the next day
What we had carv'd we did deface away.
Woful remembrance ! Nor time nor place
Of thy abodement fhadows any trace ;

But

But there to me thou fhin'ft: late glad defires,
And ye once rofes, how are ye turn'd briars!
Contentments paffed, and of pleafures chief,
Now are ye frightful horrors, hells of grief!
    When from thy native foil Love had thee driven,
(Thy fafe return prefigurating) a heaven
Of flattering hopes did in my fancy move;
Then little dreaming it fhould atoms prove.
Thefe groves preferve will I, thefe loved woods,
Thefe orchards rich with fruits, with fifh thefe floods;
My Alcon will return, and once again
His chofen exiles he will entertain;
The populous city holds him, amongft harms
Of fome fierce Cyclops, Circe's ftronger charms.
Thefe banks, faid I, he vifit will, and ftreams;
Thefe filent fhades, ne'er kifs'd by courting beams.
Far, far, off I will meet him, and I firft
Shall him approaching know, and firft be bleft
With his afpect; I firft fhall hear his voice,
Him find the fame he parted, and rejoice
To learn his paffed perils; know the fports
Of foreign fhepherds, fawns, and fairy courts.
No pleafure like the fields, an happy ftate
The fwains enjoy, fecure from what they hate:
Free of proud cares they innocently fpend
The day, nor do black thoughts their eafe offend;
Wife Nature's darlings, they live in the world
Perplexing not themfelves how it is hurl'd.
Thefe hillocks Phœbus loves, Ceres thefe plains,
Thefe fhades the Sylvans; and here Pales ftrains

Milk

Milk in the pails; the maids which haunt the springs
Dance on thefe paftures; here Amintas fings:
Hefperian gardens, Tempe's fhades, are here,
Or what the Eaftern Inde and Weft hold dear.
Come then, dear youth! the wood-nymphs twine thee
        boughs
With rofe and lily to impale thy brows.
Thus ignorant I mus'd, not confcious yet
Of what by Death was done, and ruthlefs Fate:
Amidft thefe trances Fame thy lofs doth found,
And through my ears gives to my heart a wound.
With ftretch'd-out arms I fought thee to embrace,
But clafp'd, amaz'd, a coffin in thy place;
A coffin of our joys which had the truft,
Which told that thou wert come, but chang'd to
    ' duft!
Scarce, ev'n when felt, could I believe this wrack,
Nor that thy time and glory Heavens would break.
Now, fince I cannot fee my Alcon's face,
And find nor vows nor prayers to have place
With guilty ftars, this mountain fhall become
To me a facred altar, and a tomb
To famous Alcon. Here, as days, months, years
Do circling glide, I facrifice will tears;
Here fpend my remnant time, exil'd from mirth,
Till Death at laft turn monarch of my earth.
    Shepherds on Forth, and you by Doven rocks,
Which ufe to fing and fport, and keep your flocks,
Pay tribute here of tears! ye never had
To aggravate your moans a caufe more fad.:
                        And

And to their forrows hither bring your mands,
Charged with fweeteft flow'rs, and with pure hands,
Fair nymphs, the blufhing hyacinth and rofe
Spread on the place his relics doth inclofe;
Weave garlands to his memory, and put
Over his hearfe a verfe in cyprefs cut:
Virtue did die, goodnefs but harm did give,
After the noble Alcon ceas'd to live:
Friendfhip an earthquake fuffer'd; lofing him
Love's brighteft conftellation turned dim.

MISCELLANIES.

A PASTORAL SONG.

PHILLIS and DAMON.

PHIL. SHEPHERD, doſt thou love me well?
DAM. Better than weak words can tell.
PHIL. Like to what, good ſhepherd, ſay?
DAM. Like to thee, fair cruel May.
PHIL. O how ſtrange theſe words I find!
    Yet to ſatisfy my mind,
    Shepherd, without mocking me,
    Have I any love from thee?
    Like to what, good ſhepherd, ſay?
DAM. Like to thee, fair cruel May.
PHIL. Better anſwer had it been,
    To ſay thou lov'ſt me as thine eyne.
DAM. Wo is me! theſe I love not,
    For by them love entrance got,
    At that time they did behold,
    Thy ſweet face and locks of gold.
PHIL. Like to what, dear ſhepherd, ſay?
DAM. Like to thee, fair cruel May.
PHIL. Once, dear ſhepherd, ſpeak more plain,
    And I ſhall not aſk again;
    Say, to end this gentle ſtrife,
    Doſt thou love me as thy life?
DAM. No, for it is turn'd a ſlave
    To ſad annoys, and what I have

Of life by love's ſtronger force
Is 'reft, and I'm but a dead corſe.
PHIL. Like to what, good ſhepherd, ſay?
DAM. Like to thee, fair cruel May.
PHIL. Learn I pray this, like to thee,
And ſay, I love as I do me.
DAM. Alas! I do not love myſelf,
For I'm ſplit on beauty's ſhelf.
PHIL. Like to what, good ſhepherd, ſay?
DAM. Like to thee, fair cruel May.

———————

ALL good hath left this age, all tracks of ſhame:
Mercy is baniſhed, and Pity dead;
Juſtice, from whence it came, to heav'n is fled;
Religion, maim'd, is thought an idle name.
Faith to Diſtruſt and Malice hath giv'n place;
Envy, with poiſon'd teeth, hath Friendſhip torn;
Renowned Knowledge is a deſpis'd ſcorn;
Now evil 'tis, all evil not t' embrace.
There is no life, ſave under ſervile bands;
To make Deſert a vaſſal to their crimes,
Ambition with Avarice joins hands:
O ever ſhameful, O moſt ſhameleſs times!
Save that ſun's light we ſee, of good here tell,
This earth we court ſo much were very hell.

DOTH then the world go thus, doth all thus move?
Is this the juſtice which on earth we find?
Is this that firm decree which all doth bind?
Are theſe your influences, Pow'rs above?

Thoſe

Thofe fouls which Vice's moody mifts moft blind,
Blind Fortune, blindly, moft their friend doth prove ;
And they who thee, poor idol Virtue ! love,
Ply like a feather tofs'd by ftorm and wind.
Ah ! if a Providence doth fway this All,
Why fhould beft minds groan under moft diftrefs ?
Or why fhould Pride Humility make thrall,
And injuries the innocent opprefs ?
    Heav'ns ! hinder, ftop this fate ; or grant a time
    When good may have, as well as bad, their prime.

A REPLY.

WHO do in good delight,
    That fov'reign juftice ever doth reward ;
And though fometime it fmite,
Yet it doth them regard :
For ev'n amidft their grief
They find a ftrong relief,
And death itfelf can work them no defpite.
Again, in evil who joy,
And do in it grow old,
In midft of mirth are charg'd with fin's annoy,
Which is in confcience fcroll'd ;
And when their life's frail thread is cut by time,
They punifhment find equal to each crime.

LOOK how in May the rofe,
    At fulphur's azure fumes,
In a fhort fpace her crimfon blufh doth lofe,

                    And,

And, all amaz'd, a pallid white assumes.
So time our best consumes,
Makes youth and beauty pass,
And what was pride turns horror in our glass.

T O

A SWALLOW BUILDING NEAR THE STATUE OF MEDEA.

FOND Progne, chattering wretch,
That is Medea! there
Wilt thou thy younglings hatch?
Will she keep thine, her own who could not spare?
Learn from her frantic face
To seek some fitter place.
What other may'st thou hope for, what desire,
Save Stygian spells, wounds, poison, iron, fire?

VENUS ARMED.

TO practice new alarms
In Jove's great court above,
The wanton Queen of Love
Of sleeping Mars put on the horrid arms;
Where gazing in a glass
To see what thing she was,
To mock and scoff the blue-eyed maid did move;
Who said, Sweet queen, thus should you have been
dight
When Vulcan took you napping with your knight.

THE BOAR'S HEAD.

A MIDST a pleasant green
Which sun did seldom see,
Where play'd Anchises with the Cyprian Queen,
The head of a wild boar hung on a tree:
And, driven by Zephyrs' breath,
Did fall, and wound the lovely youth beneath;
On whom yet scarce appears
So much of blood as Venus' eyes shed tears.
But, ever as she wept, her anthem was,
Change, cruel change, alas!
My Adon, whilst thou liv'd, was by thee slain;
Now dead, this lover must thou kill again?

TO AN OWL.

A SCALAPHUS, tell me,
So may night's curtain long time cover thee,
So ivy ever may
From irksome light keep thy chamber and bed;
And, in moon's liv'ry clad,
So may'st thou scorn the choristers of day—
When plaining thou dost stay
Near to the sacred window of my dear,
Dost ever thou her hear
To wake, and steal swift hours from drowsy sleep?
And, when she wakes, doth e'er a stolen sigh creep
Into thy listening ear?
If that deaf god doth yet her careless keep,
In louder notes my grief with thine express,
Till by thy shrieks she think on my distress.

                              DAPHNIS.

DAPHNIS.

NOW Daphnis' arms did grow
 In flender branches; and her braided hair,
Which like gold waves did flow,
In leafy twigs was ftretched in the air;.
The grace of either foot
Transform'd was to a root;·
A tender bark enwraps her body fair.
He who did caufe her ill
Sore wailing ftood, and from his blubber'd eyne
Did fhow'rs of tears upon the rind diftil,
Which, water'd thus, did bud and turn more green..
 O deep defpair! O heart-appalling grief!
 When that doth woe increafe fhould bring relief..

THE BEAR OF LOVE..

IN woods and defart bounds
 A beaft abroad doth roam;·
So loving fweetnefs and the honey-comb,
It doth defpife the arms of bees and wounds:.
I, by like pleafure led,
To prove what heav'ns did place
Of fweet on your fair face,
Whilft therewith I am fed,
Reft carelefs (bear of love) of hellifh fmart,
And how thofe eyes afflict and wound my heart.

FIVE

FIVE SONNETS

FOR

GALATEA.

STREPHON, in vain thou bring'ft thy rhimes and
    fongs,
Deck'd with grave Pindar's old and wither'd flow'rs;
In vain thou count'ft the fair Europa's wrongs,
And her whom Jove deceiv'd in golden fhow'rs.
Thou haft flept never under myrtle's fhed;
Or, if that paffion hath thy foul opprefs'd,
It is but for fome Grecian miftrefs dead,
Of fuch old fighs thou doft difcharge thy breaft;
How can true love with fables hold a place?
Thou who with fables doft fet forth thy love,
Thy love a pretty fable needs muft prove:
Thou fueft for grace, in fcorn more to difgrace.
    I cannot think thou wert charm'd by my looks,
    O no! thou learn'ft thy love in lovers' books.

II.

NO more with candid words infect mine ears;
    Tell me no more how that you pine in anguifh;
When found you fleep, no more fay that you languifh;
No more in fweet defpite fay you fpend tears.
Who hath fuch hollow eyes as not to fee,
How thofe that are hair-brain'd boaft of Apollo,
And bold give out the Mufes do them follow,
Though in Love's library, yet no lovers be.

If

If we, poor fouls! leaft favour but them fhew,
That ftraight in wanton lines abroad is blaz'd;
Their names doth foar on our fame's overthrow;
Mark'd is our lightnefs, whilft their wits are prais'd.
  In filent thoughts who can no fecret cover,
  He may, fay we, but not well, be a lover.

III.

YE who with curious numbers, fweeteft art,
  Frame Dedal nets our beauty to furprife,
Telling ftrange caftles builded in the fkies,
And tales of Cupid's bow and Cupid's dart;
Well, howfoe'er ye act your feigned fmart,
Molefting quiet ears with tragic cries,
When you accufe our chaftity's beft part,
Nam'd cruelty, ye feem not half too wife;
Yea, ye yourfelves it deem moft worthy praife,
Beauty's beft guard; that dragon, which doth keep
Hefperian fruit, the fpur in you does raife,
That Delian wit that otherways may fleep,
  To cruel nymphs your lines do fame afford,
  Oft many pitiful, not one poor word.

IV.

IF it be love, to wake out all the night,
  And watchful eyes drive out in dewy moans,
And, when the fun brings to the world his light,
To wafte the day in tears and bitter groans;
If it be love, to dim weak reafon's beam
With clouds of ftrange defire, and make the mind
In hellifh agonies a heav'n to dream,
Still feeking comforts where but griefs we find;

If

If it be love, to ftain with wanton thought
A fpotlefs chaftity, and make it try
More furious flames than his whofe cunning wrought
That brazen bull, where he intomb'd did fry;
  Then fure is love the caufer of fuch woes,
  Be ye our lovers, or our mortal foes.

V.

AND would you then fhake off Love's golden chain,
    With which it is beft freedom to be bound?
And, cruel! do you feek to heal the wound
Of love, which hath fuch fweet and pleafant pain?
All that is fubject unto Nature's reign
In fkies above, or on this lower round,
When it its long and far-fought end hath found,
Doth in decadens fall and flack remain.
Behold the Moon, how gay her face doth grow
Till fhe kifs all the Sun, then doth decay!
See how the feas tumultuoufly do flow
. Till they embrace lov'd banks, then poft away;
  So is 't with love; unlefs you love me ftill,
  O do not think I'll yield unto your will!

SONNET.

CARE's charming fleep, fon of the fable night,
    Brother to death, in filent darknefs born,
Deftroy my languifh ere the day be light,
With dark forgetting of my care's return;
And let the day be long enough to mourn
The fhipwreck of my ill-adventur'd youth;

Let

Let wat'ry eyes fuffice to wail their fcorn,
Without the troubles of the night's untruth.
Ceafe, dreams, fond image of my fond defires!
To model forth the paffions of to-morrow;
Let never rifing fun approve your tears,
To add more grief to aggravate my forrow:
 Still let me fleep, embracing clouds in vain,
 And never wake to feel the day's difdain.

TO THAUMANTIA, SINGING.

IS it not too, too much
 Thou late didft to me prove
A bafilifk of love,
And didft my wits bewitch?
Unlefs, to caufe more harm,
Made fyren too thou with thy voice me charm?
Ah! though thou fo my reafon didft controul,
That to thy looks I could not prove a mole,
Yet do me not that wrong,
As not to let me turn afp to thy fong.

UPON A GLASS.

IF thou wouldft fee threads purer than the gold,
 Where love his wealth doth fhew,
But take this glafs, and thy fair hair behold.
If whitenefs thou wouldft fee more white than fnow,
And read on wonder's book,
Take but this glafs, and on thy forehead look.
        Wouldft

Wouldſt thou in winter ſee a crimſon roſe,
Whoſe thorns do hurt each heart,
Look but in glaſs how thy ſweet lips do cloſe.
Wouldſt thou ſee planets which all good impart,
Or meteors divine,
But take this glaſs, and gaze upon thine eyne.
No—planets, roſe, ſnow, gold, cannot compare
With you, dear eyes, lips, brows, and amber hair !

OF A BEE.

A S an audacious knight,
Come with ſome foe to fight,
His ſword doth brandiſh, makes his armour ring ;
So this proud bee, at home perhaps a king,
Did buzzing fly about,
And, tyrant, after thy fair lip did ſting.
O champion ſtrange as ſtout !
Who haſt by nature found
Sharp arms, and trumpet ſhrill, to ſound and wound.

OF THE SAME.

O Do not kill that bee
That thus hath wounded thee !
Sweet, it was no deſpite,
But hue did him deceive :
For when thy lips did cloſe,
He deemed them a roſe.
What wouldſt thou further crave ?
He wanting wit, and blinded with delight,
Would fain have kiſs'd, but mad with joy did bite.

OF A KISS.

AH! of that cruel bee
Thy lips have fuck'd too much;
For when they mine did touch,
I found that both they hurt and fweeten'd me:
This by the fting they have,
And that they of the honey do receive:
Dear kifs! elfe by what art
Couldft thou at once both pleafe and wound my
heart?

IDMON TO VENUS.

IF, Acidalia's queen,
Thou quench in me thy torch,
And with the farre Thaumantia's heart fhalt fcorch,
Each year a myrtle tree
Here I do vow to confecrate to thee:
And, when the meads grow green,
I will of fweeteft flowers
Weave thoufand garlands to adorn thy bow'rs.

A LOVER's PLAINT.

IN midft of filent night,
When men, birds, beafts, do reft,
With love and fear poffeft,
To Heav'n, and Flore, I count my heavy plight.
Again, with rofeate wings
When morn peeps forth, and Philomela fings,

Then,

Then, void of all relief,
Do I renew my grief:
Day follows night, night day, whilſt ſtill I prove
That Heaven is deaf, Flore careleſs of my love.

HIS FIREBRAND.

LEAVE, page, that ſlender torch,
   And in this gloomy night
Let only ſhine the light
Of Love's hot brandon, which my heart doth ſcorch:
A ſigh, or blaſt of wind,
My tears, or drops of rain,
May that at once make blind;
Whilſt this like Ætna burning ſhall remain.

DAPHNIS' VOW.

WHEN ſun doth bring the day
   From the Heſperian ſea,
Or moon her coach doth roll
Above the northern pole,
When ſerpents cannot hiſs,
And lovers ſhall not kiſs,
Then may it be, but in no time till then,
That Daphnis can forget his Orienne.

THE STATUE OF VENUS SLEEPING.

BREAK not my ſweet repoſe,
   Thou, whom free will, or chance, brings to this
      place;
Let lids theſe comets cloſe,
O do not ſeek to ſee their ſhining grace:

For

For when mine eyes thou feeft, they thine will blind ;
And thou fhalt part, but leave thy heart behind.

ANTHEA's GIFT.

THIS virgin lock of hair
 To Idmon Anthea gives,
Idmon, for whom fhe lives,
Though oft fhe mix his hopes with cold defpair :
This now ; but, abfent if he conftant prove,
With gift more dear fhe vows to meet his love.

TO THAUMANTIA.

COME, let us live, and love,
 And kifs, Thaumantia mine ;
I fhall the elm be, be to me the vine ;
Come, let us teach new billing to the dove :
Nay, to augment our blifs,
Let fouls e'en other kifs.
Let Love a workman be,
Undo, diftemper, and his cunning prove,
Of kiffes three make one, of one make three :
Though moon, fun, ftars, be bodies far more bright,
Let them not vaunt they match us in delight.

A LOVER's DAY AND NIGHT.

BRIGHT meteor of day,
 For me in Thetis' bow'rs for ever ftay ;
Night, to this flow'ry globe
Ne'er fhew for me thy ftar-embroider'd robe.

Q

My

My night, my day, do not proceed from you,
But hang on Mira's brow:
For when she low'rs, and hides from me her eyes,
'Midst cleareſt day I find black night ariſe ;
When ſmiling ſhe again thoſe twins doth turn,
In midſt of night I find noon's torch to burn.

THE STATUE OF ADONIS.

WHEN Venus, 'longſt that plain,
  This Parian Adon ſaw,
She ſigh'd, and ſaid, What pow'r breaks Deſtine's
    law,
World-mourned boy, and makes thee live again ?
Then with ſtretch'd arms ſhe ran him to enfold.
But when ſhe did behold
The boar whoſe ſnowy tuſks did threaten death,
Fear cloſed up her breath.
Who can but grant then that theſe ſtones do live,
Sith this bred love, and that a wound did give ?

CLORUS TO A GROVE.

OLD oak, and you thick grove,
  I ever ſhall you love,
With theſe ſweet-ſmelling briers :
For briers, oak, grove, ye crowned my deſires,
When underneath your ſhade
I left my woe, and Flore her maidenhead.

A COUPLET

A COUPLET ENCOMIASTIC.

L OVE, Cypris, Phœbus, will feed, deck, and
crown,

Thy heart, brows, verse, with flames, with flow'rs,
renown.

ANOTHER.

T HY Muse not-able, full, il-lustred rhymes,
Make thee the poetaster of our times.

UPON A BAY TREE NOT LONG SINCE GROWING IN THE RUINS OF VIRGIL's TOMB.

T HOSE stones which once had trust
Of Maro's sacred dust,
Which now of their first beauty spoil'd are seen, .
That they due praise not want,
Inglorious and remain,
A Delian tree (fair Nature's only plant)
Now courts, and shadows with her tresses green:
Sing Io Pæan, ye of Phœbus' train ;
Though envy, av'rice, time, your tombs throw down,
With maiden laurels Nature will them crown.

FLORA's FLOWER.

VENUS doth love the rofe ;
    Apollo thofe dear flow'rs
Which were his paramours;
The queen of fable fkies
The fubtile lunaries :
But Flore likes none of thofe ;
For fair to her no flow'r feems fave the lily ;
And why ? Becaufe one letter turns it P——.

MELAMPUS's EPITAPH.

ALL that a dog could have
    The good Melampus had :
Nay, he had more than what in beafts we crave,
For he could play the brave ;
And often, like a Thrafo ftern, go mad :
And if ye had not feen, but heard him bark,
Ye would have fworn he was your parifh clerk.

THE HAPPINESS OF A FLEA.

HOW happier is that Flea,
    Which in thy breaft doth play,
Than that pied butterfly
Which courts the flame, and in the fame doth die!
That hath a light delight,
Poor fool ! contented only with a fight ;
When this doth fport, and fwell with deareft food,
And, if he die, he knight-like dies in blood.

OF

OF THE SAME.

POOR flea! then thou didſt die;
   Yet by ſo fair a hand,
That thus to die was deſtine to command:
Thou didſt die, yet didſt try
A lover's laſt delight,
To vault on virgin plains, her kiſs and bite:
Thou diedſt, yet haſt thy tomb
Between thoſe paps, O dear and ſtately room!
Flea happier far, more bleſt,
Than Phœnix burning in his ſpicy neſt.

LINA's VIRGINITY.

WHO Lina weddeth, ſhall moſt happy be;
   For he a maid ſhall find,
Though maiden none be ſhe,
A girl or boy beneath her waiſt confin'd:
And though bright Ceres' locks be never ſhorn,
He ſhall be ſure this year to lack no corn.

LOVE NAKED.

AND would ye, lovers, know
   Why Love doth naked go?
Fond, waggiſh, changeling lad!
Late whilſt Thaumantia's voice
He wond'ring heard, it made him ſo rejoice,
That he o'erjoy'd ran mad:
And in a frantic fit threw clothes away,
And ſince from lip and lap hers cannot ſtray.

Q 3   NIOBE.

NIOBE.

WRETCH'D Niobe I am ;
    Let wretches read my cafe,
Not fuch who with a tear ne'er wet their face.
Seven daughters of me came,
And fons as many, which one fatal day,
Orb'd mother ! took away.
Thus reft by heavens unjuft,
Grief turn'd me ftone, ftone too me doth entomb ;
Which if thou doft miftruft,
Of this hard rock but ope the flinty womb,
And here thou fhalt find marble, and no duft.

CHANGE OF LOVE.

ONCE did I weep and groan,
    Drink tears, draw loathed breath,
And all for love of one
Who did affect my death :
But now, thanks to difdain !
I live reliev'd of pain.
For fighs I finging go,
I burn not as before—no, no, no, no !

WILD BEAUTY.

IF all but ice thou be,
    How doft thou thus me burn ?
Or how at fire which thou doft raife in me,
Sith ice, thyfelf in ftreams doft thou not turn ?

                                               But

But rather, plaintful cafe!
Of ice art marble made, to my difgrace.
O miracle of love, not heard till now!
Cold ice doth burn, and hard by fire doth grow.

CONSTANT LOVE.

TIME makes great ftates decay,
    Time doth May's pomp difgrace,
Time draws deep furrows in the faireft face,
Time wifdom, force, renown, doth take away;
Time doth confume the years,
Time changes works in heaven's eternal fpheres;
Yet this fierce tyrant, which doth all devour,
To leffen love in me fhall have no pow'r.

TO CHLORIS.

SEE, Chloris, how the clouds
    Tilt in the azure lifts;
And how with Stygian mifts
Each horned hill his giant forehead fhrouds.
Jove thund'reth in the air;
The air, grown great with rain
Now feems to bring Deucalion's days again:
I fee thee quake: come, let us home repair;
Come, hide thee in mine arms,
If not for love, yet to fhun greater harms.

THYRSIS IN DISPRAISE OF BEAUTY.

THAT which fo much the doting world doth
        prize,
Fond ladies only care, and fole delight,
Soon-fading beauty, which of hues doth rife,

Is but an abject let of Nature's might ;
Moſt woful wretch, whom ſhining hair and eyes
Lead to love's dungeon, traitor'd by a ſight,
   Moſt woful! for he might with greater eaſe
   Hell's portals enter, and pale Death appeaſe.

As in delicious meads beneath the flowr's,
And the moſt wholeſome herbs that May can ſhew,
In cryſtal curls the ſpeckled ſerpent low'rs ;
As in the apple, which moſt fair doth grow,
The rotten worm is clos'd, which it devours ;
As in gilt cups, with Gnoſſian wine which flow,
Oft poiſon pompouſly doth hide its ſours ;
   So lewdneſs, falſehood, miſchief them advance,
   Clad with the pleaſant rays of beauty's glance.

Good thence is chas'd where beauty doth appear ;
Mild lowlineſs, with pity, from it fly ;
Where beauty reigns, as in their proper ſphere ;
Ingratitude, diſdain, pride, all deſcry ;
The flow'r and fruit, which virtue's tree ſhould bear,
With her bad ſhadow beauty maketh die :
   Beauty a monſter is, a monſter hurl'd
   From angry heaven, to ſcourge this lower world.

As fruits which are unripe, and ſour of taſte,
To be confect'd more fit than ſweet we prove ;
For ſweet, in ſpite of care, themſelves will waſte,
When they long kept the appetite do move :
So, in the ſweetneſs of his nectar, Love
The foul confects, and ſeaſons of his feaſt :
   Sour is far better, which we ſweet may make,
   Than ſweet, which ſweeter ſweetneſs will not take.
                             Foul

Foul may my lady be ; and may her nose,
A Tenerif, give umbrage to her chin ;
May her gay mouth, which she no time may close,
So wide be, that the moon may turn therein :
May eyes and teeth be made conform to those ;
Eyes set by chance and white, teeth black and thin :
   May all what seen is, and is hid from sight,
   Like unto these rare parts be framed right.

I shall not fear thus, though she stray alone,
That others her pursue, entice, admire ;
And, though she sometime counterfeit a groan,
I shall not think her heart feels uncouth fire ;
I shall not style her ruthless to my moan,
Nor proud, disdainful, wayward to desire :
   Her thoughts with mine will hold an equal line,
   I shall be hers, and she shall all be mine.

EURYMEDON's PRAISE OF MIRA.

GEM of the mountains, glory of our plains !
    Rare miracle of nature, and of love !
Sweet Atlas, who all beauty's heavens sustains,
No, beauty's heaven, where all her wonders move ;
   The sun, from east to west who all doth see,
   On this low globe sees nothing like to thee.

One phœnix only liv'd ere thou wast born;
And earth but did one Queen of Love admire,
Three Graces only did the world adorn,
But thrice three Muses sung to Phœbus' lyre ;
   Two phœnixes be now, Love's Queens are two,
   Four Graces, Muses ten, all made by you.

For

For thofe perfections which the bounteous heaven
To divers worlds in divers times affign'd,
With thoufands more, to thee at once were given,
Thy body fair, more fair they made thy mind :
   And, that thy like no age fhould more behold,
   When thou waft fram'd, they after brake the mould.

Sweet are the blufhes on thy face which fhine,
Sweet are the flames which fparkle from thine eyes,
Sweet are his torments who for thee doth pine,
Moft fweet his death for thee who fweetly dies ;
   For, if he die, he dies not by annoy,
   But too much fweetnefs and abundant joy.

What are my flender lays to fhew thy worth !
How can bafe words a thing fo high make known ?
So wooden globes bright ftars to us fet forth,
So in a cryftal is fun's beauty fhewn :
   More of thy praifes if my mufe fhould write,
   More love and pity muft the fame indite.

THAUMANTIA AT THE DEPARTURE OF IDMON.

FAIR Dian, from the height
   Of heaven's firft orb who chear'ft this lower place,
Hide now from me thy light ;
And, pitying my cafe,
Spread with a fcarf of clouds thy blufhing face.

Come

Come with your doleful fongs,
Night's fable birds, which plain when others fleep ;
Come, folemnize my wrongs,
And concert to me keep,
Sith heaven, earth, hell, are fet to caufe me weep.

This grief yet I could bear,
If now by abfence I were only pin'd ;
But, ah! worfe evil I fear ;
Men abfent prove unkind,
And change, unconftant like the moon, their mind.

If thought had fo much pow'r
Of thy departure, that it could me flay ;
How will that ugly hour
My feeble fenfe difmay,
" Farewel, fweet heart," when I fhall hear thee fay !

Dear life! fith thou muft go,
Take all my joy and comfort hence with thee ;
And leave with me thy woe,
Which, until I thee fee,
Nor time, nor place, nor change fhall take from me.

ERYCINE AT THE DEPARTURE OF ALEXIS.

AND wilt thou then, Alexis mine, depart,
And leave thefe flow'ry meads and cryftal
ftreams,
Thefe hills as green as great with gold and gems,
                                        Which

Which court thee with rich treafure in each part ?
Shall nothing hold thee ? Not my loyal heart,
That burfts to lofe the comforts of thy beams ?
Nor yet this pipe, which wildeft fatyrs tames ?
Nor lambkins wailing, nor old Dorus' fmart ?
O ruthlefs fhepherd ! forefts ftrange among
What canft thou elfe but fearful dangers find ?
But, ah ! not thou, but honour, doth me wrong ; .
O cruel honour ! tyrant of the mind.
 This faid fad Erycine, and all the flowers
Impearled as fhe went with eyes' falt fhowers.

C O M P A R I S O N.

OF HIS

THOUGHTS TO PEARLS.

WITH open fhells in feas, on heavenly dew
   A fhining oyfter lufcioufly doth feed ;
And then the birth of that etherial feed
Shews, when conceiv'd, if fkies look dark or blue :
So do my thoughts, celeftial twins ! of you,
At whofe afpect they firft begin and breed,
When they came forth to light, demonftrate true
If ye then fmil'd, or low'r'd in mourning weed.
Pearls then are orient fram'd, and fair in form,
If heavens in their conceptions do look clear ;
But if they thunder, or do threat a ftorm,
They fadly dark and cloudy do appear :
 Right fo my thoughts, and fo my notes do change ;
 Sweet if ye fmile, and hoarfe if ye look ftrange.

ALL

ALL CHANGETH.

THE angry winds not aye
　　Do cuff the roaring deep;
And, though heavens often weep,
Yet do they fmile for joy when comes difmay;
Frofts do not ever kill the pleafant flow'rs;
And love hath fweets when gone are all the fours.
This faid a fhepherd, clofing in his arms
His dear, who blufh'd to feel love's new alarms.

SILENUS TO KING MIDAS.

THE greateft gift that from their lofty thrones
　　The all-governing pow'rs to man can give,
Is, that he never breathe; or, breathing once,
A fuckling end his days, and leave to live;
For then he neither knows the woe nor joy
Of life, nor fears the Stygian lake's annoy.

TO HIS AMOROUS THOUGHT.

SWEET wanton thought, who art of beauty born,
　　And who on beauty feed'ft, and fweet defire,
Like taper fly, ftill circling, and ftill turn
About that flame, that all fo much admire,
That heavenly fair which doth out-blufh the morn,
Thofe ivory hands, thofe threads of golden wire,
Thou ftill furroundeft, yet dar'ft not afpire;
　　　　　　　　　　　　　　Sure

Sure thou doſt well that place not to come near,
Nor fee the majeſty of that fair court ;
For if thou faw'ſt what wonders there refort,
The pure intelligence that moves that fphere,
Like fouls afcending to thofe joys above,
Back never wouldſt thou turn, nor thence remove.
What can we hope for more ? what more enjoy ?
Since faireſt things thus fooneſt have their end,
And as on bodies fhadows do attend,
Soon all our blifs is follow'd with annoy :
Yet fhe's not dead, fhe lives where fhe did love ;
Her memory on earth, her foul above.

P H I L L I S

ON THE

DEATH OF HER SPARROW.

AH! if ye aſk, my friends, why this falt fhow'r
My blubber'd eyes upon this paper pour,
Gone is my fparrow ! he whom I did train,
And turn'd fo toward, by a cat is flain :
No more with trembling wings fhall he attend
His watchful miſtrefs. Would my life could end !
No more fhall I him hear chirp pretty lays ;
Have I not caufe to loath my tedious days ?
A Dedalus he was to catch a fly ;
Nor wrath nor rancour men in him could fpy.
To touch or wrong his tail if any dar'd,
He pinch'd their fingers, and againſt them warr'd :

Then

Then might that creft be feen fhake up and down,
Which fixed was unto his little crown ;
Like Hector's, Troy's ftrong bulwark, when in ire
He rag'd to fet the Grecian fleet on fire.
But ah, alas ! a cat this prey efpies,
Then with a leap did thus our joys furprife.
Undoubtedly this bird was kill'd by treafon,
Or otherways had of that fiend had reafon.
Thus was Achilles by weak Paris flain,
And ftout Camilla fell by Aruns vain ;
So that falfe horfe, which Pallas rais'd 'gainft Troy,
King Priam and that city did deftroy.
Thou, now whofe heart is big with this frail glory,
Shalt not live long to tell thy honour's ftory.
If any knowledge refteth after death
In ghofts of birds, when they have left to breathe,
My darling's ghoft fhall know in lower place
The vengeance falling on the cattifh race.
For never cat nor catling I fhall find,
But mew fhall they in Pluto's palace blind.
Ye who with gaudy wings, and bodies light,
Do dint the air, turn hitherwards your flight.
To my fad tears comply thefe notes of yours,
Unto his idol bring an harv'ft of flow'rs ;
Let him accept from us, as moft divine
Sabæan incenfe, milk, food, fweeteft wine ;
And on a ftone let us thefe words engrave :
" Pilgrim, the body of a fparrow brave
" In a fierce glutt'nous cat's womb clos'd remains,
" Whofe ghoft now graceth the Elyfian plains."

2   ON

ON THE

PORTRAIT

OF THE

COUNTESS OF PERTH.

SONNET.

THE goddefs that in Amathus doth reign
  With filver trammels, fapphire-colour'd eyes,
When naked from her mother's cryftal plain
She firft appear'd unto the wond'ring fkies;
Or when, the golden apple to obtain,
Her blufhing fnow amazed Ida's trees—
Did never look in half fo fair a guife,
As fhe here drawn (all other ages ftain).
O God, what beauties to inflame the foul,
And hold the hardeft hearts in chains of gold!
Fair locks, fweet face, love's ftately capitol,
Pure neck, which doth that heavenly frame uphold!
  If virtue would to mortal eyes appear,
  To ravifh fenfe, fhe would your beauty wear.

SONNET.

IF heaven, the ftars, and nature did her grace
  With all perfections found the moon above,
And what excelleth in this lower place
Found place in her to breed a world of love;

If

If angels gleams fhine on her faireft face,
Which makes heaven's joy on earth the gazer prove,
And her bright eyes (the orbs which beauty move)
As Phœbus dazzle in his glorious race ;
What pencil paint, what colour to the fight
So fweet a fhape can fhew? The blufhing Morn
The red muft lend, the Milky-way the white,
And Night the ftars which her rich crown adorn.
    To draw her right then, and make all agree,
    The heaven the table, Zeuxis Jove muft be.

ON THE SAME DRAWN WITH A PENCIL.

SONNET.

WHEN with brave art the curious painter drew
        This heavenly fhape, the hand why made he
    bear,
With golden veins, that flow'r of purple hue,
Which follows on the planet of the year?
Was it to fhew how in our hemifphere
Like him fhe fhines? nay, that effects more true
Of pow'r and wonder do in her appear,
While he but flow'rs, and fhe doth minds fubdue?
Or would he elfe to virtue's glorious light,
Her conftant courfe make known? or is 't that he
Doth parallel her blifs with Clitra's plight?
Right fo ; and thus he reading in her eye
Some lover's end, to grace what he did grave,
For cyprefs tree this mourning flow'r he gave.

R   MADRI-

MADRIGAL.

IF light be not beguil'd,
　And eyes right play their part,
This flow'r is not of art, but faireſt nature's child ;
And though, when Titan's from our world exil'd,
She doth not look, her leaves, his loſs to moan,
To wonder earth finds now more ſuns than one.

EPIGRAMS.

I.

THE Scottiſh kirk the Engliſh *church* do name ;
　The Engliſh church the Scots a *kirk* do call ;
Kirk and not *church*, *church* and not *kirk*, O ſhame !
Your *kappa* turn in *chi*, or periſh all.
Aſſemblies meet, poſt biſhops to the court :
If theſe two nations fight, 'tis ſtrangers ſport.

II.

AGAINST the King, ſir, now why would you
　　fight ?
Forſooth, becauſe he dubb'd me not a knight.
And ye, my lords, why arm ye 'gainſt king Charles ?
Becauſe of lords he would not make us earls.
Earls, why do ye lead forth theſe warlike bands ?
Becauſe we will not quit the church's lands.
Moſt holy churchmen, what is your intent ?
The king our ſtipends largely did augment.
　　　　　　　　　　　　　　Commons,

Commons, to tumult thus why are you driven?
Priefts us perfuade it is the way to heaven.
   Are thefe juft caufe of war; good people, grant?
' Ho! Plunder! thou ne'er fwore our covenant.

Give me a thoufand covenants; I'll fubfcrive
Them all, and more, if more ye can contrive
Of rage and malice; and let every one
Black treafon bear, not bare rebellion.
I'll not be mock'd, hifs'd, plunder'd, banifh'd hence,
For more years ftanding for a * * * * prince.
His caftles all are taken, and his crown,
His fword, and fceptre, enfigns of renown,
With that lieutenant Fame did fo extol;
And captives carried to the capital.
I'll not die martyr for a mortal thing;
'Tis 'nough to be confeffor for a king.
Will this you give contentment, honeft men?
I've written *rebels*—pox upon the pen!

III.

THE king a negative voice moft juftly hath,
   Since the kirk hath found out a negative faith.

IV.

IN parliament one voted for the king;
   The crowd did murmur he might for it fmart;
His voice again being heard, was no fuch thing; .
For that which was miftaken, was a fart.

BOLD

V.

BOLD Scots, at Barnnockburn ye kill'd your king,
   Then did in parliament approve the fact ;
And would ye Charles to such a nonplus bring,
To authorize rebellion by an Act ?
   Well, what ye crave, who knows but granted
      may be ?
But, if he do't, cause swaddle him for a baby.

VI.

A REPLY.

SWADDLED is the baby, and almost two years
   (His swaddling time) did neither cry nor stir ;
But star'd, smil'd, did lie still, void of all fears,
And sleep'd, though barked at by every cur :
   Yea, had not wak'd, if Lesly, that hoarse nurse,
   Had not him hardly rock'd—old wives him curse !

VII.

THE king nor band nor host had him to
   follow,
Of all his subjects ; they were given to thee,
Lesly. Who is the greatest ? By Apollo,
The emperor thou ; some Palsegrave scarce seems he.
Couldst thou pull lords, as we do bishops, down,
Small distance were between thee and a crown.

VIII.

VIII.

WHEN lately Pym defcended into hell,
Ere he the cups of Lethe did caroufe,
What place that was, he called loud to tell;
To whom a devil—This is the Lower Houfe.

IX.

THE STATUE OF ALCIDES.

FLORA, upon a time,
Naked Alcides' ftatue did behold;
And with delight admir'd each am'rous limb;
Only one fault, fhe faid, could be of't told.
For, by right fymmetry,
The craftfman had him wrong'd;
To fuch tall joints a taller club belong'd—
The club hung by his thigh.
To which the ftatuary did reply:
Fair nymph, in ancient days, your * * * by fár
Were not fo hugely vaft as now they are.

X.

GREAT lies they tell, preach our church can-
not err;
Lefs lies, who fay the king's not head of her;
Great lies, who cry we may fhed other's blood,
Lefs lies, who fwear dumb bifhops are not good;
Great lies they vent, fay we for God do fight,
Lefs lies, who guefs the king does nothing right;
Great lies and lefs lies all our aims defcry;
To pulpits fome, to camp the reft apply.

XI.

A SPEECH

At the KING's Entry into the
TOWN of LINLITHGOW;

PRONOUNCED BY MR. JAMES WISEMAN,

SCHOOLMASTER there,

Inclofed in a Plafter made in the Figure of a LION.

THRICE, royal Sir, here I do you befeech,
Who art a lion, to hear a lion's fpeech.
A miracle; for, fince the days of Æfop,
No lion till thefe times his voice dar'd raife up
To fuch a majefty: then, king of men,
The king of beafts fpeaks to thee from his den;
Who, though he now inclofed be in plafter,
When he was free, was Lithgow's wife fchool-
    mafter.

XII.

A COUNTRY maid Amazon-like did ride,
To fit more fure, with leg on either fide:
Her mother, who her fpied, faid that ere long
She fhould juft penance fuffer for that wrong;
For when time fhould on her more years beftow,
That horfes hair between her thighs would grow.
Scarce winter twice was come, as was her told,
When fhe found all to frizzle there with gold;
Which firft made her afraid, then turn'd her fick,
And forc'd her keep her bed almoft a week.

    2   At

At laſt her mother calls, who ſcarce for laughter
Could hear the pleaſant ſtory of her daughter;
But, that this phrenzy ſhould no more her vex,
She ſwore thus bearded were their weaker ſex;
Which when denied, Think not, ſaid ſhe, I ſcorn;
Behold the place, poor fool, where thou waſt born.
The girl that ſeeing cried, now void of pain,
Ah! mother, you have ridden on the mane!

XIII.

GOD's judgments ſeldom uſe to ceaſe, unleſs
The ſins which them procur'd men do confeſs.
Our cries are Baal's prieſts, our faſting vain;
Our pray'rs not heard, nor anſwer'd us again:
Till perjury, wrong, rebellion, be confeſt,
Think not on peace, nor to be freed of peſt.

XIV.

THE king gives yearly to his ſenate gold;
Who can deny but juſtice then is ſold?

XV.

HERE Rixus lies, a novice in the laws,
Who 'plains he came to hell without a cauſe.

THE

CHARACTER

OF AN

ANTI-COVENANTER, or MALIGNANT.

WOULD you know thefe royal knaves,
    Of free men would turn us flaves ;
Who our union do defame
With rebellion's wicked name ?
Read thefe verfes, and ye 'll fpring 'em,
Then on gibbets ftraight caufe hing 'em.

They complain of fin and folly ;
In thefe times fo paffing holy,
They their fubftance will not give,
Libertines that we may live.
Hold thofe fubjects too, too wanton,
Under an old king dare canton.

Neglect they do our circ'lar tables,
Scorn our acts and laws as fables ;
Of our battles talk but meekly,
With four fermons pleas'd are weekly ;
Swear king Charles is neither papift,
Arminian, Lutheran, or atheift.

But that in his chamber pray'rs,
Which are pour'd 'midft fighs and tears,
To avert God's fearful wrath,
Threat'ning us with blood and death ;
Perfuade they would the multitude,
This king too holy is and good.

They

They avouch we 'll weep and groan
When hundred kings we ferve for one ;
That each fhire but blood affords,
To ferve th' ambition of young lords ;
Whofe debts ere now had been redoubled,
If the ftate had not been troubled.

Slow they are our oath to fwear,
Slower for it arms to bear :
They do concord love, and peace,
Would our enemies embrace ,
Turn men profelytes by the word,
Not by mufket, pike, and fword.

They fwear that for religion's fake
We may not maffacre, burn, fack :
That the beginning of thefe pleas,
Sprang from the ill-fped A B C's.
For fervants that it is not well
Againft their mafters to rebel.

That that devotion is but flight,
Doth force men firft to fwear, then fight.
That our confeffion is indeed
Not the Apoftolic Creed ;
Which of negations we contrive,
Which Turk and Jew may both fubfcrive.

That monies fhould men's daughters marry,
They on frantic war mifcarry.
Whilft dear the foldiers they pay,
At laft who will fnatch all away.
And, as times turn worfe and worfe,
Catechife us by the purfe.

That

That debts are paid with bold ftern looks ;
That merchants pray on their 'compt books;
That Juftice dumb and fullen frowns,
To fee in croflets hang'd her gowns ;
That preachers' ordinary theme
Is 'gainft monarchy to declaim.

That, fince leagues we 'gan to fwear,
Vice did ne'er fo black appear ;
Oppreffion, bloodfhed, ne'er more rife,
Foul jars between the man and wife ;
Religion fo contemn'd was never,
Whilft all are raging in a fever.

They tell by devils, and fome fad chance,
That that deteftable league of France,
Which coft fo many thoufand lives,
And two kings, by religious knives,
Is amongft us, though few defcry ;
Though they fpeak truth, yet fay they lie.

He who fays that night is night,
That cripple folk walk not upright,
That the owls into the fpring
Do not nightingales out-fing,
That the feas we may not plough,
Ropes make of the rainy bow,
That the foxes keep not fheep,
That men waking do not fleep,
That all's not gold doth gold appear—
Believe him not, although he fwear.

To fuch fyrens ftop your ear,
Their focieties forbear.

Ye

Ye may be toffed like a wave,
Verity may you deceive ;
Juft fools they may make of you ;
Then hate them worfe than Turk or Jew..

Were it not a dangerous thing,
Should we again obey the king ;
Lords lofe fhould fovereignty,
Soldiers hafte back to Germany;
Juftice fhould in our towns remain,
Poor men poffefs their own again ;
Brought out of hell that word of Plunder,
More terrible than devil, or thunder,
Should with the covenant fly away,
And charity amongft us ftay ;
Peace and plenty fhould us nourifh,
True religion 'mongft us flourifh ?

When you find thefe lying fellows,
Take and flower with them the gallows.
On others you may too lay hold,
In purfe or cheft, if they have gold.
Who wife or rich are in this nation,
Malignants are by proteftation.

THE FIVE SENSES.

1. SEEING.

FROM fuch a face, whofe excellence
    May captivate my fovereign's fenfe,
And make him (Phœbus like) his throne,
Refign to fome young Phaëton,

Whofe

Whofe fkillefs and unftayed hand
May prove the ruin of the land,
Unlefs great Jove, down from the fky,
Beholding earth's calamity,
Strike with his hand that cannot err
The proud ufurping charioter;
And cure, though Phœbus grieve, our woe—
From fuch a face as can work fo,
Wherefoever thou 'ft a being,
Blefs my Sovereign and his Seeing.

2. HEARING.

FROM jefts prophane and flattering tongues,
    From bawdy tales and beaftly fongs,
From after-fupper fuits, that fear
A parliament or council's ear;
From Spanifh treaties, that may wound
The country's peace, the gofpel's found;
From Job's falfe friends, that would entice
My fovereign from heaven's paradife;
From prophets fuch as Achab's were,
Whofe flatterings foothe my fovereign's ear;
His frowns more than his Maker's fearing,
Blefs my Sovereign and his Hearing.

3. TASTING.

FROM all fruit that is forbidden,
    Such for which old Eve was chidden;
From bread of labours, fweat, and toil;
From the poor widow's meal and oil;

From

From blood of innocents oft wrangled
From their eftates, and from that's ftrangled;
From the candid poifon'd baits
Of Jefuits, and their deceits;
Italian fallads, Romifh drugs,
The milk of Babel's proud whore's dugs;
From wine, that can deftroy the brain;
And from the dangerous figs of Spain;
At all banquets, and all feafting,
Blefs my Sovereign and his Tafting.

4. FEELING.

FROM prick of confcience, fuch a fting
    As flays the foul, heav'n blefs the king;
From fuch a bribe as may withdraw
His thoughts from equity or law;
From fuch a fmooth and beardlefs chin
As may provoke or tempt to fin;
From fuch a hand, whofe moift palm may
My fovereign lead out of the way;
From things polluted and unclean,
From all things beaftly and obfcene;
From that may fet his foul a reeling,
Blefs my Sovereign and his Feeling.

5. SMELLING.

WHERE myrrh and frankincenfe are thrown,
    The altar's built to gods unknown,
O let my fovereign never dwell;
Such damn'd perfumes are fit for hell.

Let

Let no fuch fcent his noftrils ftain ;
From fmells that poifon can the brain
Heav'ns ftill preferve him.   Next I crave,
Thou wilt be pleas'd, great God ! to fave
My fov'reign from a Ganymede,
Whofe whorifh breath hath pow'r to lead
His Excellence which way it lift—
O let fuch lips be never kifs'd !
From a breath fo far excelling,
Blefs my Sovereign and his Smelling.

THE ABSTRACT.

SEEING.

A ND now, juft God, I humbly pray,
    That thou wilt take the flime away
That keeps my fovereign's eyes from feeing
The things that will be our undoing.

HEARING.

T HEN let him hear, good God, the founds
    As well of men as of his hounds.

TASTE.

G IVE him a tafte, and truly too,
    Of what his fubjects undergo.

FEELING AND SMELLING.

G IVE him a feeling of their woes,
    And then no doubt his royal nofe

                                        Will

Will quickly fmell the rafcals forth,
Whofe black deeds have eclips'd his worth :
They found, and fcourg'd for their offences,
Heavens blefs my Sovereign and his Senfes.

POLEMO-MIDDINIA

INTER VITARVAM ET NEBERNAM.

NYMPHÆ, quæ colitis highiffima monta Fifæa,
Seu vos Pittenwema tenent, feu Crelia crofta,
Sive Anftræa domus, ubi nat Haddocus in undis,
Codlineufque ingens, ubi Fleucca & Sketta pererrant
Per coftam, & fcopulis Lobfter monifootus in udis
Creepat, & in mediis ludit Whitenius undis :
Et vos Skipperii, foliti qui per mare breddum
Valde procul lanchare foris, iterumque redire,
Linquite fkellatas botas, fhippafque picatas,
Whiftlantefque fimul fechtam memorate bloodæam,
Fechtam terribilem, quam marvellaverat omnis
Banda Deûm, quoque Nympharum Cockelfhelearum,
Maia ubi Sheepifeda, atque ubi Solgoofifera Baffa
Swellant in pelago, cum Sol bootatus Edenum
Foftabat radiis madidis & fhouribus atris,

. . . .

. . . .

Quo vifo·ad fechtæ noifam cecidere volucres.
Ad terram cecidere grues, plifh-plafhque dedere
Solgoofæ in pelago, prope littora Bruntiliana ;
Sea-futor obftupuit, fummique in margine faxi
Scartavit præluftre caput, wingafque flapavit.

Quodque

Quodque magis, alte volitans Heronius ipfe
Ingeminans clig-clag mediis fhitavit in undis.

    Namque a principio ftoriam tellabimus omnem,
Muckrelium ingentem turbam Vitarva per agros
Nebernæ marchare fecit, & dixit ad illos,
" Ite hodie armati greppis, drivate caballos
" Nebernæ per crofta, atque ipfas ante feneftras.
" Quod fi forte ipfa Neberna venerit extra,
" Warrantabo omnes, & vos bene defendebo."

    Hic aderant Geordy Akinhedius, & little Johnus,
Et Jamy Richæus, & ftout Michel Henderfonus,
Qui jolly tryppas ante alios danfare folebat,
Et bobbare bene, & laffas kiffare bonæas;
Duncan Olyphantus, valde ftalvartus, & ejus
Filius eldeftus jolyboyus, atque oldmoudus,
Qui pleugham longo gaddo drivare folebat;
Et Rob Gib, wantonus homo, atque Oliver Hutchin,
Et ploucky-fac'd Waty Strang, atque inkneed Alcknda
        Atken,
Et Willy Dick, heavy-arftus homo, pigerrimus om-
     nium,
Qui tulit in pileo magnum rubrumque favorem,
Valde lethus pugnare, fed hunc Corngrevius heros
Noutheadum vocavit, atque fllum forcit ad arma.
Infuper hic aderant Tom. Taylor, & Hen. Watfonus,
Et Tomy Gilchriftus, & fool Jocky Robinfonus,
Andrew Alfhenderus, & Jamy Tomfonus, & unus
Norland bornus homo, valde valde Anticovenanter,
Nomine Gordonus, valde blackmoudus, & alter
(Deil ftick it! ignoro nomen) flavry beardius homo,
Qui pottas dightavit, & affas jecerat extra.
                Denique

Denique præ reliquis Geordeum affatur, & inquit,
Geordi mi formane, inter ftoutiffimus omnes,
Huc ades & crook faddelos, hemmafquue, creilefque,
Brechemmefque fimul omnes bindato jumentis ;
Amblentemque meum naggum, fattumqne mariti
Curforem, & reliquos trottantes fumito averos.
In cartis yokkato omnes, extrahito muckam
Crofta per & riggas, atque ipfas ante feneftras
Nebernæ ; & aliquid fin ipfa contra loquatur,
In fydis tu pone manus, & dicito fart jade.
  Nec mora, formannus cunctos flankavit averos,
Workmannofque ad workam omnes vocavit, & illi
Extemplo cartas bene fillavere jigantes :
Whiftlavere viri, workhorfofque ordine fwieros,
Drivavere foras, donec iterumque iterumque
Fartavere omnes, & fic turba horrida muftrat,
Haud aliter quam fi cum multis Spinola troupis
Proudus ad Oftendam marchaffet fortiter urbem :
Interea ante alios dux Piper Laius heros
Præcedens, magnamque gerens cum burdine pypam
Incipit Harlai cunctis fonare batellum.
Tunc Neberna furens yettam ipfa egreffa, videnfque
Muck-cartas tranfire viam, valde angria facta
Non tulit affrontam tantam ; verum, agmine facto,
Convocat extemplo Barowmannos atque Ladæos,
Iackmannumque, Hiremannos, Pleughdrivfters, atque
        Pleughmannos
Tumlantefque fimul reekofo ex kitchine boyos,
Hunc qui dirtiferas terfit cum difhclouty difhas,
Hunc qui gruelias fcivit bene lickere plettas,
            S   Et

Et faltpannifumos, & widebricatos fifheros,
Hellæofque etiam falteros duxit ab antris,
Coalheughos nigri girnantes more Divelli,
Lifeguardamque fibi fævas vocat improba laffas,
Maggæam magis doctam milkare cowæas,
Et doctum fweepare flooras, & fternere beddas,
Quæque novit· fpinnare, & longas ducere threedas;
Naufæam, claves bene quæ keepaverat omnes,
Yellantemque Elpen, longo bardamque Anapellam,
Fartantemque fimul Gyllam, gliedamque Katæam
Egregie indutam blacko caput footy clouto;
Mammæamque fimul vetulam, quæ fciverat apte
Infantum teneras blande ofcularier arfas;
Quæque lanam cardare folet greafyfingria Betty.
   Tum deum hungræos ventres Neberna gruelis
Farfit, & guttas rawfuinibus implet amaris,
Poftea newbarmæ ingentem dedit omnibus hauftum,
Staggravere omnes, grandefque ad fidera riftas
Barmifumi attollunt, & fic ad prælia marchant.
Nec mora marchavit foras longo ordine turma,
Ipfa prior Neberna fuis ftout facta ribaldis,
Ruftæum manibus geftans furibunda gulæum:
Tandem muckreilios vocat ad pell-mellia flaidos.
" Ite, ait, uglæi fellows, fi quis modo pofthac
" Muckifer has noftras tentet croffare feneftras,
" Juro quod ego ejus longum extrahabo thrapellum,
" Et totam rivabo faciem, luggafque gulæo hoc
" Ex capite cuttabo ferox, totumque videbo
" Heartbloodum fluere in terram." Sic verba finivit.
Obftupit Vitarva diu dirtfluida, fed inde

                                        Couragium

Couragium accipiens, muckreilos ordine cunctos
Middini in medio faciem turnare coëgit.
  O qualem primo fleuram guftaffes in ipfo
Battelli onfetto ! Pugnat muckreillius heros
Fortiter, & muckam per pofteriora cadentem
In creilibus fhoolare ardet. Sic dirta volavit.
  O quale hoc hurly hurly fuit, fi forte vidiffes
Pypantes arfes, & flavo fanguine breeckas
Dripantes, hominumque heartas ad prælia faintas!
  O qualis firy fary fuit, namque alteri nemo
Ne vel footbreddum yerdæ yieldare volebat,
Stout erat ambo quidem, valdeque hardhearta caterva!
Tum vero è medio muckdryvfter profilit unus
Gallantæus homo, & greppam minatur in ipfam
Nebernam (quoniam mifere fcaldaverat omnes),
Dirtavitque totam peticotam gutture thicko,
Pearlineafque ejus fkirtas, filkamque gownæam,
Vafquineamque rubram muckfherda begariavit.
Et tunc ille fuit valde faintheartus, & ivit
Valde procul, metuens fhottam woundumque profundum.
Sed nec valde procul fuerat revengia in illum ;
Extemplo Gillæa ferox invafit, & ejus
In faciem girnavit atrox, & tigrida facta
Boublentem grippans berdam, fic dixit ad illum :
Vade domum, filthæe nequam, aut te interficiabo.
Tunc cum gerculeo magnum fecit Gilly whippum,
Ingentemque manu fherdam levavit, & omnem
Gallantæi hominis gafhbeardam befmeariavit ;
Sume tibi hoc, inquit, fneefing valde operativum,
Pro premio, fwingere, tuo ; tum denique fleido
Ingentem Gillywamphra dedit, validamque nevellam,

          S 2   Inge-

Ingeminatque iterum, donec bis fecerit ignem
Ambobus fugere ex oculis ; fic Gylla triumphat.
Obſtupuit bombaizdus homo ; backumque repente
Turnavit, veluti naſus bloodaſſet ; et, O fy !
Ter quater exclamat, et O quam fœde neezavit !
Disjuniumque omne evomuit valde hungrius homo,
Lauſavitque ſupra atque infra, miſerabile viſu,
Et luggas necko imponens, ſic cucurit abſens ;
Non audens gimpare iterum, nennworſa tuliſſet.
    Hæc Neberna videns yellavit turpia verba,
Et fy, fy ! exclamat, prope nunc victoria loſta eſt.
Nec mora, terribilem fillavit dira canonem,
Elatiſque hippis magno cum murmure fartam
Barytonam emiſit, veluti Monſmegga cracaſſet.
Tum vero quackarunt hoſtes, flightamque repente
Sumpſerunt ; retroſpexit Jackmannus, & ipſe
Sheepheadus metuit ſonitumque ictumque buleti.
    Quod ſi king Spanius, Philippus nomine, ſeptem
Hiſce confimiles habuiſſet forte canones
Batterare Sluiſſam, Sluiſlam dingaſſet in aſſam.
Aut ſi tot magnus Ludivocus forte dediſſet
Ingentes fartas ad mœnia Montalbana,
Ipſam continuo townam dingaſſet in yerdam.
    Exit corngrevius, wracco omnia tendere videns,
Confiliumque meum ſi non accipitis, inquit,
Pulchras ſcartabo facies, & vos worriabo :
Sed needlo per feuſtram broddatus, inque privatas
Partes ſtobbatus, greitans ookanſque grivate,
Barlafumle clamat, & dixit, O Deus ! O God !
Quid multis ? Sic fraya fuit, ſic guiſa peracta eſt,
Una nec interea ſpilata eſt droppa cruoris.

                                        E P I.

EPITAPHS.

ON A DRUNKARD.

NOR amaranths nor rofes do bequeath
  Unto this hearfe, but tamarifts and wine;
For that fame thirft, though dead, yet doth him pine,
Which made him fo caroufe while he drew breath.

ON ONE NAMED *MARGARET*.

IN fhells and gold pearls are not kept alone,
  A Margaret here lies beneath a ftone;
A Margaret that did excel in worth
All thofe rich gems the Indies both fend forth;
Who, had fhe liv'd when good was lov'd of men,
Had made the Graces four, the Mufes ten;
And forc'd thofe happy times her days that claim'd,
From her, to be the Age of Pearl ftill nam'd;
She was the richeft jewel of her kind,
Grac'd with more luftre than fhe left behind,
All goodnefs, virtue, bounty; and could cheer
The faddeft minds: now Nature knowing here
  How things but fhewn, then hidden, are lov'd beft,
  This Margaret 'fhrin'd in this marble cheft.

ON

ON A YOUNG LADY.

THIS beauty fair, which death in duſt did turn,
  And clos'd ſo ſoon within a coffin ſad,
Did paſs like lightning, like the thunder burn,
So little life, ſo much of worth it had.
Heav'ns, but to ſhew their might, here made it ſhine;
And, when admir'd, then in the world's diſdain,   .
O tears! O grief! did call it back again,
Left earth ſhould vaunt ſhe kept what was divine.
What can we hope for more, what more enjoy,
Sith.faireſt things thus fooneſt have their end;
And, as on bodies ſhadows do attend,
Sith all our blifs is follow'd with annoy?
  She is not dead, ſhe lives where ſhe did love,
  Her memory on earth, her ſoul above.

ARETINUS's EPITAPH.

HERE Aretine lies, moſt bitter gall,
  Who whilſt he liv'd ſpoke evil of all;
Only of God the arrant Scot
Nought ſaid, but that he knew him not.

VERSES ON THE LATE
WILLIAM EARL OF PEMBROKE.

I.

THE doubtful fears of change ſo fright my mind,
  Though raiſed to the higheſt joy in love,
As in this ſlippery ſtate more grief I find
Than they who never ſuch a blifs did prove;

                                        But,

But, fed with ling'ring hopes of future gain,
Dream not what 'tis to doubt a lofer's pain.

II.

Defire a fafer harbour is than fear,
And not to rife lefs danger than to fall;
The want of jewels we far better bear,
Than, fo poffeft, at once to lofe them all :   ●
  Unfatisfied hopes time may repair,
  When ruin'd faith muft finifh in defpair.

III.

Alas ! ye look but up the hill on me,
Which fhews to you a fair and fmooth afcent ;
The precipice behind ye cannot fee,
On which high fortunes are too pronely bent :
  If there I flip, what former joy or blifs
  Can heal the bruife of fuch a fall as this ?

E. P.

A   REPLY.

I.

WHO love enjoys, and placed hath his mind
  Where fairer virtues faireft beauties grace ;
Then in himfelf fuch ftore of worth doth find,
That he deferves to find fo good a place ;
  To chilling fears how can he be fet forth
  Whofe fears condemn his own, doubt others worth ?

II.

Defire, as flames of zeal, fear, horrors meets,
They rife who fall of falling never prov'd.
Who is fo dainty, fatiate with fweets,
To murmur when the banquet is remov'd ?

The

The faireft hopes time in the bud deftroys,
When fweet are memories of ruin'd joys.

III.

It is no hill, but heaven, where you remain ;
And whom defert advanced hath fo high
To reach the guerdon of his burning pain,
Muft not repine to fall, and falling die :
  His hopes are crown'd. What years of tedious
    breath
  Can them compare with fuch a happy death ?

UPON THE DEATH OF

JOHN EARL OF LAUDERDALE.

OF thofe rare worthies who adorn'd our North,
    And fhone like conftellations, thou alone
Remainedft laft, great Maitland ! charg'd with worth
Second in Virtue's theatre to none.
But finding all eccentric in our times,
Religion into fuperftition turn'd,
Juftice filenc'd, exiled, or in-urn'd ;
Truth, Faith, and Charity reputed crimes ;
The young men deftinate by fword to fall,
And trophies of their country's fpoils to rear ;
Strange laws the ag'd and prudent to appal,
And forc'd fad yokes of tyranny to bear ;
  And for no great nor virtuous minds a room—
  Difdaining life, thou fhouldft into thy tomb.

II. WHEN

II.

WHEN mifdevotion every where fhall take place,
And lofty orators, in thund'ring terms,
Shall move you, people, to arife in arms,
And churches hallow'd policy deface ;
When you fhall but one general fepulchre
(As Averroes did one general foul)
On high, on low, on good, on bad confer,
And your dull predeceffors rites controul—
Ah ! fpare this monument, great guefts ! it keeps
Three great Jufticiars, whom true worth did raife ;
The Mufes' darlings, whofe lofs Phœbus weeps ;
Beft men's delight, the glory of their days.
More we would fay, but fear, and ftand in awe
To turn idolaters, and break your law.

III.

DO not repine, blefs'd foul, that humble wits
Do make thy worth the matter of their verfe:
No high-ftrain'd mufe our times and forrows fits ;
And we do figh, not fing, to crown thy hearfe.
The wifeft prince e'er manag'd Britain's ftate
Did not difdain, in numbers clear and brave,
The virtues of thy fire to celebrate,
And fix a rich memorial on his grave.
Thou didft deferve no lefs ; and here in jet,
Gold, touch, brafs, porphyry, or Parian ftone,
That by a prince's hand no lines are fet
For thee—the caufe is, now this land hath none.
Such giant moods our parity forth brings,
We all will nothing be, or all be kings.

ON

ON THE DEATH OF

A NOBLEMAN IN SCOTLAND,

BURIED AT AITHEN.

AITHEN, thy pearly coronet let fall ;
     Clad in sad robes, upon thy temples set
The weeping cyprefs, or the fable jet.

Mourn this thy nurfeling's lofs, a lofs which all
Apollo's choir bemoans, which many years
Cannot repair, nor influence of fpheres.

Ah ! when fhalt thou find fhepherd like to him,
Who made thy banks more famous by his worth,
Than all thofe gems thy rocks and ftreams fend forth?

His fplendour others glow-worm light did dim :
Sprung of an ancient and a virtuous race,
He virtue more than many did embrace.

He fram'd to mildnefs thy half-barbarous fwains ;
The good man's refuge, of the bad the fright,
Unparallell'd in friendfhip, world's delight !

For hofpitality along thy plains
Far-fam'd a patron ; and a pattern fair
Of piety ; the Mufes' chief repair ;

Moft

Moft debonna're, in courtefy fupreme;
Lov'd of the mean, and honour'd by the great.;
Ne'er dafh'd by Fortune, nor caft down by Fate;
To prefent and to after times a theme.

Aithen, thy tears pour on this filent grave,
And drop them in thy alabafter cave,
And Niobe's imagery here become;
And, when thou haft diftilled here a tomb,
Enchafe in it thy pearls, and let it bear,
" Aithen's beft gem and honour fhrin'd lies here."

FAME, regifter of time,
    Write in thy fcroll that I,
Of wifdom lover, and fweet poefy,
Was cropped in my prime;
And ripe in worth, though green in years, did die.

JUSTICE, Truth, Peace, and Hofpitality,
    Friendfhip, and Love, being refolv'd to die,
In thefe lewd times, have chofen here to have
With juft, true, pious ——— their grave;
Them cherifh'd he fo much, fo much did grace,
That they on earth would chufe none other place.

WHEN

WHEN Death, to deck his trophies, ſtopt thy
    breath,
Rare ornament and glory of theſe parts !
All with moiſt eyes might ſay, and ruthful hearts,
That things immortal vaſſal'd were to death.

What good in parts on many ſhar'd we ſee,
From Nature, gracious Heaven, or Fortune flow ;
To make a maſter-piece of worth below,
Heaven, Nature, Fortune gave in groſs to thee.

In honour, bounty, rich—in valour, wit,
In courteſy ; born of an ancient race ;
With bays in war, with olives crown'd in peace ;
Match'd great with offspring for great actions fit.

No ruſt of times, nor change, thy virtue wan
With times to change ; when truth, faith, love, decay'd,
In this new age, like Fate thou fixed ſtaid,
Of the firſt world an all-ſubſtantial man.

As erſt this kingdom given was to thy ſire,
The prince his daughter truſted to thy care,
And well the credit of a gem ſo rare
Thy loyalty and merit did require.

Years cannot wrong thy worth, that now appears
By others ſet as diamonds among pearls ;
A queen's dear foſter, father to three earls,
Enough on earth to triumph are o'er years.

                    Life

Life a fea voyage is, death is the haven,
And freight with honour there thou haft arriv'd ;
Which thoufands feeking, have on rocks been driven :
That good adorns thy grave which with thee liv'd.

For a frail life, which here thou didft enjoy,
Thou now a lafting haft, freed of annoy.

TO THE

OBSEQUIES

OF THE

BLESSED PRINCE JAMES,

KING OF GREAT BRITAIN.

LET holy David, Solomon the wife,
    That king whofe breaft Egeria did inflame,
Auguftus, Helen's fon, great in all eyes,
Do homage low to thy maufolean frame ;
And bow before thy laurel's anadem ;
Let all thofe facred fwans, which to the fkies
By never-dying lays have rais'd their name,
From north to fouth, where fun doth fet and rife.
Religion, orphan'd, waileth o'er thy urn ;
Juftice weeps out her eyes, now truly blind ;
To Niobes the remnant virtues turn ;
Fame but to blaze thy glories ftays behind
    J' th' world, which late was golden by thy breath,
    Is iron turn'd, and horrid by thy death.

FOND

FOND wight, who dream'ft of greatnefs, glory,
    ftate;
And worlds of pleafures, honours, doft devife ;
Awake, learn how that here thou art not great
Nor glorious : by this monument turn wife.

One it enfhrineth fprung of ancient ftem,
And (if that blood nobility can make)
From which fome kings have not difdain'd to take
Their proud defcent, a rare and matchlefs gem.

A beauty here it holds by full affurance,
Than which no blooming rofe was more refin'd,
Nor morning's blufh more radiant ever fhin'd ;
Ah ! too, too like to morn and rofe at laft !

It holds her who in wit's afcendant far
Did years and fex tranfcend ; to whom the heaven
More virtue than to all this age had given ;
For virtue meteor turn'd, when fhe a ftar.

Fair mirth, fweet converfation, modefty,
And what thofe kings of numbers did conceive
By Mufes nine, and Graces more than three,
Lie clos'd within the compafs of this grave.

    Thus death all earthly glories doth confound,
    Lo ! how much worth a little duft doth bound.

                                    FAR

FAR from thefe banks exiled be all joys,
   Contentments, pleafures, mufic (care's relief) !
Tears, fighs, plaints, horrors, frightments, fad annoys,
Inveft thefe mountains, fill all hearts with grief.

Here, nightingales and turtles, vent your moans ;
Amphrifian fhepherd, here come feed thy flock,
And read thy Hyacinth amidft our groans ;
Plain, Echo, thy Narciffus from our rocks.

Loft have our meads their beauty, hills their gems,
Our brooks their cryftal, groves their pleafant fhade :
The faireft flow'r of all our anadems
Death cropped hath ; the Lefbia chafte is dead !

   Thus figh'd the Tyne, then fhrunk beneath his urn ;
And meads, brooks, rivers, hills, about did mourn.

———————

THE flow'r of virgins, in her prime of years,
   By ruthlefs Deftinies is ta'en away,
And rap'd from earth, poor earth ! before this day
Which ne'er was rightly nam'd a vale of tears.

Beauty to heaven is fled, fweet modefty
No more appears ; fhe whofe harmonious founds
Did ravifh fenfe, and charm mind's deepeft wounds,
Embalm'd with many a tear now low doth lie !

                                          FAIR

Fair hopes now vanifh'd are. She would have grac'd
A prince's marriage-bed ! but, lo ! in heaven
Bleft paramours to her were to be given !
She liv'd an angel, now is with them plac'd.

Virtue is but a name abftractly trimm'd,
Interpreting what fhe was in effect ;
A fhadow from her frame which did reflect,
A portrait by her excellences limm'd.

Thou whom free-will or chance hath hither brought,
And read'ft, here lies a branch of Maitland's ftem,
And Seyton's offspring ; know that either name
Defigns all worth yet reach'd by human thought.

Tombs elfewhere ufe life to their guefts to give,
Thefe afhes can frail monuments make live.

ANOTHER ON THE SAME SUBJECT.

LIKE to the garden's eye, the flow'r of flow'rs,
  With purple pomp that dazzle doth the fight ;
Or, as among the leffer gems of night,
The ufher of the planet of the hours ;
Sweet maid, thou fhinedft on this world of ours,
Of all perfections having trac'd the height ;
Thine outward frame was fair, fair inward pow'rs,
A fapphire lanthorn, and an incenfe light.
Hence the enamour'd heaven, as too, too good
On earth's all-thorny foil long to abide,

Tranf-

Tranſplanted to their fields ſo rare a bud,
Where from thy ſun no cloud thee now can hide.
  Earth moan'd her loſs, and wiſh'd ſhe had the grace
Not to have known, or known thee longer ſpace.

———————

HARD laws of mortal life!
    To which made thralls we come without conſent,
Like tapers, lighted to be early ſpent,
Our griefs are always rife,
When joys but halting march, and ſwiftly fly,
Like ſhadows in the eye:
The ſhadow doth not yield unto the ſun,
But joys and life do waſte e'en when begun.

———————

WITHIN the cloſure of this narrow grave
    Lie all thoſe graces a good wife could have :
But on this marble they ſhall not be read,
For then the living envy would the dead

———————

THE daughter of a king of princely parts,
    In beauty eminent, in virtues chief;
Loadſtar of love, and loadſtone of all hearts,
Her friends' and huſband's only joy, now grief;
Is here pent up within a marble frame,
Whoſe parallel no times, no climates claim.

T   VERSE

VERSES frail records are to keep a name,
   Or raife from duft men to a life of fame;
The fport and fpoil of ignorance; but far
More frail the frames of touch and marble are,
Which envy, avarice, time, ere long confound,
Or mifdevotion equals with the ground.
Virtue alone doth laft, frees man from death;
And, though defpis'd and fcorned here beneath,
Stands grav'n in angels' diamantine rolls,
And blazed in the courts above the poles.
Thou waft fair virtue's temple, they did dwell,
And live ador'd in thee; nought did excel,
But what thou either didft poffefs or love,
The Graces' darling, and the maids of Jove;
Courted by Fame for bounties, which the Heaven
Gave thee in great; which, if in parcels given,
Too many fuch we happy fure might call;
How happy then waft thou, who enjoy'dft them all?
A whiter foul ne'er body did inveft,
And now, fequefter'd, cannot be but bleft;
Enrob'd in glory, midft thofe hierarchies
Of that immortal people of the fkies,
Bright faints and angels, there from cares made free,
Nought doth becloud thy fovereign good from thee.
Thou fmil'ft at earth's confufions and jars,
And how for Centaurs' children we wage wars:
Like honey flies, whofe rage whole fwarms confumes,
Till duft thrown on them makes them veil their
    plumes.
                      Thy

Thy friends to thee a monument would raife,
And limn thy virtues ; but dull grief thy praife
Breaks in the entrance, and our tafk proves vain ;
What duty writes, that woe blots out again :
Yet Love a pyramid of fighs thee rears,
And doth embalm thee with farewels and tears.

ROSE.

THOUGH marble porphyry, and mourning
touch,
May praife thefe fpoils, yet can they not too much ;
For beauty laft, and   this ftone doth clofe,
Once earth's delight, Heaven's care, a pureft rofe.
And, Reader, fhouldft thou but let fall a tear
Upon it, other flow'rs fhall here appear,
Sad violets and hyacinths, which grow
With marks of grief, a public lofs to fhow.

II.

Relenting eye, which deigneft to this ftone
To lend a look, behold here laid in one,
The living and the dead interr'd ; for dead
The turtle in its mate is ; and fhe fled
From earth, her   choos'd this place of grief
To bound   thoughts, a fmall and fad relief.
His is this monument, for hers no art
Could frame ; a pyramid rais'd of his heart.

III. Inftead

III.

Inftead of epitaphs and airy praife,
This monument a lady chafte did raife
To her lord's living fame; and after death
Her body doth unto this place bequeath,
To reft with his, till God's fhrill trumpet found,
Though time her life, no time her love could bound.

T O

SIR WILLIAM ALEXANDER.

With the AUTHOR's Epitaph.

THOUGH I have twice been at the doors of death,
And twice found fhut thofe gates which ever mourn,
This but a lightning is, truce ta'en to breathe,
For late-born forrows augur fleet return.

Amidft thy facred cares, and courtly toils,
Alexis, when thou fhalt hear wand'ring fame
Tell, Death hath triumph'd o'er my mortal fpoils,
And that on earth I am but a fad name;

If thou e'er held me dear, by all our love,
By all that blifs, thofe joys heaven here us gave,
I conjure thee, and by the maids of Jove,
To grave this fhort remembrance on my grave:

Here Damon lies, whofe fongs did fometime grace
The murmuring Efk:—may rofes fhade the place.

DIVINE

DIVINE POEMS.

A TRANSLATION.

I.

AH, filly foul! what wilt thou fay
When He, whom earth and heaven obey,
Comes man to judge in the laft day?

II.

When He a reafon afks, why grace
And goodnefs thou wouldft not embrace,
But fteps of vanity didft trace!

III.

That day of terror, vengeance, ire,
Now to prevent thou fhouldft defire,
And to thy God in hafte retire.

IV.

With wat'ry eyes, and figh-fwoll'n heart,
O beg, beg in his love a part,
Whilft confcience with remorfe doth fmart.

V.

That dreaded day of wrath and fhame
In flames fhall turn this world's huge frame,
As facred prophets do proclaim.

VI.

O! with what grief fhall earthlings groan
When that great Judge, fet on his throne,
Examines ftrictly every one!

T 3   VII. Shrill-

VII.

Shrill-founding trumpets through the air
Shall from dark fepulchres each where
Force wretched mortals to appear.

VIII.

Nature and Death amaz'd remain
To find their dead arife again,
And procefs with their Judge maintain.

IX.

Difplay'd then open books fhall lie,
Which all thofe fecret crimes defcry
For which the guilty world muft die.

X.

The Judge enthron'd, whom bribes not gain,
The clofeft crimes appear fhall plain,
And none unpunifhed remain.

XI.

O! who then pity fhall poor me?
Or who mine advocate fhall be?
When fcarce the jufteft pafs fhall free...

XII.

All wholly holy, dreadful King,
Who freely life to thine doft bring,
Of mercy fave me, mercy's fpring!

XIII.

Then, fweet Jefu, call to mind
How of thy pains I was the end,
And favour let me that day find.

XIV. In

XIV.

In fearch of me Thou, full of pain,
Didft fweat blood, death on crofs fuftain:
Let not thefe fuff'rings be in vain.

XV.

Thou fupreme Judge, moft juft and wife,
Purge me from guilt, which on me lies,
Before that day of thine affize.

XVI.

Charg'd with remorfe, lo! here I groan,
Sin makes my face a blufh take on;
Ah! fpare me, proftrate at thy throne.

XVII.

Who Mary Magdalen didft fpare,
And lend'ft the thief on crofs thine ear,
Shew me fair hopes I fhould not fear.

XVIII.

My prayers imperfect are and weak,
But worthy of thy grace them make,
And fave me from hell's burning lake.

XIX.

On that great day, at thy right hand,
Grant I amongft thy fheep may ftand,
Sequefter'd from the goatifh band.

XX.

When that the reprobates are all
To everlafting flames made thrall,
O to thy chofen, Lord, me call!

T 4 XXI. That

XXI.

That I one of thy company,
With thofe whom thou doft juftify,
May live bleft in eternity.

SONNETS.

TOO long I follow'd have my fond defire,
And too long painted on the ocean ftreams;
Too long refrefhment fought amidft the fire,
Purfu'd thofe joys which to my foul are blames.
Ah! when I had what moft I did admire,
And feen of life's delights the laft extremes,
I found all but a rofe hedg'd with a brier,
A nought, a thought, a mafquerade of dreams.
Henceforth on thee, my only good, I'll think;
For only thou canft grant what I do crave;
Thy nail my pen fhall be; thy blood, mine ink:
Thy winding-fheet, my paper; ftudy, grave:
  And, till my foul forth of this body flee,
  No hope I'll have but only, only thee.

TO fpread the azure canopy of heaven,
And fpangle it all with fparks of burning gold;
To place this pond'rous globe of earth fo even,
That it fhould all, and nought fhould it uphold;
With motions ftrange t' endue the planets feven,
And Jove to make fo mild, and Mars fo bold;
To temper what is moift, dry, hot, and cold,
Of all their jars that fweet accords are given;
Lord,

Lord, to thy wifdom's nought, nought to thy might :
But that thou fhouldft, thy glory laid afide,
Come bafely in mortality to 'bide,
And die for thofe deferv'd an endlefs night ;
  A wonder is, fo far above our wit,
  That angels ftand amaz'd to think on it.

WHAT haplefs hap had I for to be born
    In thefe unhappy times, and dying days,
Of this now doting world, when good decays,
Love's quite extinct, and virtue's held a fcorn !
When fuch are only priz'd by wretched ways,
Who with a golden fleece them can adorn ;
When avarice and luft are counted praife,
And braveft minds live, orphan like, forlorn !
Why was not I born in that golden age,
When gold was not yet known, and thofe black arts
By which bafe worldlings vilely play their parts,
With horrid acts ftaining earth's ftately ftage ?
  To have been then, O heaven ! 't had been my blifs ;
  But blefs me now, and take me foon from this.

ASTREA in this time
  Now doth not live, but is fled up to heaven ;
Or if fhe live, it is not without crime
That fhe doth ufe her power,
And fhe is no more virgin, but a whore ;

                        Whore,

Whore, proſtitute for gold:
For ſhe doth never hold her balance even;
And when her ſword is roll'd,
  The bad, injurious, falſe, ſhe not o'erthrows,
  But on the innocent lets fall her blows.

WHAT ſerves it to be good? Goodneſs by
    thee,
The holy-wife, is thought a fool to be;
For thee, the man to temperance inclin'd
Is held but of a baſe and abject mind;
The continent is thought, for thee, but cold:
Who yet was good, that ever died old?
The pitiful, who others fears to kill,
Is kill'd himſelf, and goodneſs doth him ill;
The meek and humble man who cannot brave,
By thee is to ſome giant's brood made ſlave.
Poor Goodneſs, thine thou to ſuch wrongs ſet'ſt forth,
That, O! I fear me, thou art nothing worth.
  And when I look to earth, and not to heaven,
  Ere I were turned dove, I would be raven.

BRIGHT portals of the ſky,
    Emboſs'd with ſparkling ſtars;
Doors of eternity,
With diamantine bars,
Your arras rich uphold;

                              Looſe

Loofe all your bolts and fpiings,
  Ope wide your leaves of gold;
  That in your roofs may come the King of kings.
Scarf'd in a rofy cloud,
  He doth afcend the air;
  Straight doth the moon him fhroud
  With her refplendent hair:
  The next encryftall'd light
  Submits to him its beams;
  And he doth trace the height
  Of that fair lamp which flames of beauty ftreams.
He towers thofe golden bounds
  He did to fun bequeath;
  The higher wand'ring rounds.
  Are found his feet beneath:
  The Milky-way comes near,
  Heaven's axle feems to bend,.
  Above each turning fphere
  That, rob'd in glory, Heaven's King may afcend.
O Well-fpring of this All!
  Thy Father's image vive;
  Word, that from nought did call.
  What is, doth reafon, live!
  The foul's eternal food,
  Earth's joy, delight of heaven,
  All truth, love, beauty, good,
  To Thee, to Thee, be praifes ever given.
What was difmarfhall'd late
  In this thy noble frame,
  And loft the prime eftate,
  Hath re-obtain'd the fame,

Is now moſt perfeᴄt ſeen ;
Streams, which diverted were
(And, troubled, ſtray'd unclean)
From their firſt ſource, by Thee home turned are.
By Thee, that blemiſh old
    Of Eden's leprous prince,
    Which on his race took hold,
    And him exil'd from thence,
    Now put away is far ;
    With ſword, in ireful guiſe,
    No cherub more ſhall bar
Poor man the entrance into Paradiſe.
By Thee, thoſe ſpirits pure,
    Firſt children of the light,
    Now fixed ſtand, and ſure,
    In their eternal right ;
    Now human companies
    Renew their ruin'd wall ;
    Fall'n man, as Thou mak'ſt riſe,
Thou giv'ſt to angels, that they ſhall not fall.
By Thee, that prince of ſin,
    That doth with mifchief fwell,
    Hath loſt what he did win,
    And ſhall endungeon'd dwell ;
    His ſpoils are made the prey,
    His fanes are ſack'd and torn,
    His altars raz'd away,
And what ador'd was late, now lies a ſcorn.
Theſe manſions pure and clear,
    Which are not made by hands,
    Which once by him 'joy'd were,
                                        And

And his, then not ſtain'd, bands,
Now forfeit'd, diſpoſſeſt,
And headlong from them thrown,
Shall Adam's heirs make bleſt,
By Thee, their great Redeemer, made their own.
O! Well-ſpring of this All!
Thy Father's image vive;
Word, that from nought did call
What is, doth reaſon, live!
Whoſe work is but to will;
God's co-eternal Son,
Great Baniſher of ill,
By none but Thee could theſe great deeds be
done.
Now each ethereal gate
To him hath open'd been;
And Glory's King in ſtate
His palace enters in:
Now come is this High Prieſt
In the moſt holy place,
Not without blood addreſt,
With glory heaven, the earth to crown with grace.
Stars, which all eyes were late,
And did with wonder burn,
His name to celebrate,
In flaming tongues them turn;
Their orby cryſtals move
More active than before,
And entheate from above,
Their Sovereign Prince laud, glorify, adore.

The

The choirs of happy fouls,
  Wak'd with that mufic fweet,
  Whofe defcant care controuls,
  Their Lord in triumph meet;
· The fpotlefs fp'rits of light
  His trophies do extol,
  And, arch'd in fquadrons bright,
  Greet their great Victor in his capitol.
O glory of the heaven!
  O fole delight of earth!
  To thee all power be given,
  God's uncreated birth;
  Of mankind lover true,
  Endurer of his wrong,
  Who doft the world renew,
  Still be thou our falvation, and our fong.
From top of Olivet fuch notes did rife,
When man's Redeemer did tranfcend the fkies.

———————

MORE oft than once Death whifper'd in mine
      ear,
Grave what thou hear'ft in diamond and gold;
I am that monarch whom all monarchs fear,
Who have in duft their far-ftretch'd pride uproll'd.
All, all is mine beneath moon's filver fphere;
And nought, fave Virtue, can my power withhold:
This, not believ'd, experience true thee told,
By danger late when I to thee came near.

                                        As

As bugbear then my vifage I did fhow,
That of my horrors thou right ufe might'ft make,
And a more facred path of living take :
Now ftill walk armed for my ruthlefs blow ;
  Truft flattering life no more, redeem time paft,
  And live each day, as if it were thy laft.

THE SHADOW OF THE JUDGMENT.

ABOVE thofe boundlefs bounds, where ftars do
      move,
The ceiling of the cryftal round above,
And rainbow-fparkling arch of diamond clear,
Which crowns the azure of each underfphere,
In a rich manfion, radiant with light,
To which the fun is fcarce a taper bright,
Which, though a body, yet fo pure is fram'd,
That almoft fpiritual it may be nam'd,
Where blifs aboundeth, and a lafting May,
All pleafures heightening, flourifheth for aye,
The King of Ages dwells. About his throne,
Like to thofe beams day's golden lamp hath on,
Angelic fplendours glance, more fwift than aught
Reveal'd to fenfe, nay, than the winged thought,
His will to practife : here do feraphim
Burn with immortal love ; there cherubim,
With other noble people of the light,
As eaglets in the fun, delight their fight ;
Heaven's ancient denizens, pure active powers,
Which, freed of death, that cloifter high embowers,

                                            Ethereal

Ethereal princes, ever-conquering bands,
Bleſt ſubjeĉts, aĉting what their king commands ;
Sweet choriſters, by whoſe melodious ſtrains
Skies dance, and earth untir'd their brawl ſuſtains.
Mixed among whoſe ſacred legions dear,
The ſpotleſs ſouls of humanes do appear,
Diveſting bodies which did cares diveſt,
And there live happy in eternal reſt.

    Hither, ſurcharg'd with grief, fraught with annoy,
(Sad ſpeĉtacle into that place of joy !)
Her hair diſorder'd, dangling o'er her face,
Which had of pallid violets the grace ;
The crimſon mantle, wont her to adorn,
Caſt looſe about, and in large pieces torn ;
Sighs breathing forth, and from her heavy eyne,
Along her cheeks diſtilling cryſtal brine,
Which downward to her ivory breaſt was driven,
And had bedew'd the milky-way of heaven,
Came Piety : at her left hand near by,
A wailing woman bare her company,
Whoſe tender babes her ſnowy neck did clip,
And now hang on her pap, now by her lip :
Flames glanc'd her head above, which once did glow,
But late look pale, a poor and ruthful ſhow !
She, ſobbing, ſhrunk the throne of God before,
And thus began her caſe to him deplore :

    Forlorn, wretch'd, deſolate ! to whom ſhould I
My refuge have, below or in the ſky,
But unto thee ? See, all-beholding King,
That ſervant, no, that darling thou didſt bring
On earth, loſt man to ſave from hell's abime,
And raiſe unto thoſe regions above time ;

Who made thy name fo truly be implor'd,
And by the reverend foul fo long ador'd,
Her banifh'd now fee from thefe lower bounds;
Behold her garments' fhreds, her body's wounds:
Look how her fifter Charity there ftands,
Profcrib'd on earth, all maim'd by wicked hands:
Mifchief there mounts to fuch an high degree,
That there now none is left that cares for me.
There dwells idolatry, there atheifm reigns;
There man in dumb, yet roaring, fins him ftains;
So foolifh, that he puppets will adore
Of metal, ftone, and birds, beafts, trees, before
He once will to Thy holy fervice bow,
And yield Thee homage. Ah, alas! yet now
To thofe black fp'rits which thou doft keep in chains
He vows obedience, and with fhameful pains
Infernal horrors courts; cafe fond and ftrange!
To bane than blifs defiring more the change.
Thy Charity, of graces once the chief,
Did long time find in hofpitals relief;
Which now lie levell'd with the loweft ground,
Where fad memorials fcarce are of them found.
Then (vagabonding) temples her receiv'd,
Where my poor cells afforded what fhe crav'd;
But now thy temples raz'd are, human blood
Thofe places ftains, late where thy altars ftood:
Times are fo horrid, to implore thy name
That it is held now on the earth a blame.
Now doth the warrior, with his dart and fword,
Write laws in blood, and vent them for thy word:

U   Religion,

Religion, faith pretending to make known,
All have, all faith, religion quite o'erthrown!
Men awlefs, lawlefs live; moft woful cafe!
Men no more men, a God-contemning race.

Scarce had fhe faid, when, from the nether world
(Like to a lightning through the welkin hurl'd,
That fcores with flames the way, and every eye
With terror dazzles as it fwimmeth by),
Came Juftice; to whom angels did make place,
And Truth her flying footfteps ftraight did trace.
Her fword was loft, the precious weights fhe bare
Their beam had torn, fcales rudely bruifed were:
From off her head was reft her golden crown;
In rags her veil was rent, and ftar-fpangl'd gown;
Her tear-wet locks hang'd o'er her face, which made
Between her and the Mighty King a fhade;
Juft wrath had rais'd her colour (like the morn
Portending clouds moift embryos to be born),
Of which, fhe taking leave, with heart fwoll'n great,
Thus ftrove to 'plain before the throne of ftate.

Is not the earth thy workmanfhip, great King?
Didft thou not all this All from nought once bring
To this rich beauty, which doth on it fhine;
Beftowing on each creature of thine
Some fhadow of thy bounty? Is not man
Thy vaffal, plac'd to fpend his life's fhort fpan
To do thee homage? And then didft not thou
A queen inftall me there, to whom fhould bow
Thy earth's indwellers, and to this effect
Put in my hand thy fword? O high neglect!

Now

Now wretched earthlings, to thy great difgrace,
Perverted have my pow'r, and do deface
All reverent tracts of juftice ; now the earth
Is but a frame of fhame, a funeral hearth,
Where every virtue hath confumed been,
And nought (no, not their duft) refts to be feen :
Long hath it me abhorr'd, long chafed me ;
Expell'd at laft, here I have fled to Thee,
And forthwith rather would to hell repair,
Than earth, fince juftice execute is there.
All live on earth by fpoil, the hoft his gueft
Betrays ; the man of her lies in his breaft
Is not affur'd ; the fon the father's death
Attempts ; and kindred kindred reave of breath
By lurking means, of fuch age few makes fick,
Since hell difgorg'd her baneful arfenic.
Whom murders, foul affaffinates defile,
Moft who the harmlefs innocents beguile,
Who moft can ravage, rob, ranfack, blafpheme,
Is held moft virtuous, hath a worthy's name ;
So on embolden'd malice they rely,
That, madding, thy great puiffance they defy :
Erft man refembled thy portrait, foil'd by fmoke
Now like thy creature hardly doth he look.
Old Nature here (fhe pointed where there ftood
An aged lady in a heavy mood)
Doth break her ftaff, denying human race
To come of her, things born to her difgrace !
The dove the dove, the fwan doth love the fwan ;
Nought fo relentlefs unto man as man.

U 2   O ! if

O! if thou mad'ft this world, govern'ft it all,
Deferved vengeance on the earth let fall:
The period of her ftanding perfect is;
Her hour-glafs not a minute fhort doth mifs.
The end, O Lord, is come; then let no more
Mifchief ftill triumph, bad the good devour;
But of thy word fince conftant, true thou art,
Give good their guerdon, wicked due defert.

She faid: throughout the fhining palace went
A murmur foft, fuch as afar is fent
By mufked zephyrs' fighs along the main;
Or when they curl fome flow'ry lee and plain:
One was their thought, one their intention, will;
Nor could they err, Truth there refiding ftill:
All, mov'd with zeal, as one with cries did pray,
Haften, O Lord! O haften the laft day!

Look how a generous prince, when he doth hear
Some loving city, and to him moft dear,
Which wont with gifts and fhows him entertain
(And, as a father's, did obey his reign),
A rout of flaves and rafcal foes to wrack,
Her buildings overthrow, her riches fack,
Feels vengeful flames within his bofom burn,
And a juft rage all refpects overturn:
So feeing earth, of angels once the inn,
Manfion of faints, deflower'd all by fin,
And quite confus'd, by wretches here beneath,
The world's great Sovereign moved was to wrath.
Thrice did he roufe himfelf, thrice from his face
Flames fparkle did throughout the heavenly place.

The

The ſtars, though fixed, in their rounds did quake;
The earth, and earth-embracing ſea, did ſhake:
Carmel and Hæmus felt it; Athos' tops
Affrighted ſhrunk; and near the Ethiops,
Atlas, the Pyrenees, the Apennine,
And lofty Grampius, which with ſnow doth ſhine.
Then to the ſynod of the ſp'rits he ſwore,
Man's care ſhould end, and time ſhould be no more;
By his own Self he ſwore of perfect worth,
Straight to perform his word ſent angels forth.

There lies an iſland, where the radiant ſun,
When he doth to the northern tropics run,
Of ſix long moneths makes one tedious day;
And when through ſouthern ſigns he holds his way,
Six moneths turneth in one loathſome night
(Night neither here is fair, nor day hot-bright,
But half white, and half more); where, ſadly clear,
Still coldly glance the beams of either Bear—
The froſty Groen-land. On the lonely ſhore
The ocean in mountains hoarſe doth roar,
And over-tumbling, tumbling over rocks,
Caſts various rainbows, which in froth he chokes:
Gulphs all about are ſhrunk moſt ſtrangely ſteep,
Than Nilus' cataracts more vaſt and deep.
To the wild land beneath to make a ſhade,
A mountain lifteth up his creſted head:
His locks are icicles, his brows are ſnow;
Yet from his burning bowels deep below,
Comets, far-flaming pyramids, are driven,
And pitchy meteors, to the cope of heaven.

No fummer here the lovely grafs forth brings,
Nor trees, no, not the deadly cyprefs fprings.
Cave-loving Echo, daughter of the Air,
By human voice was never waken'd here :
Inftead of night's black bird, and plaintful owl,
Infernal furies here do yell and howl.
A mouth yawns in this height fo black obfcure
With vapours, that no eye it can endure :
Great Ætna's caverns never yet did make
Such fable damps, though they be hideous black ;
Stern horrors here eternally do dwell,
And this gulf deftine for a gate to hell :
Forth from this place of dread, earth to appal,
Three furies rufhed at the angel's call.
One with long treffes doth her vifage mafk,
Her temples clouding in a horrid cafk ;
Her right hand fwings a brandon in the air,
Which flames and terror hurleth every where ;
Pond'rous with darts, her left doth bear a fhield,
Where Gorgon's head looks grim in fable field :
Her eyes blaze fire and blood, each hair 'ftills blood,
Blood thrills from either pap, and where fhe ftood
Blood's liquid coral fprang her feet beneath ;
Where fhe doth ftretch her arm is blood and death.
Her Stygian head no fooner fhe uprears,
When earth of fwords, helms, lances, ftraight ap-
    pears
To be deliver'd ; and from out her womb,
In flame-wing'd thunders, artillery doth come ;
Floods filver ftreams do take a blufhing dye,
The plains with breathlefs bodies buried lie ;

                                        Rage,

Rage, wrong, rape, facrilege, do her attend,
Fear, difcord, wrack, and woes which have no end:
Town is by town, and prince by prince withftood;
Earth turns an hideous fhamble, a lake of blood.

 The next with eyes funk hollow in her brains,
Lean face, fnarl'd hair, with black and empty veins,
Her dry'd-up bones fcarce cover'd with her fkin,
Bewraying that ftrange ftructure built within;
Thigh-bellylefs, moft ghaftly to the fight,
A wafted fkeleton refembleth right.
Where fhe doth roam in air faint do the birds,
Yawn do earth's ruthlefs brood and harmlefs herds,
The wood's wild forragers do howl and roar,
The humid fwimmers die along the fhore:
In towns, the living do the dead up-eat,
Then die themfelves, alas! and wanting meat;
Mothers not fpare the birth of their own wombs,
But turn thofe nefts of life to fatal tombs.

 Laft did a faffron-colour'd hag come out,
With uncomb'd hair, brows banded all about
With dufky clouds, in ragged mantle clad,
Her breath with ftinking fumes the air befpread;
In either hand fhe held a whip, whofe wires
Still'd poifon, blaz'd with Phlegethontal fires.
Relentlefs, fhe each ftate, fex, age, defiles,
Earth ftreams with gores, burns with envenom'd boils;
Where fhe repairs, towns do in deferts turn,
The living have no paufe the dead to mourn;
The friend, ah! dares not lock the dying eyes
Of his belov'd; the wife the hufband flies;

Men bafilifks to men prove, and by breath,
Than lead or fteel, bring worfe and fwifter death:
No cyprefs, obfequies, no tomb they have;
The fad heaven moftly ferves them for a grave.
    Thefe over earth tumultuoufly do run,
South, North, from rifing to the fetting fun;
They fometime part, yet, than the winds more fleet,
Forthwith together in one place they meet.
Great Quinzay, ye it know, Sufania's pride,
And you where ftately Tiber's ftreams do glide;
Memphis, Parthenope, ye too it know,
And where Euripus' feven-fold tide doth flow:
Ye know it, empreffes, on Thames, Rhone, Seine;
And ye, fair queens, by Tagus, Danube, Rhine;
Though they do fcour the earth, roam far and large,
Not thus content, the angels leave their charge:
We of her wreck thefe flender figns may name,
By greater they the judgment do proclaim.
    This center's center with a mighty blow
One bruifeth, whofe crack'd concaves louder low,
And rumble, than if all th' artillery
On earth difcharg'd at once were in the fky;
Her furface fhakes, her mountains in the main
Turn topfy-turvy, of heights making plain:
Towns them ingulph; and late where towers did ftand
Now nought remaineth but a wafte of fand:
With turning eddies feas fink under ground,
And in their floating depths are valleys found;
Late where with foamy crefts waves tilted waves,
Now fifhy bottoms fhine, and moffy caves.
                                        The

The mariner cafts an amazed eye
On his wing'd firs, which bedded he finds lie,
Yet can he fee no fhore ; but whilft he thinks,
What hideous crevice that huge current drinks,
The ftreams rufh back again with ftorming tide,
And now his fhips on cryftal mountains glide,
Till they be hurl'd far beyond feas and hope,
And fettle on fome hill or palace top ;
Or, by triumphant furges over-driven,
Shew earth their entrails, and their keels the heaven.
  Sky's cloudy tables fome do paint, with fights
Of armed fquadrons, juftling fteeds and knights,
With fhining croffes, judge, and fapphire throne,
Arraigned criminals to howl and groan,
And plaints fent forth are heard: new worlds feen
        fhine
With other funs and moons, falfe ftars decline,
And dive in feas ; red comets warm the air,
And blaze, as other worlds were judged there.
Others the heavenly bodies do difplace,
Make fun his fifter's ftranger fteps to trace ;
Beyond the courfe of fpheres he drives his coach,
And near the cold Arcturus doth approach ;
The Scythian amaz'd is at fuch beams,
The Mauritanian to fee icy ftreams ;
The fhadow which ere while turn'd to the Weft,
Now wheels about, then reeleth to the Eaft :
New ftars above the eighth heaven fparkle clear,
Mars chops with Saturn, Jove claims Mars's fphere ;
Shrunk nearer earth, all blacken'd now and brown,
In mafk of weeping clouds appears the moon.
                                          There

There are no feafons, Autumn, Summer, Spring,
All are ftern Winter, and no birth forth bring :
Red turns the fky's blue curtain o'er this globe,
As to propine the Judge with purple robe.
   At firft, entranc'd, with fad and curious eyes,
Earth's pilgrims ftare on thofe ftrange prodigies :
The ftar-gazer this round finds truly move
In parts and whole, yet by no fkill can prove
The firmament's ftay'd firmnefs. They which dream
An everlaftingnefs in world's vaft frame,
Think well fome region where they dwell may wrack,
But that the whole nor time nor force can fhake ;
Yet, frantic, mufe to fee heaven's ftately lights,
Like drunkards, waylefs reel amidft their heights.
Such as do nations govern, and command
Vafts of the fea and emperies of land,
Repine to fee their countries overthrown,
And find no foe their fury to make known :
Alas ! they fay, what boots our toils and pains,
Of care on earth is this the furtheft gains ?
No riches now can bribe our angry fate ;
O no ! to blaft our pride the heavens do threat:
In duft now muft our greatnefs buried lie,
Yet is it comfort with the world to die.
As more and more the warning figns increafe,
Wild dread deprives loft Adam's race of peace ;
From out their grand-dame earth they fain would fly,
But whither know not, heavens are far and high :
Each would bewail and mourn his own diftrefs ;
But public cries do private tears fupprefs :

                         Laments,

Laments, plaints, fhrieks of woe, difturb all ears,
And fear is equal to the pain it fears.
   Amidft this mafs of cruelty and flights,
This galley full of God-defpifing wights,
This jail of fin and fhame, this filthy ftage,
Where all act folly, mifery, and rage;
Amidft thofe throngs of old prepar'd for hell,
Thofe numbers which no Archimede can tell,
A filly crew did lurk, a harmlefs rout,
Wand'ring the earth, which God had chofen out
To live with Him (few rofes which did blow
Among thofe weeds earth's garden overgrow,
A dew of gold ftill'd on earth's fandy mine,
Small diamonds in world's rough rocks which fhine),
By purple tyrants which purfu'd and chas'd,
Liv'd reclufes, in lonely iflands plac'd;
Or did the mountains haunt, and forefts wild,
Which they than towns more harmlefs found and
      mild;
Where many an hymn they, to their Maker's praife,
Teach'd groves and rocks, which did refound their
      lays.
Nor fword, nor famine, nor plague-poifoning air,
Nor prodigies appearing every where,
Nor all the fad diforder of this All,
Could this fmall handful of the world appal;
But as the flow'r, which during winter's cold
Runs to the root, and lurks in fap uproll'd,
So foon as the great planet of the year
Begins the Twins' dear manfion to clear,
                       Lifts

Lifts up its fragrant head, and to the field
A fpring of beauty and delight doth yield :
So at thofe figns and apparitions ftrange,
Their thoughts, looks, geftures, did begin to change;
Joy makes their hands to clap, their hearts to dance,
In voice turns mufic, in their eyes doth glance.
　　What can, fay they, thefe changes elfe portend,
Of this great frame, fave the approaching end ?
Paft are the figns, all is perform'd of old,
Which the Almighty's heralds us foretold.
Heaven now no longer fhall of God's great power
A turning temple be, but fixed tower ;
Burn fhall this mortal mafs amidft the air,
Of Divine Juftice turn'd a trophy fair ;
Near is the laft of days, whofe light embalms
Paft griefs, and all our ftormy cares becalms.
O happy day ! O cheerful, holy day !
Which night's fad fables fhall not take away !
Farewel complaints, and ye yet doubtful thought
Crown now your hopes with comforts long time fought;
Wip'd from our eyes now fhall be every tear,
Sighs ftopt, fince our falvation is fo near.
What long we long'd for, God at laft hath given,
Earth's chofen bands to join with thofe of heaven.
Now noble fouls a guerdon juft fhall find,
And reft and glory be in one combin'd ;
Now, more than in a mirror, by thefe eyne,
Even face to face, our Maker fhall be feen.
O welcome wonder of the foul and fight !
O welcome object of all true delight !

　　　　　　　　　　　　　　　　Thy

Thy triumphs and return we did expect,
Of all paſt toils to reap the dear effect:
Since thou art juſt, perform thy holy word;
O come ſtill hop'd for, come long wiſh'd for, Lord.
   While thus they pray, the heavens in flames appear,
As if they ſhew fire's elemental ſphere;
The earth ſeems in the ſun, the welkin gone;
Wonder all huſhes; ſtraight the air doth groan   .
With trumpets, which thrice louder ſounds do yield
Than deaf'ning thunders in the airy field.
Created nature at the clangor quakes;
Immur'd with flames, earth in a palſy ſhakes,
And from her womb the duſt in ſeveral heaps
Takes life, and muſt'reth into human ſhapes:
Hell burſts, and the foul priſoners there bound
Come howling to the day, with ſerpents crown'd.
Millions of angels in the lofty height,
Clad in pure gold, and the electre bright,
Uſhering the way ſtill where the Judge ſhould move,
In radiant rainbows vault the ſkies above;
Which quickly open, like a curtain driven,
And beaming glory ſhews the KING OF HEAVEN.
   What Perſian prince, Aſſyrian moſt renown'd,
What Scythian with conquering ſquadrons crown'd,
Ent'ring a breached city, where conſpire
Fire to dry blood, and blood to quench out fire;
Where cutted carcaſſes quick members reel,
And by their ruin blunt the reeking ſteel,
Reſembleth now the ever-living King?
What face of Troy which doth with yelling ring,
                                        And

And Grecian flames tranſported in the air;
What dreadful ſpectacle of Carthage fair;
What picture of rich Corinth's tragic wrack,
Or of Numantia the hideous ſack;
Or theſe together ſhewn, the image, face,
Can repreſent of earth, and plaintful caſe,
Which muſt lie ſmoking in the world's vaſt womb,
And to itſelf both fuel be and tomb?
   Near to that ſweet and odoriferous clime,
Where the all-cheering emperor of time
Makes ſpring the caſſia, nard, and fragrant balms,
And every hill, and Collin crowns with palms;
Where incenſe ſweats, where weeps the precious
      myrrh,
And cedars overtop the pine and fir;
Near where the aged phœnix, tir'd of breath,
Doth build her neſt, and takes new life in death;
A valley into wide and open fields
Far it extendeth * * * * *

The reſt is wanting.

HYMNS.

I.

SAVIOUR of mankind! Man Emanuel!
   Who ſinleſs died for ſin, who vanquiſh'd hell,
The firſt fruits of the grave, whoſe life did give
Light to our darkneſs, in whoſe death we live—
O ſtrengthen thou my faith, correct my will,
That mine may thine obey: protect me ſtill,

So

So that the latter death may not devour
My foul feal'd with thy feal ; fo in the hour
When thou, whofe body fanctified thy tomb,
(Unjuftly judg'd) a glorious judge fhalt come,
To judge the world with juftice ; by that fign
I may be known and entertain'd for thine.

II.

HIM, whom the earth, the fea, and fky
Worfhip, adore, and magnify,
And doth this threefold engine fteer,
Mary's pure clofet now doth bear :

Whom fun and moon, and creatures all,
Serving at times, obey his call,
Pouring from heaven his facred grace,
I' th' virgin's bowels hath ta'en place.

Mother moft bleft by fuch a dower,
Whofe Maker, Lord of higheft power,
Who this wide world in hand contains,
In thy womb's ark himfelf reftrains.

Bleft by a meffage from heaven brought,
Fertile with Holy Ghoft full fraught,
Of nations the defired King,
Within thy facred womb doth fpring.

Lord, may thy glory ftill endure,
Who born waft of a virgin pure ;
The Father's and the Sp'rit's love,
Which endlefs worlds may not remove.

III. JESU,

III.

JESU, our prayers with mildnefs hear,
  Who art the crown which virgins decks,
Whom a pure maid did breed and bear,
The fole example of her fex.

Thou feeding there where lilies fpring,
While round about the virgins dance,
Thy fpoufe doft to glory bring,
And them with high rewards advance.

The virgins follow in thy ways
Whitherfoever thou doft go,
They trace thy fteps with fongs of praife,
And in fweet hymns thy glory fhew.

Caufe thy protecting grace, we pray,
In all our fenfes to abound,
Keeping from them all harms which may
Our fouls with foul corruption wound.

  Praife, honour, ftrength, and glory great,
  To God the Father, and the Son,
  And to the holy Paraclete,
  While time lafts, and when time is done.

IV.

BENIGN Creator of the ftars,
  Eternal Light of faithful eyes,
Chrift, whofe redemption none debars,
Do not our humble prayers defpife.

   6.   Who

Who for the ftate of mankind griev'd,
That it by death deftroy'd fhould be,
Haft the difeafed world reliev'd,
And given the guilty remedy.

When th' evening of the world drew near,
Thou as a bridegroom deign'ft to come
Out of thy wedding chamber dear,
Thy Virgin Mother's pureft womb :

To the ftrong force of whofe high reign
All knees are bow'd with gefture low,
Creatures which heav'n or earth contain
With rev'rence their fubjection fhew.

O holy Lord ! we thee defire,
Whom we expect to judge all faults,
Preferve us, as the times require,
From our deceitful foes' affaults.

Praife, honour, ftrength, and glory great,
To God the Father, and the Son,
And to the Holy Paraclete,
Whilft time lafts, and when time is done,

HYMN FOR SUNDAY.

O BLEST Creator of the light,
    Who bringing forth the light of days,
With the firft work of fplendour bright
The world didft to beginning raife ;

Who

Who morn with evening join'd in one
Commandedſt ſhould be call'd the day :
The foul confuſion now is gone ;
O hear us when with tears we pray :

Leſt that the mind, with fears full fraught,
Should loſe beſt life's eternal gains,
While it hath no immortal thought,
But is enwrapt in ſinful chains.

O may it beat the inmoſt ſky,
And the reward of life poſſeſs !
May we from hurtful actions fly,
And purge away all wickedneſs !

Dear Father, grant what we entreat,
And only Son, who like pow'r haſt,
Together with the Paraclete,
Reigning whilſt times and ages laſt.

HYMN FOR MONDAY.

GREAT Maker of the heavens wide,
Who, leſt things mix'd ſhould all confound,
The floods and waters didſt divide,
And didſt appoint the heav'ns their bound;

Ordering where heav'nly things ſhall ſtay,
Where ſtreams ſhall run on earthly ſoil,
That waters may the flames allay,
Leſt they the globe of earth ſhould ſpoil.

Sweet

Sweet Lord, into our minds infufe
The gift of everlafting grace,
That no old faults which we did ufe.
May with new frauds our fouls deface.

May our true faith obtain the light,
And fuch clear beams our hearts poffefs,
That it vain things may banifh quite,
And that no falfehood it opprefs. ⁻
  Dear Father, grant what we entreat, &c.

HYMN FOR TUESDAY.

GREAT Maker of man's earthly realm,
  Who didft the ground from waters take
Which did the troubled land o'erwhelm,
And it immovable didft make;

That there young plants might fitly fpring,
While it with golden flow'rs attir'd,
Might forth ripe fruit in plenty bring,
And yield fweet fruit by all defir'd:

With fragrant greennefs of thy grace,
Our blafted fouls of wounds releafe,
That tears foul fins away may chafe,
And in the mind bad motions ceafe.

May it obey thy heav'nly voice,
And never drawing near to ill,
T' abound in goodnefs may rejoice,
And may no mortal fin fulfil.
  Dear Father, &c.

X 2   HYMN

HYMN FOR WEDNESDAY.

O HOLY God of heav'nly frame,
   Who mak'ft the pole's wide center bright,
And paint'ft the fame with fhining flame,
Adorning it with beauteous light;

Who framing, on the fourth of days,
The fiery chariot of the fun,
Appoint'ft the moon her changing rays,
And orbs in which the planets run;

That thou might'ft by a certain bound
'Twixft night and day divifion make;
And that fome fure fign might be found
To fhew when months beginning take;

Men's hearts with lightfome fplendour blefs,
Wipe from their minds polluting fpots,
Diffolve the bond of guiltinefs,
Throw down the heaps of finful blots.
   Dear Father, &c.

HYMN FOR THURSDAY.

O GOD, whofe forces far extend,
   Who creatures which from waters fpring
Back to the flood doft partly fend,
And up to th' air doft partly bring;

Some in the waters deeply div'd,
Some playing in the heav'ns above,

                                    That

That natures from one ftock deriv'd
May thus to feveral dwellings move :

Upon thy fervants grace beftow,
Whofe fouls thy bloody waters clear,
That they no finful falls may know,
Nor heavy grief of death may bear;

That fin no foul oppreft may thrall,
That none be lifted high with pride,
That minds caft downwards do not fall,
Nor raifed up may backward flide.

    Dear Father, &c.

HYMN FOR FRIDAY.

G OD, from whofe work mankind did fpring,
   Who all in rule doft only keep,
Bidding the dry land forth to bring
All kind of beafts which on it creep ;

Who haft made fubject to man's hand.
Great bodies of each mighty thing,
That, taking life from thy command,
They might in order ferve their King ;

From us thy fervants, Lord, expel
Thofe errors which uncleannefs breeds,.
Which either in our manners dwell,
Or mix themfelves among our deeds.

Give

Give the rewards of joyful life ;
The plenteous gifts of grace increafe ;
Diffolve the cruel bonds of ftrife ;
Knit faft the happy league of peace.
 Dear Father, &c.

HYMN FOR SATURDAY.

O TRINITY ! O bleffed light !
 O Unity, moft principal !
The fiery fun-now leaves our fight ;
Caufe in our hearts thy beams to fall :

Let us with fongs of praife divine
At morn and evening thee implore ;
And let our glory, bow'd to thine,
Thee glorify for evermore.

 To God the Father glory great,
 And glory to his only Son,
 And to the Holy Paraclete,
 Both now, and ftill while ages run.

HYMN UPON THE NATIVITY.

CHRIST, whofe redemption all doth free,
 Son of the Father, who alone,
Before the world began to be,
Didft fpring from him by means unknown ;

 Thou

Thou his clear brightnefs, thou his light,
Thou everlafting hope of all,
Obferve the pray'rs which in thy fight
Thy fervants through the world let fall:

O deareft Saviour, bear in mind,
That of our body thou, a child,
Didft whilom take the natural kind,
Born of the Virgin undefil'd.

This much the prefent day makes known,
Paffing the circuit of the year,
That thou from thy high Father's throne
The world's fole fafety didft appear.

The higheft heaven, the earth, and feas,
And all that is within them found,
Becaufe he fent thee us to eafe,
With mirthful fongs his praife refound.

We alfo, who redeemed are
With thy pure blood from finful ftate,
For this thy birth-day will prepare
Now hymns this feaft to celebrate.

Glory, O Lord, be given to thee,
Whom the unfpotted Virgin bore;
And glory to thee, Father, be,
And th' Holy Ghoft, for evermore.

HYMN

HYMN UPON THE INNOCENTS.

HAIL you, ſweet babes! that are the flow'rs,
    Whom, when you life begin to taſte,
The enemy of Chriſt devours,
As whirlwinds down the roſes caſt:

Firſt ſacrifice to Chriſt you went,
Of offer'd lambs a tender ſort;
With palms and crowns, you innocent
Before the ſacred alter ſport.

UPON THE SUNDAYS IN LENT.

HYMN.

O MERCIFUL Creator, hear
    Our pray'rs to thee devoutly bent,
Which we pour forth with many a tear
In this moſt holy faſt of Lent.

Thou mildeſt ſearcher of each heart,
Who know'ſt the weakneſs of our ſtrength,
To us forgiving grace impart,
Since we return to thee at length.

Much have we ſinned, to our ſhame;
But ſpare us, who our ſins confeſs;
And, for the glory of thy name,
To our ſick ſouls afford redreſs.

Grant

Grant that the flesh may be so pin'd
By means of outward abstinence,
As that the sober watchful mind
May fast from spots of all offence.

Grant this, O blessed Trinity !
Pure Unity, to this incline—
That the effects of fasts may be
A grateful recompence for thine.

ON THE ASCENSION DAY.

O JESU, who our souls dost save,
   On whom our love and hopes depend ;
God from whom all things being have,
Man when the world drew to an end ;

What clemency thee vanquish'd so,
Upon thee our foul crimes to take,
And cruel death to undergo,
That thou from death us free might make ?

Let thine own goodness to thee bend,
That thou our sins may'st put to flight ;
Spare us—and, as our wishes tend,
O satisfy us with thy sight !

May'st thou our joyful pleasures be,
Who shall be our expected gain;
And let our glory be in thee,
While any ages shall remain.

HYMN

HYMN FOR WHITSUNDAY.

CREATOR, Holy Ghoſt, defcend;
   Vifit our minds with thy bright flame;
And thy celeſtial grace extend
To fill the hearts which thou didſt frame :

Who Paraclete art faid to be,
Gift which the higheſt God beſtows;
Fountain of life, fire, charity,
Ointment whence ghoſtly bleſſing flows.

Thy fevenfold grace thou down doſt fend,
Of God's right hand thou finger art;
Thou, by the Father promifed,
Unto our mouths doſt fpeech impart.

In our dull fenfes kindle light;
Infufe thy love into our hearts;
Reforming with perpetual light
Th' infirmities of fleſhly parts.

Far from our dwelling drive our foe,
And quickly peace unto us bring;
Be thou our guide, before to go,
That we may ſhun each hurtful thing.

Be pleafed to inſtruct our mind,
To know the Father and the Son;
The Spirit who them both doth bind
Let us believe while ages run.

To

To God the Father glory great,
And to the Son who from the dead
Arofe, and to the Paraclete,
Beyond all time imagined.

ON THE TRANSFIGURATION OF OUR LORD,

THE SIXTH OF AUGUST.

A HYMN.

ALL you that feek Chrift, let your fight
    Up to the height directed be,
For there you may the fign moft bright
Of everlafting glory fee.

A radiant light we there behold,
Endlefs, unbounded, lofty, high ;
Than heaven or that rude heap more old
Wherein the world confus'd did lie.

The Gentiles this great prince embrace;
The Jews obey this king's command,
Promis'd to Abraham and his race
A blefling while the world fhall ftand.

By mouths of prophets free from lyes,
Who feal the witnefs which they bear,
His Father bidding teftifies
That we fhould him believe and hear.

Glory

Glory, O Lord, be given to thee,
Who haft appear'd upon this day;
And glory to the Father be,
And to the Holy Ghoft, for aye.

ON THE FEAST OF ST. MICHAEL THE ARCHANGEL.

TO thee, O Chrift! thy Father's light,
  Life, virtue, which our heart infpires,
In prefence of thine angels bright,
We fing with voice and with defires :
Ourfelves we mutually invite,
To melody with anfwering choirs.

With reverence we thefe foldiers praife,
Who near the heavenly throne abide ;
And chiefly him whom God doth raife,
His ftrong celeftial hoft to guide—
Michael, who by his power difmays
And beateth down the Devil's pride.

PETER, AFTER THE DENIAL OF HIS MASTER.

LIKE to the folitary pelican,
  The fhady groves I haunt, and deferts wild,
Amongft wood's burgeffes; from fight of man,
From earth's delight, from mine own felf exil'd.

But

But that remorfe, which with my fall began,
Relenteth not, nor is by change turn'd mild ;
But rends my foul, and, like a famifh'd child,
Renews its cries, though nurfe does what fhe can.
Look how the fhrieking bird that courts the night
In ruin'd wall doth lurk, and gloomy place :
Of fun, of moon, of ftars, I fhun the light,
Not knowing where to ftay, what to embrace :
How to heaven's lights fhould I lift thefe of mine,
Sith I denied him who made them fhine !

ON THE VIRGIN MARY.

THE woful Mary, 'midft a blubber'd band
 Of weeping virgins, near unto the tree
Where God death fuffer'd, man from death to free,
Like to a plaintful nightingale did ftand,
  Which fees her younglings reft before her eyes,
  And hath nought elfe to guard them, fave her
   cries :
Love thither had her brought, and mifbelief
Of thefe fad news, which charg'd her mind to fears ;
But now her eyes, more wretched than her tears,
Bear witnefs (ah, too true !) of feared grief :
  Her doubts made certain did her hopes deftroy,
  Abandoning her foul to black annoy.
Long fixing downcaft eyes on earth, at laft
She longing them did raife (O torturing fight !)
To view what they did fhun, their fole delight
Imbrued in his own blood, and naked plac'd

To

To finful eyes; naked, fave that black veil
Which heaven him fhrouded with, that did bewai
It was not pity, pain, grief, did poffefs
The mother, but an agony more ftrange :
Cheeks' rofes in pale lilies ftraight did change;
Her fp'rits, as if fhe bled his blood, turn'd lefs.
     When fhe him faw, woe did all words deny,
     And grief her only fuffer'd figh, O my!
O my dear Lord and Son! then fhe began;
Immortal birth, tho' of a mortal born;
Eternal bounty, which doth heav'n adorn;
Without a mother, God; a father, man.!
     Ah! what haft thou deferv'd? what haft tho
          done,
     Thus to be treat? Woe's me, my fon, my fon!
Who bruis'd thy face, the glory of this All?
Who eyes engor'd, load-ftars to Paradife?
Who, as thou wert a trimmed facrifice,
Did with that cruel crown thy brows impale?
     Who rais'd thee, whom fo oft the angels ferv'd,
     Between thofe thieves who that foul death deferv'd
Was it for this thou bred waft in my womb?
Mine arms a cradle ferv'd thee to repofe?
My milk thee fed, as morning dew the rofe?
Did I thee keep till this fad time fhould come,
     That wretched men fhould nail thee to a tree,
     And I a witnefs of thy pangs muft be?
It is not long, the way's beftrew'd with flow'rs,
With fhouts to echoing heav'ns and mountains roll'd,
                                        Since

Since, as in triumph, I thee did behold
In royal pomp approach proud Sion's tow'rs :
   Lo, what a change ! Who did thee then embrace,
   Now at thee fhake their heads, inconftant race !
Eternal Father ! from whofe piercing eye
Hid nought is found that in this All is form'd,
Deign to vouchfafe a look unto this round,
This round, the ftage of a fad tragedy :
   Look but if thy dear pledge thou here canft know,
   On an unhappy tree a fhameful fhow !
Ah ! look if this be he, Almighty King,
Before heav'ns fpangled were with ftars of gold,
Ere world a center had it to uphold,
Whom from eternity thou forth didft bring ;
   With virtue, form, and light who did adorn
   Sky's radiant globes—fee where he hangs a fcorn!
Did all my prayers tend to this ? Is this
The promife that celeftial herald made
At Nazareth, when full of joy he faid,
I happy was, and from thee did me blefs ?
   How am I bleft ? No, moft unhappy I
   Of all the mothers underneath the fky.
How true and of choice, oracles the choice
Was that bleft Hebrew, whofe dear eyes in peace
Mild death did clofe ere they faw this difgrace,
When he forefpake with more than angel's voice ;
The Son fhould (malice fign) be fet apart,
   Then that a fword fhould pierce the mother's
     heart!

But

But whither doft thou go, life of my foul?
O ftay a little till I die with thee!
And do I live thee languifhing to fee?
And cannot grief frail laws of life controul?
    If grief prove weak, come, cruel fquadrons, kill
    The Mother, fpare the Son, he knows no ill:
He knows no ill; thofe pangs, bafe men, are due
To me, and all the world, fave him alone;
But now he doth not hear my bitter moan;
Too late I cry, too late I plaints renew:
    Pale are his lips, down doth his head decline,
    Dim turn thofe eyes once wont fo bright to fhine.
The heavens which in their manfions conftant move,
That they may not feem guilty of this crime,
Benighted have the golden eye of time.
Ungrateful earth, canft thou fuch fhame approve,
    And feem unmov'd, this done upon thy face?
    Earth trembled then, and fhe did hold her peace.

COMPLAINT OF THE BLESSED VIRGIN.

THE mother ftood, with grief confounded,
    Near the crofs; her tears abounded,
      While her dear fon hanged was,
Through whofe foul her fighs forth venting,
Sadly mourning and lamenting,
    Sharpeft points of fwords did pafs:
O how fad and how diftrefs'd
Was the mother, ever-blefs'd,

                            Who

Who God's only Son forth brought!
She in grief and woes did languiſh,
Quaking to behold what anguiſh
To her noble Son was wrought.

DEDICATION OF A CHURCH.

JERUSALEM, that place divine,
The viſion of ſweet peace is nam'd,
In heaven her glorious turrets ſhine,
Her walls of living ſtones are fram'd;
    While angels guard her on each ſide,
    Fit company for ſuch a bride.
She, deck'd in new attire from heaven,
Her wedding chamber now deſcends,
Prepar'd in marriage to be given
To Chriſt, on whom her joy depends.
    Her walls wherewith ſhe is incloſ'd,
    And ſtreets, are of pure gold compos'd.
The gates, adorn'd with pearls moſt bright,
The way to hidden glory ſhew;
And thither, by the bleſſed might
Of faith in Jeſus' merits, go
    All theſe who are on earth diſtreſs'd,
    Becauſe they have Chriſt's name profeſs'd,
Theſe ſtones the workmen dreſs and beat,
Before they throughly poliſh'd are;
Then each is in his proper ſeat
Eſtabliſh'd by the builder's care,
    In this fair frame to ſtand for ever,
    So join'd that them no force can ſever.

Y   To

To God, who fits in higheft feat,
Glory and power given be ;
To Father, Son, and Paraclete,
Who reign in equal dignity ;
  Whofe boundlefs pow'r we ftill adore,
  And fing their praife for evermore.

———————

*The following Poems were not publifhed in the Octavo
Edition.*

SONNET.

L ET Fortune triumph now, and Io fing,
  Sith I muft fall beneath this load of care ;
Let her what moft I prize of ev'ry thing
Now wicked trophies in her temple rear.
She who high palmy empires doth not fpare,
And tramples in the duft the proudeft king ;
Let her vaunt how my blifs fhe did impair,
To what low ebb fhe now my flow doth bring :
Let her count how (a new Ixion) me
She in her wheel did turn ; how high or low
I never ftood, but more to tortur'd be.
Weep foul, weep plaintful foul, thy forrows know;
  Weep, of thy tears till a black river fwell,
  Which may Cocytus be to this thy hell.

SONNET

SONNET.

O NIGHT, clear night, O dark and gloomy day !
  O woeful waking ! O foul-pleafing fleep !
O fweet conceits which in my brains did creep !
Yet four conceits which went fo foon away.
A fleep I had more than poor words can fay ;
For, clos'd in arms, methought I did thee keep,
A forry wretch plung'd in misfortunes deep.
Am I not wak'd, when light doth lyes bewray ?
O that that night had ever ftill been black !
O that that day had never yet begun !
And you, mine eyes, would ye no time faw fun !
To have your fun in fuch a zodiac :
    Lo, what is good of life is but a dream,
    When forrow is a never ebbing ftream.

SONNET.

SO grievous is my pain, fo painful life,
  That oft I find me in the arms of death ;
But, breath half gone, that tyrant called Death,
Who others kills, reftoreth me to life :
For while I think how woe fhall end with life,
And that I quiet peace fhall 'joy by death,
That thought ev'n doth o'erpow'r the pains of death,
And call me home again to loathed life :
Thus doth mine evil tranfcend both life and death,
While no death is fo bad as is my life,

Nor

Nor no life fuch which doth not end by death,
And Protean changes turn my death and life :
  O happy thofe who in their birth find death,
  Sith but to languifh heaven affordeth life.

S O N N E T.

I CURSE the night, yet do from day me hide,
  The Pandionian birds I tire with moans ;
The echoes even are wearied with my groans,
Since abfence did me from my blifs divide.
Each dream, each toy, my reafon doth affright ;
And when remembrance reads the curious fcroll
Of paft contentments caufed by her fight,
Then bitter anguifh doth invade my foul,
While thus I live eclipfed of her light.
O me ! what better am I than the mole ?
Or thofe whofe zenith is the only pole,
Whofe hemifphere is hid with fo long night ?
  Save that in earth he refts, they hope for fun ;
  I pine, and find mine endlefs night begun.

M A D R I G A L.

POOR turtle, thou bemoans
  The lofs of thy dear love,
And I for mine fend forth thefe fmoaking groans.
Unhappy widow'd dove !
While all about do fing,
I at the root, thou on the branch above,
Even weary with our moans the gaudy fpring ;
                        Yet

Yet thefe our plaints we do not fpend in vain,
Sith fighing zephyrs anfwer us again.

SONNET.

A S, in a dufky and tempeftuous night,
  A ftar is wont to fpread her locks of gold,
And while her pleafant rays abroad are roll'd,
Some fpiteful cloud doth rob us of her fight:
Fair foul, in this black age fo fhin'd thou bright,
And made all eyes with wonder thee behold;
Till ugly death, depriving us of light,
In his grim mifty arms thee did enfold.
Who more fhall vaunt true beauty here to fee?
What hope doth more in any heart remain,
That fuch perfections fhall his reafon rein,
If beauty, with thee born, too died with thee?
    World, plain no more of Love, nor count his harms;
    With his pale trophies Death has hung his arms.

MADRIGAL.

I FEAR not henceforth death,
  Sith after this departure yet I breathe.
Let rocks, and feas, and wind,
Their higheft treafons fhew;
Let fky and earth combin'd
Strive (if they can) to end my life and woe;
Sith grief cannot, me nothing can o'erthrow;
    Or, if that aught can caufe my fatal lot,
    It will be when I hear I am forgot.

                                    MADRI-

M A D R I G A L.

TRITONS, which bounding dive
　　Through Neptune's liquid plain,
When as ye ſhall arrive
With tilting tides where ſilver Ora plays,
And to your king his wat'ry tribute pays,
　Tell how I dying live,
　And burn in midſt of all the coldeſt main.

F ' I   N   I   S.'

www.ingramcontent.com/pod-product-compliance
Lightning Source LLC
Chambersburg PA
CBHW020939030726
47496CB00005B/1258